MOBILIZING POLITICS AND SOCIETY?

The EU Convention represents an innovative political architecture to structure the debate on the future Constitution of the European Union. Its key aim was to spawn a large debate on the future of the Union in the member states. Specifically, the Convention contained mechanisms for the participation of domestic politicians, the civil society, intellectuals and the youth.

Mobilizing Politics and Society? raises the question of whether the EU Convention has really generated participation and debate beyond the technocratic circles of EU policy making. Chapters examine both current member states and countries outside the EU in the South of Europe, focussing on a range of countries such as Portugal, Spain, Italy, Greece, Malta, Cyprus and Turkey. The contributors compare discourses, forms of mobilization, types of participation – and also the lack thereof. A timely and useful map to show how the South of Europe is discussing the future of the EU, this book also demonstrates that the participation and engagement of social actors in EU affairs remains limited and explains why. The book contains an Appendix section with documentation on the EU Convention and South European participants.

A timely analysis of the European Union Convention's impact on the domestic political systems, and civil society in Southern Europe, this book will be of interest to students and academics of Politics and the European Union.

This book is a special issue of the journal *South European Society and Politics*.

Sonia Lucarelli is currently Adjunct Professor of International Relations at the Universities of Bologna at Forlì and at the University of Siena. Her areas of interest include IR theory, European security and EU foreign policy.
Claudio M. Radaelli is Professor of Public Policy, Jean Monnet Chair in EU Policy Analysis and Director of the Centre for European Studies at Bradford University. His research interests lie in the theory of the public process, new modes of governance, EU public policy, international tax policy, and the politics of regulation.

MOBILIZING POLITICS AND SOCIETY?

The EU Convention's Impact on Southern Europe

Edited by Sonia Lucarelli and Claudio M. Radaelli

Routledge
Taylor & Francis Group
LONDON AND NEW YORK

First published 2005 by Routledge

2 Park Square, Milton Park, Abingdon, Oxon OX14 4RN
711 Third Avenue, New York, NY 10017, USA

Routledge is an imprint of the Taylor & Francis Group, an informa business

First issued in paperback 2016

Transferred to Digital Printing 2006

Copyright © 2005 Routledge

Typeset Sabon 10/12pt in Europe
by the Alden Group, Oxford

British Library Cataloguing in Publication Data
A catalogue record for this book is available from
the British Library

Library of Congress Cataloging in Publication Data

ISBN 0-415-34799-8

ISBN 978-0-415-34799-0 (hbk)
ISBN 978-1-138-97621-4 (pbk)

CONTENTS

v

    European Institutional Changes   97
    FRANCISCO TORRES AND ANA FRAGA

7   Greece: On New, European Tracks?   121
    NICOS YANNIS

8   The Debate on the Future of Europe in Malta: Moving to
    Centre Stage   142
    PETER G. XUEREB

9   Old and New Patterns of Domestic Politics in the European
    Perspective: The Debate in the Republic of Cyprus   152
    KALLIOPE AGAPIOU-JOSEPHIDES

10 Turkey on the Edges of the Convention on the
    'Future of Europe'   173
    KEMAL KİRİŞCİ AND ZEYNEP GÜLŞAH ÇAPAN

11 Regions and the Convention on the Future of Europe   192
    MICHAEL KEATING

12 The Participation and Representation of Women in the
    Debate on the Future of the European Union   208
    MERCEDES MATEO DIAZ

    Annex 1–3   223

    Index   239

Kalliope Agapiou-Josephides is a Lecturer and Jean Monnet Chair Holder at the University of Cyprus, Department of Social and Political Sciences. Her research interests and publications include: institutional aspects of European integration, women and politics, women and science.

Carlos Closa Montero is Associated Researcher at the Real Instituto Elcano de Estudios Internacionales y Estratégicos. His publications include *Sistema Político de la Unión Europea* (1997); *Spain and the EU* (with Paul Heywood, 2004); and *La europeización del sistema político español* (editor, 2001).

Ana Fraga has been a senior advisor to the committee on European affairs of Assembleia da República since 1991. Her most recent publications include *Os Parlamentos Nacionais e a Legitimidade da União Europeia* (2001).

Zeynep Gülşah Çapan is Research Assistant at Istanbul Bilgi University. Her areas of interest are the European Union, migration, IR theory, citizenship and identity.

Michael Keating is Professor of Regional Studies at the European University Institute, Italy, and Professor of Scottish politics at the University of Aberdeen, Scotland. He has published numerous books and articles on urban and regional politics, nationalism and European politics. Currently he is working on regional development policies in Europe, on stateless nations in the changing international order, and on devolution in the United Kingdom. He is co-director of the ECPR Standing Group on Regionalism and co-editor of *Regional and Federal Studies*.

Kemal Kirişci is professor at the Department of Political Science and International Relations at Boğaziçi University, Istanbul. He holds a Jean Monnet chair in European Integration and is also the director of the Centre for European Studies at the university. His areas of research interest include European integration, Middle Eastern politics, ethnic conflicts, and refugee movements and international migration. His publications include *Justice and Home Affairs Issues in Turkish-EU Relations* (2001); *Turkey in World Politics: An Emerging Multi-Regional Power* (co-editor with B. Rubin, 2001); *The Political Economy of Cooperation in the Middle East* (co-author, 1998); *Turkey and the Kurdish Question: An Example of a Trans-State Ethnic Conflict* (co-author, 1997); and *The PLO and World Politics, (1986)*. Kirisci has also published numerous articles and chapters on identity issues, Turkish foreign policy, northern Iraq and refugee movements in academic journals and edited books.

Margarita León holds a post-doctoral Marie Curie Fellowship at the Robert Schuman Centre for Advanced Studies, European University Institute, Italy.

Sonia Lucarelli is currently Adjunct Professor of International Relations at the University of Bologna at Forlì (undergraduate programme) and at the University of Siena (Master and PhD programmes). Her areas of interest include IR theory, European security and EU foreign policy. Among her recent publications: *Europe and the Breakup of Yugoslavia. A Political Failure in Search of a Scholarly Explanation* (2000); *La polis europea. L'Unione europea oltre l'euro* (editor, 2002); *Studi internazionali: i luoghi del sapere in Italia* (co-editor with Roberto Menotti, 2002). She is author of articles and book chapters on the areas of interest mentioned above.

Mercedes Mateo Diaz holds a post-doctoral Jean Monnet/Vincent Wright Fellowship in Comparative Politics and Marie Curie Fellowship at the Robert Schuman Centre for Advanced Studies, European University Institute, Italy.

Covadonga Meseguer holds a post-doctoral Jean Monnet Fellow/Vincent Wright Fellowship in Comparative Politics at the Robert Schuman Centre for Advanced Studies, European University Institute, Italy.

Daniela Piana is Jean Monnet Fellow at the European University Institute of Fiesole, where she is working on the constitution of the EU. She collaborates with the Centre of Public Policy Analysis at the University of Bologna, where her main research field deals with decisional processes and institutional changes. She has published several articles in Italian and foreign journals concerning decisional rationality, European public policy and deliberative processes in political arenas.

Claudio M. Radaelli is Professor of Public Policy, Jean Monnet Chair in EU Policy Analysis, and Director of the Centre for European Studies at Bradford University. His research interests lie in the theory of the policy process, new modes of governance, EU public policy, international tax policy, and the politics of regulation. Recent publications include *Technocracy in the European Union* (1999), *Regulatory Impact Analysis in Comparative Perspective* (2001), and *The Politics of Europeanisation* (co-editor, 2003).

Jesse Scott is a PhD Researcher at the European University Institute, is assistant to Convention Vice-President Giuliano Amato on projects for public debate on the future of Europe, is Co-ordinator of European University Institute Convention Watch, and has written on the Convention and public debate in the *EUSA Review* (15:4, 2002), in the College of Europe Convention papers (*Making a Constitution for the European Union*, forthcoming, 2004), and for the European Parliament (STOA) study by the European University Institute (*Evaluation of the Use of New Technologies in order to facilitate Democracy in Europe*, forthcoming Autumn 2003).

Francisco Torres is Professor and head of research at the IEE, Universidade Católica, Visiting Associate Professor of Economics at Universidade de Aveiro and Senior Economist at the Portuguese Central Bank. He has published extensively on European Union issues. His most recent publications include *EMU and Cohesion: Theory and Policy* (co-author with Brian Ardy, Iain Begg and Waltraud Schelkle, 2003) and *Governing EMU* (co-editor with Amy Verdun, Chiara Zilioli and Hubert Zimmermann, forthcoming).

Filippo Vergara Caffarelli is Research Fellow in Economics at La Sapienza University, Rome. He is also a PhD Researcher in Economics at the European University Institute, Florence, and is a member both of the Osservatorio sulla Convenzione Europea of the Italian EC Affairs Ministry and the European University Institute Convention Watch. He is a Scientific Co-Director of the Thesmos Centre of European Studies and has written on Economic Theory and European Economic Policy issues in *Rivista di Politica Economica* (88:12, 1998) and *I quaderni di Thesmos II* (eds. S. da Empoli and F. Arcelli, 2003).

Peter Xuereb is Professor of European and Comparative Law, and Chairman of the European Documentation and Research Centre at the University of Malta. He has published widely in European and Comparative Law.

Nicos Yannis is the Press Officer of DG Development in the European Commission. His recent publications include *Τι είναι η κοινωνία πολιτών* [What is civil society?] (2002), 'Federal Ideas and Greek Responses' in *Greece in the European Union: the New Role and the New Agenda* (ed. P. K. Ioakimides, 2002) and 'The Parliament of Greece: Slow but Constant Moves Towards European Integration?' in *National Parliaments on their Ways to Europe: Losers or Latecomers?* (eds. W. Vessels and A. Maurer, 2001).

ACRONYMS

ABGS	Avrupa Birliği Genel Sekreterligi (Secretariat General For the European Union Affairs) [Turkey]
AEGEE	Association des Etats Generaux des Etudiants de L'Europe (European Students General Forum)
AER	Assembly of European Regions
AKEL	Anorthotiko Komma Ergazomenoulaov (Progressive Party of the Working People) [Greece]
AKP	Adalet ve Kalkınma Partisi (Justice and development Party) [Turkey]
ANAP	Anavatan Partisi (Motherland Party) [Turkey]
ATTAC	Association pour une Taxation des Transaction financières pour l'Aide au Citoyens – International Movement for democratic control of financial market and their institutions
CALRE	Conferenza delle Assemblee Legislative Regionali (Conference of the European Legislative Assemblies)
CAP	Common Agricultural Policy
CDS-PP	Centro Democrático Social – Partido Popular (Christian Democratic Party) [Portugal]
CECOP	European Confederation of workers. Co-operatives, sociales co-operatives and participatives enterprises
CEMR	Council of European Municipalities and Regions
CFDP	Common Foreign Defence Policy
CFSP	Common Foreign Security Policy
CGIL	Confederazione Generale Italiana del Lavoro (General Confederation of Labour)
CGT	Confédération Générale du Travail
CHP	Cumhuriyet Halk Partisi (Republican People's Party) [Turkey]
CISL	Confederazione Italiana Sindacati Lavoratori (Confederation of Workers' Union)
COBAS	Comitati di Base [Italy]
CoR	Committee of the Regions
COSAC	Conférence des Organes Spécialisées aux Affaires Communautaires (Conference of European Affairs Committees of the EU)
CPRM	Conference of Peripheral Maritime Regions
DGB	Deutsche Gewerkschaftbund (Federal German Trade Union)
DIKO	Dimokratiko Komma (Democratic Party) [Greece]

DİSK	Türkiye Devrimci İşçi Sendikaları Konfederasyonu (Confederation of Progressive Trade Unions of Turkey)
DISY	Dimocratikos Synagermos (Democratic Rally) [Turkey]
DSP	Demokratik Sol Partisi (Democratic Left Party) [Turkey]
DYP	Doğru Yol Partisi (True Path Party) [Turkey]
E(E)C	European (Economic) Community
ECJ	European Court of Justice
EDI	Enomenoi Dimokrates (United Democrats)
EDRC	European Documentation and Research Center
EEC	European Economic Community
EESC	European Economic and Social Committee
EKEM	Ελληνικό Κέντρο Ευρωπαϊκών Μελετών (Hellenic Center for European Studies)
EKEME	Ελληνικό Κέντρο Ευρωπαϊκών Μελετών και Ερευνών (Greek Center of European Studies and Research)
ELDR	European Liberal, Democratic and Reformist Group [Turkey]
EMS	European Monetary System
EMU	Economic and Monetary Union
ENEES	Ενωση Νέων Ερευνητών Ευρωπαϊκών Σπουδών (Young Researchers Association For European Studies) [Greece]
EP	European Parliament
EPIN	European Policy Institutes Network
EPP	European People's Party
EU	European Union
GSEE	Γενική Συνομοσπονδία Εργατών Ελλάδος (General Confederation of Greek Workers)
IGC	Intergovernmental Conference
IHD	Insan Hakları Dernegi (Human Rights Association of Turkey)
İKV	İktisadi Kalkınma Vakfı (Economic Development Foundation) [Turkey]
KESK	Kamu Emekçileri Sendikaları Konfederasyonu (Confederation of Public Service Employees' Union) [Turkey]
KKE	Κομμουνιστικό Κόμμα Ελλάδος (Communist Party) [Greece]
MEP	Member of European Parliament
MFA	Ministry of Foreign Affairs
MHP	Milliyetçi Hareket Partisi (Nationalist Action Party) [Turkey]
MIC	Malta-European Union Information Centre
MPs	Members of National Parliaments
ND	New Democracy [Greece]
NGO	Non Governmental Organization

OMC	Open Method of Coordination
PASOK	Panhellenion Sosialistiko Kenema (Panhellenic Socialist Movement)
PCP	Partido Comunista Português (Portuguise Communist Party)
PES	Party of European Socialists
PEV	Partido Ecologista os Verdes (Ecologist and Greens Party) [Portugal]
PS	Partido Socialista (Socialist Party) [Portugal]
PSD	Partido Social Democrata (Social Democratic Party) [Portugal]
RIE	Real Instituto Elcano
RIEAS	Research Institute for European and American Studies
SEV	Syndesmos Ellinikon Viomihanion (Greek Industries Association)
SSEA	Secretary of State for European Affairs
TEPSA	Trans-European Policy Studies Association
TESEV	Türkiye Ekonomik ve Sosyal Etüdler Vakfi (Turkish Economic and Social Studies Foundation)
TMMOB	Türk Mühendis ve Mimar Odaları Birliği (Turkish Union of Chambers of Turkish Engineers and Architects)
TÜMTİS	Türkiye Motorlu Taşıt İşçileri Sendikası (Turkish Road Transport Workers Trade Union)
TÜRKİS	Türk İşçi Sendikaları Konfederasyonu (Confederation of Trade Unions of Turkey)
TUSİAD	Türk Sanayiciler ve İş Adamları Dernegi (Turkish Industrialists' and Businessmen's Association)
UIL	Unione Italiana del Lavoro (Union of Italian Labour)
UN	United Nations
UNICE	Union of Industrial and Employer's Confederations of Europe
WG	Working Group

The discussion of constitutional reform in the European Union (EU) remains lively and contentious. Faced with enlargement, with a set of tricky policy challenges, and with the pressures of domestic politics, it is no mean task to attempt to craft a consensus around ambitious proposals for constitutional change. During 2002 and 2003 the European Convention laboured to devise a pathway to reform, handing over the baton in autumn 2003 to the Intergovernmental Conference (IGC) to negotiate the fine print, and in the knowledge that subsequently the final text would have to go for ratification in all the member states, both the 'old' 15 and the 'new' ten. In December 2003 the IGC was suspended under the Italian presidency of the Council after a failure to find agreement on key proposals as regards the institutional rules. It is all the more important therefore that we have a good understanding of the different ingredients in this discussion, that we refine our insights into the different perspectives of different member states and of different political and societal groups, and that we be able to assess what the role of the experimental Convention has been in preparing the most recent negotiations over treaty reform. Research on this subject is a priority in the Robert Schuman Centre for Advanced Studies, where the idea for this volume was born.

This volume makes a valuable contribution to our understanding in a number of ways. First, the authors focus on the process of the Convention as such in contrast to the several studies that focus on the outputs of the Convention. This is particularly useful in so far as they highlight which political actors were mobilized – and how and why – in order to comment on what differences the varied patterns of mobilization make in terms of domestic political processes. The stories told by the authors about this provide excellent lenses through which to view subsequent reactions in and to the IGC.

Secondly, and crucially, this volume thoroughly surveys the debates in the southern European members of the EU. This focus is especially valuable because so much – perhaps too much – attention has traditionally been given to the roles and preferences of northern member states, and currently much of the spotlight is on the eastern new members. Moreover – facts speak for themselves – the arguments in the IGC included a robust approach from Spanish negotiators, and the task of attempting mediation fell to the Italian government. Many clues can be found in the contributions that follow to the dynamics of domestic debate across southern Europe. It is indeed interesting to compare and contrast both similarities and differences among these southern EU member countries, and to benefit from the systematic efforts of the authors to develop a convincing and well-grounded comparative frame.

Thirdly, the authors argue that there are some interesting shared features in the experiences of all the countries covered as they responded to the European Convention. They suggest that, whatever the limits to political mobilization around the Convention, nonetheless this experiment produced more transparency, more extensive consultation and more emphasis on political communication with citizens than is typically associated with the political processes of these countries. Thus the claim is that by southern European standards there was a net gain in terms of 'good governance'. This claim is in particular about the way the Convention operated as a process, as distinct from the outputs or subsequent political negotiating positions of individual governments.

Fourthly, it appears to be the case in the countries covered here that the Convention in some senses triggered forms of Europeanization of domestic discourses, in so far as some of the overarching European issues were brought into domestic political debates and went beyond the often much narrower preoccupations with immediate local benefits from EU integration. Even though it may be argued that this discursive impact was greater among those groups and actors most routinely involved in European debates, nonetheless some of the Conventions's subject matter was domesticated by being incorporated in domestic party and electoral politics. We shall all need to reflect a great deal more on the question of what indeed are the patterns of domestication of Europe, and how these feed back into the way that the European debate on constitutional reform is taken forward.

HELEN WALLACE
Robert Schuman Centre for Advanced Studies
European University Institute, Florence
December 2003

The European Convention: A Process of Mobilization?

SONIA LUCARELLI and CLAUDIO M. RADAELLI

INTRODUCTION: A NEW DISCOURSE AND PRACTICE OF EUROPEAN GOVERNANCE?

It would be wrong to see the European Convention on the Future of Europe as a simple transmission belt between one treaty negotiation and another.[1] In fact, it represented a discontinuity in European Union (EU) patterns of governance. Although one of the main tasks of the Convention was to pave the way for the intergovernmental conference (IGC) opened under the Italian Presidency of the EU on 4 October 2003, one cannot place it in parenthesis and trace a straight line between Nice and the 2003 IGC. And it would be wrong to reduce the Convention to its output – that is, the draft constitution.[2] In this essay, we set out to examine the Convention as a political process, specifically a process of mobilization.

There are several elements that make the Convention – at least potentially – an episode of discontinuity in European governance. Not a total discontinuity – as one of the aims of this essay is to situate the Convention in recent shifts in European discourses and practice of governance – but certainly an innovation with major potential. In this essay we discuss the form and content of innovation and distinguish between the potential and results of the Convention as a process of mobilization. In doing so, we situate the reports contained in this volume in relation to the main questions in our project.

Let us start with the ambitions of the exercise in the context of challenges from 'within' and from the 'outside'. The European

This essay and the project of the special issue were undertaken during a stay at the EUI, Robert Schuman Centre for Advanced Studies. The authors wish to thank Helen Wallace for her suggestions on who to contact for this project. Susannah Verney provided formidable support, encouragement, first-class peer review and enthusiasm throughout the project. The authors would also like to thank the Forum on the Problems of Peace and War in Florence, and particularly Giorgio Cheli, Marco De Bernardi and Christian Palmieri, for assistance, and the referees for their comments and suggestions on the draft essays. The contributors provided comments on this introduction. Their help is appreciated, although the authors remain responsible for the mistakes and inaccuracies presented in this section.

Convention held its opening session on 28 February 2002 with the hard task of working out the European response to two major challenges: to bring the EU closer to its citizens and make it able to 'shoulder its responsibilities in the governance of globalization' (European Council, 2001; see *Laeken Declaration on the Future of the European Union* in Annex 1). The two tasks were closer than it might appear at first glance, if one follows the European Council's claim that European citizens call for 'a clear, open, effective, democratically controlled Community ... which points the way ahead for the world' (European Council 2001). Put differently, the major task of the Convention – according to its mandate – was to rethink the EU and to shape an international actor with a democratic legitimacy to be strengthened both in terms of input and output (drawing on the distinction made by Scharpf 1997). In short, responsiveness and effectiveness were required.

In order to achieve this aim, the Laeken European Council listed 56 questions regarding key aspects of institutional transformation, but, most importantly, Laeken set an unprecedented process of transformation. The Convention's peculiar composition (see Annex 2) and working method were shaped to mark a difference with the exclusively inter-governmental method of Treaty revision, dominated by the member states and predominantly focused on technical issues. Pressures from within (the challenge of democratizing a post-national polity, adapting to the needs of an enlarged Europe, and efficiency) and from outside (globalization and foreign policy crises) demanded a qualitative step with respect to the previous attempt at shaping the Union for enlargement (the Treaty of Nice). This led to the big question of 'what kind of Europe do we want?'

Such a new constitutive momentum could not be confined to a group of state representatives and technocrats. It had to involve and mobilize a larger public. The convention that produced the Charter of Fundamental Rights (Eriksen, Fossum and Menéndez 2001; Menéndez 2002) was rather successful. Thus, a similar quasi-constitutive assembly was organized. It was decided that the chairman of the Convention would be Mr Valery Giscard d'Estaing, and the vice-chairmen Mr Giuliano Amato and Mr Jean-Luc Dehaene. The Assembly would be composed of 15 representatives of the heads of state or government of the member states, 30 members of national parliaments (two from each Member State), 16 members of the European Parliament (EP) and two Commission representatives. The accession candidate countries would be represented in the same way as the member states, but would not be able to prevent any consensus which might emerge among the member states. Additionally, three representatives of the Economic and Social

Committee, three of the European social partners, six of the Committee of the Regions (CoR) and the European Ombudsman would attend as observers. The creation of a more restricted praesidium (composed of the chairman, vice-chairmen and nine members of the plenum) and of working groups would facilitate the work of such a large assembly. A parallel Convention of the Youth would elaborate proposals to the main Convention, thereby securing the participation of the new generation of European citizens.

However, the idea of social participation was not limited to the composition of the Convention and to the Youth Convention. A forum open to organizations representing civil society (the social partners, the business world, non-governmental organizations (NGOs), academia, etc.) was established. The aim was to articulate the Forum as a network of organizations and individuals in regular contact with the Convention. One should not be misled, though, by the purely consultative character of the Forum. True, it would be difficult to claim that the Forum played a substantial role in shaping the final result (that is, the Draft Constitutional Treaty). However, the Forum should be assessed in terms of process. In this vein, it provided a useful channel for public debate on the themes of the Convention.

There was also – in the Forum and in the whole of the Convention process – a commitment to 'listen' to the society. Only after having listened would the Convention turn to 'reflection' and ultimately 'making proposals'. Undeniably, this represented an important innovation, a discontinuity with the technocratic tradition of EU politics (Radaelli 1999).

Overall, the Convention was designed as a political body with two essential aims. One was a goal defined in terms of output – that is, the constitutional draft. The other was all about process – that is, 'mobilizing politics and society'. One can also see the latter goal as an attempt to create a European public sphere in which citizens discuss Europe and thereby construct their identity as Europeans (following Habermas 2001). Indeed, Habermas argued that a constitutional debate is the best instrument to start the process that would eventually lead to a European *demos*. From this perspective, identity, political community and institutions are in a process of mutual construction and cannot be considered independently from each other (see also Cerutti 2001; 2003).

In this respect the Convention was a crucial discontinuity – as Daniela Piana argues in her essay for this volume – in terms of symbolic value. The preparation of a constitution for Europe was an exercise in identity politics in which Europeans asked themselves 'who are we?' (the political and cultural identity of 'Europe'), 'where are we going to?'

(the models most suitable for the design of the European political house) and 'what do we need to get there?' (in terms of governance capacity and specific instruments).

As a matter of fact, the Convention was not simply an exercise in terms of proposing ideas for treaty revisions but an attempt to work on the idea of a *constitution* for Europe. This ambitious aim represents a further element of discontinuity – at least potentially – of the Convention with respect to its previous record. For many years, the very notion of a possible constitution had been adamantly opposed in many quarters. Moreover, even when the Convention started, there were many who dismissed this ambition by saying that the body would simply discuss 'hypotheses on the future of Europe' and not a full constitutional draft.

The seeds of a constitutional debate are to be found, once again, in the process that led to the Charter of Fundamental Rights, which was solemnly proclaimed by the European institutions at the end of 2000. Since then, there has been a substantial discursive shift – from a technical discussion on the functioning of EU institutions to a larger debate on the broader topic of European governance. Between 2001 and 2003 the discussion on the future of the EU progressed from the rather dull discussion of Nice to the core topic of 'governance'. In July 2001 the European Commission presented its own preferences and suggestions on European governance (European Commission, 2001), thus spawning an academic and political debate on this topic (Joerges, Mény and Weiler 2001). The Convention is therefore an episode (perhaps the most important one) in a process of discursive development on governance and the role of European institutions therein. It cannot be seen in isolation from this broader discursive trend towards the 'big' questions raised by participatory governance and deliberation in a European context (on participatory governance in the EU, see Gröte and Gibpki 2002).

Furthermore, the participation of the applicant countries brought further implications in terms of the innovative potential of the Convention. In this connection, the Convention had a further political value: it increased the legitimacy of the whole integration process among the applicants' elites and public, and fostered political socialization within the EU system. The point is made in this volume by Kalliope Agapiu-Josephides regarding Cyprus, but it crops up in other cases in our sample as well (and arguably within a large portion of the applicant countries).

Taking these points together, we would argue that the Convention had considerable potential in terms of (a) the creation of a European public sphere, (b) the mobilization of politics and society at domestic level, and (c) deliberative-participatory governance. This was the main reason behind this project. However, one should not confuse potential with reality. Indeed, another reason that got us into this project was, to put it bluntly, healthy scepticism. On the one hand, all of us scholars of European integration were literally bombarded with the grandiose discourse of participation, learning from below and getting the 'peoples of Europe' into the deliberations on the 'future of governance'. On the other hand, there was evidence suggesting that the goal of mobilizing politics and society was quite hard to achieve.

Indeed, when we convened the early meetings for this project, we used to compare the Convention to the 'parallel action' described in Robert Musil's *The Man Without Qualities*. In this novel, the world of pre-First World War Vienna is suddenly excited by rumours of a colossal parallel action, to culminate in the celebration of the emperor. However, although all those who count in Vienna say they are part of the parallel action and celebrate its grandiosity, none of them can really say what the action is all about. Neither can they describe one specific way in which the parallel action will bring about some sort of real change. We do not want to pre-empt the conclusions of this project, and the reader will see how most authors remain sceptical but with shades of 'grey' rather than 'black and white' responses. At this stage, though, it is important to stress that one motivation behind this project was to check if empirical reality matched the official discourse and, had we found that the constitutional dog was not barking at all, what the reasons were for that outcome? In sum, although we were persuaded that mobilization and participatory governance were an important angle for the analysis of the Convention (better than the narrow angle of strategic behaviour), we did not want to confuse this way of approaching the Convention with a description of what was actually going on.

Another important motivation was that almost every project on the Convention we were aware of, was in one way or another concerned with the analysis of the outcome. Since the very first day in which the proposals for specific treaty articles became public, most academics were literally obsessed with the analysis of the legislation in the making, trying to assess whether a particular clause was well written or not, or raising more substantial questions about the meaning and political implications of the preamble, articles and sections. The last thing we want to do is to deny the usefulness of legal–political analysis of the outcome of the Convention (see *inter alia* de Witte 2003). However, process is at least as important as outcome in this case.

'The way to Ithaca' is probably as important as 'Ithaca', as Kalliope Agapiou-Josephides reminds us in her essay on Cyprus. Firstly, the outcome produced by the Convention is not the end of the story, as the events taking place at the IGC have now documented all too well.

Secondly, an emphasis on outcome rather than process neglects the potential of the Convention described above. A potential – we repeat – that was all about bringing society back into the debate and mobilizing domestic political systems on fundamental European issues, thereby setting the seeds for a European political identity for Europeans.

In what follows we describe our project and the ground covered by the individual essays. We report on the main results in terms of the mobilization of party politics, governments, regions, youth, gender and intellectuals. We then look at public opinion and citizens' awareness, and make some arguments about identity politics. Finally, we present our conclusions.

A PROCESS-BASED, 'BOTTOM-UP' APPROACH TO THE CONVENTION

Given our motivations and research questions, we opted for a focus on national public discourses and participation – hence, country-specific reports. We also added – as we will explain in a moment – selected horizontal studies on key issues cutting across all the countries. The focus on domestic politics and society is indicative of our preference for approaches to Europeanization sensitive to the interrelations between EU-level and domestic contexts (Featherstone and Radaelli 2003). In general, we wanted to use our cases to shed some light on the interaction between domestic and international politics, as well as look for some evidence of a relation between national public spaces and the formation of a European political identity.

The selection of countries provided these opportunities. Southern Europe, indeed, provides a fascinating geographical area for this type of analysis. To begin with, the traditional debate on the weakness of civil society and social capital in these societies makes them an ideal test to measure the 'power' of the Convention as an agent of mobilization. The power of a phenomenon can be measured only in relation to the patterns it can break and the ones that it cannot alter. Add to this that Europe has always been a fundamental actor in domestic processes of democratization, modernization and policy change in Southern Europe. It follows that the potential in terms of discourse and more generally mobilization around the issues raised by the Convention was higher than in other areas of the EU. Finally, Southern Europe presents opportunities for the analysis of the Convention because it includes a founding member and three 2nd or 3rd generation member states, as well as two accession countries and one candidate, plus a full range of geographical extents.

We therefore covered the South European EU member states – Greece, Italy, Portugal and Spain – and the two Southern European applicants due to enter the Union in 2004 – Cyprus and Malta. This volume presents country reports, commencing with EU member states (Italy, a founding member of the EU, followed by Spain, Portugal and Greece); the reports on the applicant countries (now new EU member states) follow. Of these applicant countries, we look first at the Republic of Cyprus (that is, the applicant part of the island) and then at Malta. To this group, we decided to add Turkey. Turkey is the only candidate country present at the Convention that at the time had not yet started its accession negotiations. We added Turkey precisely because of its peculiar position with respect to the EU, and set out to find out what the evidence from this contrast case could tell us. However, the contrast between member states and applicants and between applicants and Turkey are by no means the only possible comparisons. We were equally interested in tracing the possible differences between large and small states, or federal versus more centralized states.

The country reports follow a standard format. This enables us (and, hopefully, the reader) to make comparisons. The format revolves around a set of questions addressed by each country report. Specifically, we asked:

- How did the governments get ready for the Convention? How did they seek to promote a wide social debate? Did they create special task forces and units in core government, dedicated websites and initiatives for the promotion of public debate?
- What were the main proposals formulated by the government and the political parties between the start of the Convention and its termination? Was the discourse on the Convention consensual at the level of elites? If not, what were the main discursive and political cleavages?
- What did parliaments do during the Convention (special sessions, hearings and formulation of proposals for the Convention), and with what impact in terms of mobilization? Who was mobilized in the end?
- What was the role played by regions and sub-national politics in general?
- Were interest groups and NGOs mobilized?
- Did visibility and coverage of the topic in the press and the media grow during the Convention? What do opinion polls and surveys tell us?
- Did the Convention 'reach out' in relation to the mobilization of youth?

- What were the specific topics of the Convention discussed in the public debate (for example, the reference to Christianity, the name of the new entity, the so-called 'drop out' clause, the idea of double citizenship, etc.)?

Given the specific angle chosen for this project (that is, emphasis on the process rather than outcome), we also commissioned three horizontal essays and a country report specifically dealing with the mobilization of intellectuals in Spain. The horizontal contributions cover the following topics:

- the deliberative nature of the Convention as a process;
- the mobilization of regional actors; and
- the role of gender in the Convention.

These essays touch on some crucial aspects that could not be examined (at least, not fully) by reading the country reports. However, they by no means complete the range of possible cross- and transnational issues that we could deal with, but we believe they provide useful evidence. Further insights regarding, for instance, the role of the Youth Convention – another possible transnational theme – can be easily inferred by the country reports as they cover the mobilization of youth at the national and Youth Convention levels.

With these horizontal essays we venture beyond the usual chartered territory of South European society and politics, but with good reason. Firstly, in order to understand the role played by the Convention's arguments and discourses in domestic politics, it is indispensable to understand what kind of deliberative arena the Convention was – hence, Daniela Piana's contribution on discourse and deliberation within the Convention. This contribution precedes the country reports because it introduces the reader to the Convention as an agent of potential cognitive and discursive mobilization. We thought it would be useful to contrast this fundamental dimension of discursive mobilization 'at the top' with one case study on the mobilization of intellectuals in one country of our sample, a contrast which would provide the reader with a balanced assessment of this dimension. The other aspect of this contrast is provided by Carlos Closa Montero, who specifically focuses on the role of intellectuals in Spain. The reader should read his contribution in relation to the observations on intellectual mobilization contained in the country reports.

Secondly, there is an ongoing debate on how far Europeanization has empowered regions in Southern Europe. Most of the country reports comment on the regional dimension and how debates on EU federalism reverberate in domestic debates on regionalism and federalism. The horizontal essay on regions provides the full picture of regional mobilization across the whole EU. The reader can therefore situate the empirical evidence on individual countries in the broader EU-level process.

Thirdly, the impact of European gender issues in domestic debates across the South of Europe has been limited so far. However, one should also account for the degree of gender mobilization at the top. Mercedes Mateo Diaz explains how limited the potential of the Convention was in the first place. The stimulus from the 'top' was minimal, and it is not surprising to observe that South European politics and societies (traditionally lagging behind the continental and Northern European countries) have not amplified the weak gender message of the Convention.

THE EVIDENCE

Taken together, the essays in this volume show that the result of the Convention in terms of mobilization, participation and deliberative governance has been limited. The Convention 'listened' (to use the language used by its designers) and heard more from top political actors than from society. It is hard to disagree with the statement that the Convention was less interested in what was happening outside its body than in what was going on in its working groups – thus increasing inward-looking attitudes. Moreover, it is true that the participation of civic society, even in national debates, was limited.

However, the more we progressed towards the conclusions of our project, the more we became persuaded that this was not the best way to summarize the empirical findings presented here, for two reasons: the international situation at the time of the Convention and the standard with which we compare participation levels to those reached in previous rounds of EU integration.

During the work of the Convention, as many case studies in this volume show, public attention was largely captured by the so-called 'international war against terrorism' and, in particular, by the international debate on the war against Iraq. The crisis in Iraq was also significant for the domestic debates on the future of Europe for what it showed about the EU's incapacity to take a unitary position on such a crucial international crisis. Each European state, member or applicant took a position primarily dictated by national preferences, thereby leading to a serious fracture within Europe and in transatlantic relations. The seriousness and the length of this international crisis were such that public attention during the Convention was predominantly captured by the international situation rather than by the Convention itself.

Despite this, the Convention, due to its peculiar composition and working method, mobilized youth, women, intellectuals, NGOs, pressure groups and citizens to a degree that is possibly lower than the one expected at the time of the Laeken Declaration, but definitely higher than ever before. To be clear: the Convention was a sea change in comparison to past episodes of EU politics, which were dominated either by technocratic styles or – on the rare occasions in which the EU mobilized public sentiment – by hostility to integration projects, as shown by the Irish referendum on Nice. As mentioned, this was a discontinuity with the past. Add to this that for Southern European countries the Convention improved on domestic standards of participation. Let us, though, look at the evidence in detail, commencing with the mobilization of political actors.

The Mobilization of Politics: Governments and Party Politics

The mobilization of politics was, on balance, substantial. Governments and parliaments organized themselves with special committees and task forces, although in small-to-medium countries (like Portugal) formal organizational changes were far less important than informal networking among the few people working on the Convention topics. In Southern Europe, the mobilization of governments was more reactive than proactive. It was more a reaction to the emerging politics of the Convention than an attempt to shape it from the beginning. This is certainly the case with Portugal. The 'small/large countries cleavage' is also relevant as far as the substantive position of the governments is concerned. On the whole, the small-to-medium countries of our sample (Greece, Malta and Cyprus) defended the idea of a Europe where each country is equal to the others. Supranational institutions are seen as bastions against a union of the states that might turn into a 'union of the larger states'. The creation of the 'Group of 16' responded to this need.

In the Italian case, governmental mobilization was more ambiguous. The participation of Italians in the Convention was massive in purely numerical terms, as our country report documents. Italy stated from the beginning that it wanted to be a big player in the Convention, and to host the IGC on the Constitution. Throughout the Convention, however, it was not clear at all what the Italian government really wanted from the whole exercise. Party politics at home, even within the governing coalition, was more fragmented than the international press thinks. By no means was Mr Silvio Berlusconi – Italy's prime minister – the only player, and in any case his positions were in constant evolution – perhaps strategically, with the aim of playing a larger role at the IGC by maintaining an arm's-length relationship with the Convention's debates. To give an example, the Italian political elite discussed for months whether the participants in the Convention were simply in charge of formulating hypotheses for the IGC or were engaged in drafting the constitution. The language describing them ranged from '*costituenti*' (those who are making the constitutions) to 'those who are making hypotheses'. Berlusconi himself added some elements to the enigmatic position of the Italians when he tried to take the discussion on the future of Europe to prime ministerial level (with the 'BAB' connection – Blair, Aznar and Berlusconi), but without articulating a coherent discourse on EU governance.

Party politics has responded in different ways, with low degrees of mobilization in countries like Portugal and higher degrees in other countries. In most countries, domestic political cleavages reappeared in the debate on the future of Europe. More broadly, in all countries but one (Cyprus – due to lack of significant political divergences on Europe) the domestic political agenda dominated the debate on the future of Europe. Similar to what happened in Italy, the fractures within the government and between government and opposition were reproduced in the domestic discussion about Europe.

This leads to the point that domestic politics influenced both the national positions on the Convention and the internal debate about the Convention. Not surprisingly, the subsidiarity/federalism issue was at the core of the domestic debate in Spain (a federal country) and in Italy (a country where the discussion on federalization is a central political issue). The same issue was less debated in smaller or more centralized countries (Malta, Cyprus), but never completely absent (Portugal). Greece, in this respect, represents an exception to the rule.

Further evidence of the role played by domestic political agendas is provided by the cleavage between member states and applicants. In the latter group, political discourse was captured by the issue of future membership more than by the substantive transformation of the EU. This is particularly the case with Malta and Turkey. In the latter country, the disappointing failure to get a date for the start of negotiations at the Copenhagen European Council of December 2003 further weakened the participation of its citizens.

Regions, Youth, Intellectuals and Gender
Regions were quite active throughout the Convention, especially in Italy and Spain. However, in his essay, Michael Keating notes a paradox. Although European integration has been a major catalyst in the process

of regionalism over the last twenty years or so, the regional theme was not a priority at the Convention. One limitation of the Convention, he observes, was that the national debates on devolution, federalism, and regionalism did not link into the European debate. This happened despite the fact that 'Europe' is a constant discursive point of reference in the domestic politics of regionalism.

The Youth Convention triggered interesting responses, although not always and not everywhere. In Greece, youth mobilization was eventually drawn into party politics and never really took off. In Malta, students made a serious attempt to activate an original mobilization on the future of Europe, but the referendum of spring 2003 brought them into the narrower terms of the issues raised by political parties on EU membership.

Intellectuals have played an ambiguous role. In some cases (Spain) they have been mobilized from above, with governments creating the structures for their participation and even dictating the terms of academic discourse. In other contexts (Malta), they were very entrepreneurial in trying to craft a public discourse and using universities as platforms for wider social debates. There is, then, also evidence of intellectual mobilization from the bottom. On balance, however, the Convention did not manage to break the self-referential discourse of intellectuals. Put differently, the impression is that the windows were not opened and that the usual (and rather stuffy) air around the circles of experts contributing to the debate on Europe on a routine basis lingered indefinitely in the various intellectual loci of discussion. Thus, the idea that intellectuals would act as agents of wider societal mobilization and engagement did not quite work out.

Add to this that the usual suspects (lawyers and some slightly more interdisciplinary professors of European Studies) dominated the intellectual discourse on the Convention. The intellectual mobilization did not reach out to new types of intellectuals and new intellectual publics, such as film-makers, artists and novelists. Even the discussion on the possible reference to Christianity in the constitutional draft – an obvious point of controversy between countries like Spain and Italy and the other EU partners, and a focal point for the political discussion in Turkey – remained more at the political level rather than at the level of deep interrogations on ethics and theology. In Southern European countries, there was no attempt to 'dig deep' on whether there is a common religious identity in Europe or Western Europe.

Not much mobilization, then, considering that what was at stake was nothing less than 'the future of European governance'. One qualification is in order, however. Our country reports document more or less unanimously that the intellectual capacity in the South of Europe for ambitious discourses on Europe is low. In the countries of our sample, not only is the intellectual debate confined to one or two disciplines, but the overall number of academics and think tanks working professionally on European issues is low.[3] Thus, we would also argue that there are structural limitations in how far intellectual discourses can reach out.[4] In countries like Italy, there is no critical mass in terms of healthy European Studies (no matter how they are defined, although in the countries included in our sample, Law dominates) and even the more classic domain of international relations is narrow and limited to traditional approaches (Lucarelli and Menotti 2002).

Yet another disappointing result is provided by the participation of women. Perhaps the biggest mistake was to take gender mainstreaming for granted after so many years of mobilization of the Commission and the Parliament on this issue. Gender equality, Mercedes Mateo Diaz argues, 'does not just happen'. In terms of the representation of women, the Convention does not score well because of the lack of specific actions to tackle the issue.

Public Opinion

The opportunities for the Convention to get more coverage in the respective national media – thereby producing information and chances of a broader citizen participation – were very limited. The larger public was definitely not informed about the Convention. Not even as much as one might have expected, given the political and social relevance of the whole process (see Table 1). Media coverage followed agendas that were clearly national. It was higher when a country held the rotating

TABLE 1*
KNOWLEDGE OF THE EU CONVENTION HAVE YOU ALREADY HEARD OF THE EUROPEAN CONVENTION?[1]

	YES	NO
ITALY	33	67
GREECE	81	19
SPAIN	39	61
PORTUGAL	35	65
CYPRUS	54	46
MALTA	44	56

*Tables compiled with data from Standard Eurobarometers for the member states (No.56-2001, No.58-2002, No.59-2003, No.60-2003) and Candidate Eurobarometers for the Candidate Countries. We also use the Eurobarometer Flash on the Convention, 2003. NB The percentage of those that have replied 'I do not know' is not included. This is the reason why the sum of the expressed percentages does not reach 100 per cent.
[1] No data on Turkey is available.

presidency (Spain, Greece, Italy) or in connection with particular issues of direct relevance for the domestic political debate. The latter is illustrated by the Italian press coverage of the government's internal fragmentation or the public attention in Spain on the debate about the role of national parliaments (in that case, versus regional parliaments) in the EU. It is also the case of the large space reserved in Malta to debate – and media coverage – of the pros and cons of EU membership. Even part of the active participation of Greece in the Convention is to be read as a response to the country's preoccupations around the issue of the accession of Cyprus.

If little space was reserved for EU matters in the press, even less televisual airtime was reserved. Despite this gloomy picture, opinion polls on the whole show a slowly rising awareness among Europeans of EU issues. In Greece, Spain and Portugal there has been a general increase in terms of knowledge of EU institutions, such as the EP and the European Commission (during the period between autumn 2001 and spring 2003; see Table 2). The majority of Italian, Spanish, Greek and Portuguese citizens support EU policies, like the choice of a single European currency. In several cases, support increased in the same period (Table 3). The beginning of the IGC and the referendum that will take place in some countries for the adoption of the new Constitutional Treaty will inevitably raise public debate and awareness further.

Discursive Mobilization, Cognitive Innovation and Identity Politics

What about the quality of debate and possibly deliberation 'at the top', that is, within the Convention itself? In her contribution, Daniela Piana

TABLE 2
KNOWLEDGE OF THE EU: HAVE YOU EVER HEARD OF THE ...?

GREECE	AUTUMN 2001	SPRING 2003	AUTUMN 2003
European Parliament	81	88	
European Commission	73	82	
ITALY	AUTUMN 2001	SPRING 2003	AUTUMN 2003
European Parliament	94	93	
European Commission	93	77	
SPAIN	AUTUMN 2001	SPRING 2003	AUTUMN 2003
European Parliament	89	91	
European Commission	76	74	
PORTUGAL	AUTUMN 2001	SPRING 2003	AUTUMN 2003
European Parliament	90	91	
European Commission	83	84	

Note: Figures represent percentage of 'yes' responses.

TABLE 3
SUPPORT FOR EU POLICIES: WHAT IS YOUR OPINION OF EACH OF THE
FOLLOWING STATEMENTS?

ITALY	AUTUMN 2001	SPRING 2003	AUTUMN 2003
Euro	79	82	70
Common Foreign Policy	80	79	76
Enlargement	61	59	61
GREECE	AUTUMN 2001	SPRING 2003	AUTUMN 2003
Euro	79	70	64
Common Foreign Policy	81	82	75
Enlargement	74	71	65
SPAIN	AUTUMN 2001	SPRING 2003	AUTUMN 2003
Euro	69	75	70
Common Foreign Policy	69	70	66
Enlargement	61	60	62
Portugal	AUTUMN 2001	SPRING 2003	AUTUMN 2003
Euro	67	75	69
Common Foreign Policy	62	62	65
Enlargement	57	60	52

Note: Replies report favourable answers.

looks at the symbolic, discursive and cognitive dimensions. She 'reads' the texts produced by the working groups of the Convention and the Forum using the lenses of deliberative democracy and reasoned argumentation. She does not argue that the Convention was an example of deliberative democracy. Instead, she uses the literature on deliberative democracy as a heuristic method for empirical analysis. Her conclusion, indeed, is that social participation has been somewhat limited. The important point, however, is about ideational innovation and creativity. The quality of arguments and normative positions that emerged within the Convention is high, especially in the domains of social governance, subsidiarity, EU democracy and participatory governance. As such, the Convention has produced a positive discontinuity in cognitive and normative mobilization at the EU level.

At the same time, at the state level, discursive mobilization was sometimes extremely relevant. This was the case of Greece. According to Nicos Yannis, the Convention[5] has reframed the discussion on the EU, from narrow typical Greek issues to wider fundamental topics at the core of EU governance, such as federalism. Empirical evidence on public opinion in Greece, though, does not fully support the claim that there has been a comprehensive shift. The Greeks seem to favour federalism at the EU level but these principles do not percolate down to the discussion on the Greek state, which remains distant from any federal benchmark.[6]

However, according to Yannis, there is evidence of slow, incremental changes in identity politics. The Greeks now think about their position in Europe as fully fledged European citizens. Political parties, intellectuals and to some extent public opinion are concerned about the shape of EU governance and all the major political issues at the EU level. Their identity in Europe is no longer a simple matter of discussing the classic issues relevant to Greece. The Greek identity is thus on new, European tracks. Whether this was only an episode or a permanent shift is a point to bear in mind for future research.

Contrast this with Portugal, where 'reactive adaptation' – dictated by the domestic political elite – persists. At the outset, the Portuguese saw the Convention as a dangerous German plot, but eventually they fell in line with the 'politically correct' orthodoxy and argued that the Convention was a very good thing indeed. In between, there was no clear identity shift in terms of asking themselves significant and radical questions about Europe: politics and discourse 'as usual' was the final result.

Spain presents both evidence of the Europeanization of the discourse and of the 'domestication' of Europe. Let us look at 'domestication' first before proceeding to address broader issues about both this and Europeanization in the final section of this essay. Domestic political concerns played a large role in how the Convention was approached by Spanish political elites. One of the major preoccupations of the government was to avoid domestic spillover of debates on 'federalism' and 'constitution'. The government tried to pre-empt the spillover of these discussions from the EU level to the domestic level, and thus was very cautious – and often sceptical – about the use of these terms in the Convention. The territorial distribution of power at home was an issue far too important not to constrain positions on the Convention, especially under conditions of extraordinary 'regional' mobilization. The reference is to the Basque and Catalan parallel Conventions pressing the government 'from below'. There was a lively, sometimes hot, debate at home, but the official positions of the government seemed to acknowledge only the presence of CoR on crucial questions of territorial autonomy.

THE EUROPEANIZATION OR DOMESTICATION OF EUROPE?

The Spanish case shows how identity politics works in two directions – a point made by Risse in his recent analysis of the Euro's impact on national identities (Risse 2003). One direction is from the EU to domestic identity: a major constitutional debate at the Convention level forced the Spanish political elites to ask what the identity of Spain as European 'citizen' is. There was a clear discontinuity in that for many years the Spanish identity in Europe was linked to the impact of the EU on democratization in Spain.

Now all sorts of new questions, such as those related to federalism and defence policy, have come to the fore. To make the process more complicated, the Convention interacted with the war in Iraq. Spain found itself closer to the US (with the Italians) rather than Germany and France at a time in which the Convention was discussing the future of security and defence policy in the EU. As mentioned above, the Europeanization of identity was somewhat counterbalanced by the domestication of Europe. Take the issue of terrorism: it enabled the Spanish government to use 'Europe' as a discursive lever for legitimacy. In this case, it was 'Europe' that was brought into the domestic arena, not vice versa. Terrorism has been one of the major concerns of Spanish public opinion, and by playing this card the government has reframed a top domestic priority (and a clear identity fracture) as a 'European' priority.

Italy belongs to the group of European countries where the citizens trust 'Europe' more than national institutions. Despite some flavours of Euro-scepticism and national 'pride' within the Berlusconi government, the Italians already share important components of a European political identity: trust and belief in the legitimacy of European institutions, and of 'the EU as polity'. It is hard to say if the Convention has made any difference in this respect. The Italians have been very little informed on the work of the Convention and, when they have been, it has happened primarily with direct reference to domestic politics – with a few, relevant exceptions, including Giuliano Amato's 'letters from Europe' posted to the daily *Il Sole-24 Ore*. The political discourse surrounding the Convention has been – broadly speaking – split between President Ciampi's enthusiastic European rhetoric and Prime Minister Berlusconi's more ambiguous, often elusive and sometimes incoherent speeches. No specific new theme (or new approaches to old themes) has so far trickled down to the domestic political debate from the Convention.

The applicant countries have a lot in common as far as the impact on ideas and identities is concerned. In all countries, the main issue under scrutiny was not the transformation of Europe, but membership. Attention was captured by the pros and cons (Malta, Turkey) of EU membership (less so in Cyprus due to unchallenged faith in the pros of membership). However, as anticipated above, in these countries the participation of national Convention representatives has delivered the idea of a more friendly and open EU, thereby raising the perception of the legitimacy of European institutions. Furthermore, EU-related discussions – both on the Convention and, particularly, on membership – have initiated a public

TABLE 4
EUROPEAN AND NATIONAL IDENTITY 'IN THE NEAR FUTURE DO YOU SEE
YOURSELF AS ... ?'

ITALY	Autumn 2001	Spring 2003	Autumn 2003
Italian only	31	26	25
Italian and European	57	58	60
European and Italian	6	10	8
European only	3	3	4
GREECE	**Autumn 2001**	**Spring 2003**	**Autumn 2003**
Greek only	58	53	51
Greek and European	35	41	42
European and Greek	4	3	4
European only	2	3	2
SPAIN	**Autumn 2001**	**Spring 2003**	**Autumn 2003**
Spanish only	50	55	29
Spanish and European	42	39	59
European and Spanish	5	4	6
European only	2	1	4
PORTUGAL	**Autumn 2001**	**Spring 2003**	**Autumn 2003**
Portuguese only	51	49	51
Portuguese and European	43	43	43
European and Portuguese	2	4	3
European only	3	3	2
CYPRUS	**Autumn 2001**	**Spring 2003**	**Autumn 2003**
Cypriot only	34	25	37
Cypriot and European	53	63	53
European and Cypriot	7	8	5
European only	2	1	3
MALTA	**Autumn 2001**	**Spring 2003**	**Autumn 2003**
Maltese only	45	30	35
Maltese and European	49	53	54
European and Maltese	-	6	5
European only	1	1	2
TURKEY	**Autumn 2001**	**Spring 2003**	**Autumn 2003**
Turkish only	57	62	45
Turkish and European	32	42	44
European And Turkish	3	-	5
European only	6	1	3

debate on Europe that has not been limited to a cost-benefit calculation but
has included a reflection on national identities and, more broadly, on what
it means to be European. The degree of self-reflection does not even come
close to what Habermas (2001) would call for, but it is not without
significance. Looking at the candidate countries, the feeling of being
European increased a little among Cypriot, Maltese and Turkish citizens

TABLE 5
SUPPORT FOR EUROPEAN UNION MEMBERSHIP 'GENERALLY SPEAKING,
DO YOU THINK YOUR COUNTRY'S MEMBERSHIP OF THE EUROPEAN
UNION IS A ... ?'

ITALY	Autumn 2001	Spring 2003	Autumn 2003
Bad thing	5	6	10
Good thing	64	64	58
GREECE	Autumn 2001	Spring 2003	Autumn 2003
Bad thing	7	8	7
Good thing	68	61	62
SPAIN	Autumn 2001	Spring 2003	Autumn 2003
Bad thing	7	6	7
Good thing	57	62	62
PORTUGAL	Autumn 2001	Spring 2003	Autumn 2003
Bad thing	8	9	11
Good thing	63	61	55
CYPRUS	Autumn 2001	Spring 2003	Autumn 2003
Bad thing	13	4	11
Neither good nor bad	31	21	26
Good thing	51	72	59
MALTA	Autumn 2001	Spring 2003	Autumn 2003
Bad thing	31	19	17
Neither good nor bad	25	24	22
Good thing	39	51	55
TURKEY	Autumn 2001	Spring 2003	Autumn 2003
Bad thing	14	11	10
Neither good nor bad	18	14	18
Good thing	59	67	67

between autumn 2001 and spring 2003 (Table 4). Support for EU
membership (Table 5) grew in the same period. Trust in EU institutions
(Table 6) confirms a pattern of political socialization within the EU system.
All these aspects related to public opinion in these countries are
accompanied by an increase in self-assessed knowledge of the EU
(as defined in Table 7).

Finally, participation at the Convention has produced social
learning. Both Cyprus and Turkey provide evidence that interaction at
the European table fostered learning of formal and informal rules of
the game. This was not limited to top political interaction within the
Convention. For Turkish political parties, the Convention was instrumental in bringing closer – and often facilitating new contact – with their
counterparts in EU member states.

TABLE 6
TRUST IN THE EU 'DO YOU TEND TO TRUST OR NOT TO TRUST THE EU?'

ITALY	Autumn 2001	Spring 2002	Autumn 2003
Tend not to trust	17	20	25
Tend to trust	65	62	57
GREECE	Autumn 2001	Spring 2002	Autumn 2003
Tend not to trust	22	34	30
Tend to trust	70	58	65
SPAIN	Autumn 2001	Spring 2002	Autumn 2003
Tend not to trust	24	31	30
Tend to trust	66	57	57
PORTUGAL	Autumn 2001	Spring 2002	Autumn 2003
Tend not to trust	22	19	25
Tend to trust	69	66	61
CYPRUS	Autumn 2001	Spring 2003	Autumn 2003
Tend not to trust	26	13	20
Tend to trust	62	78	65
MALTA	Autumn 2001	Spring 2003	Autumn 2003
Tend not to trust	35	31	32
Tend to trust	46	54	53
TURKEY	Autumn 2001	Spring 2003	Autumn 2003
Tend not to trust	34	38	40
Tend to trust	53	49	50

TABLE 7
SELF-ASSESSED KNOWLEDGE OF THE EU 'HOW MUCH DO YOU FEEL YOU KNOW
ABOUT THE EU, ITS POLICIES, ITS INSTITUTIONS AND BODIES?'

CYPRUS	Autumn 2001	Spring 2003	Autumn 2003
Mean	4.61	5.16	4.92
MALTA	Autumn 2001	Spring 2003	Autumn 2003
Mean	4.34	5.33	4.88
TURKEY	Autumn 2001	Spring 2003	Autumn 2003
Mean	3.69	3.77	3.74

Note: Respondents were asked to use the following scale: 1-2 = nothing; 3-5 = a bit;
6-8 = quite a lot; 9-10 = a great deal.

CONCLUSIONS

Our argument in this essay and more generally in the project is that the
Convention's major potential was in terms of process rather than outcome.
Its potential in terms of mobilization was considerable. The empirical
evidence presented here shows that political mobilization was higher at
the level of political elites and party politics than at the level of society.

Indeed, social mobilization was limited and often 'absorbed' by party politics. NGOs were mobilized when they saw the Convention as an opportune structure to advance positions that were difficult to achieve in a domestic context. The Convention made governments more open in terms of information released through official websites, higher institutional transparency and some attempts to stimulate participation. As such, this was an improvement on domestic policy styles, but there was far less social participation than expected.

It is difficult to answer the question of why the dog of mobilization did not bark at the societal level. There is plenty of empirical evidence in our country reports pointing to structural problems of state-society relations, political centralization of key decisions, lack of consultative traditions, pre-eminence of informal and opaque networking of narrow elites, and intellectuals aligned to party-positions – hence limited in their ideational autonomy.

Yet – as Yannis warns us in his report on Greece – we cannot put the blame on member states. Poor results are also connected to the long-standing problem of the EU democratic deficit. In this respect, the Convention tried to innovate as much as possible in relation to past experience. It set bold goals of participation and 'listening' to society. As we have argued, judged by its own past standards, the EU has scored well with the Convention.

Despite limited (yet by no means trivial) social participation, the more interesting result of the Convention relates to identity politics. For those who, in South European countries, took part in the debate, the Convention acted as a massive interrogation of who we are, what is Europe, and what does it mean to us to be European. There has been more than one attempt to domesticate Europe and go back to the usual patterns of domestic politics and national identities, but there is also evidence of identities becoming more Europeanized. The debate on the Preamble of the Draft Constitution and reference therein to the common roots of the EU was a typical discussion in which answering the question 'what qualifies us as a political community?' was unavoidable.

The jury on the net effect of Europeanization and domestication is still out – and will be out for a while longer. The Convention was only an episode of a long-term process of co-evolution of national and European identities, but definitely not an irrelevant one.

NOTES

1. The website is www.europa.eu.int/futurum/index_en.htm.
2. The literature on European consititutionalism is large. Some recent contributions are provided by Börzel and Risse (2001); Joerges, Mény and Weiler (2000), and Weiler (1999). On the Convention see Norman (2003) and Shaw *et al.* (2003).

3. One possible exception is Malta, where there are – by the standards of a small country – numerous academics working on aspects of European Studies. Add to this that not all Maltese intellectuals necessarily live in Malta – as Peter Xuereb noted in an email exchange with us; many contribute to the national debate from their base all over Europe and beyond.

4. In small countries like Malta, however, intellectuals have a high profile and easy access to the media. Many are themselves politicians or regular contributors to newspapers and television. We are grateful to Peter Xuereb for this comment.

5. Yet the reader should also consider the impact of the Greek presidency of the EU (January–June 2003) in raising public awareness of the EU.

6. Over the last decade, however, three of the four main political parties have been supporting federalism, although admittedly not always analyzing in detail what they meant by this. We thank Susannah Verney for this observation.

REFERENCES

Börzel, T. and T. Risse (2001): 'The Post-Nice Agenda of the European Union: What's the Problem, How to Deal with It, and What to Avoid', *Policy Papers Series on Constitutional Reform of the European Union 1*, Florence: European University Institute, Robert Schuman Centre.

Cerutti, F. (2001): 'Towards the Political Identity of the Europeans. An Introduction', in F. Cerutti and E. Rudolph (eds.), *A Soul for Europe, Volume 1: On the Political and Cultural Identity of the Europeans. A Reader*, Leuven: Peeters, pp.1–32.

Cerutti, F. (2003): 'A Political Identity of the Europeans?', *Thesis Eleven 72*, pp.26–45.

de Witte, B. (ed.) (2003): *Ten Reflections on the Constitutional Treaty for Europe*, Florence: EUI, Robert Schuman Centre for Advanced Studies.

Eriksen, E.O., E.J. Fossum and J.A. Menéndez (eds.) (2001): *The Chartering of Europe. The Charter of Fundamental Rights in Context*, Report No.8, Oslo: Arena.

European Commission (2001): *White Paper on Governance* COM (2001) 428, Brussels, 25 July 2001.

European Council (2001): *Laeken Declaration on the Future of Europe*, Attachment to the Presidency Conclusions, European Council Meeting in Laeken, 14–15 December 2001 (SN300/01 ADD1).

Featherstone, K. and C.M. Radaelli (eds.) (2003): *The Politics of Europeanization*, Oxford: Oxford University Press.

Gröte J. and Gibkpi B. (eds.) (2002): *Participatory Governance. Political and Societal Implications*, Opladen: Leske & Budrich.

Habermas, J. (2001): *So, Why Does Europe Need a Constitution?*, Policy Papers Series on Constitutional Reform of the European Union No.2, Florence: EUI, Robert Schuman Centre.

Joerges, C., Y. Mény and J.H.H. Weiler (eds.) (2000): *What Kind of Constitution for What Kind of Polity? Responses to Joschka Fischer*, Florence and Cambridge, MA: Robert Schuman Centre and Harvard Law School.

Joerges, C., Y. Mény and J.H.H. Weiler (eds.) (2001): *Symposium: Responses to the European Commission's White Paper on Governance*, Florence and Cambridge, MA: Robert Schuman Centre and Harvard Law School.

Lucarelli, S. and R. Menotti (2002): 'No-Constructivists' Land. IR in Italy in the 1990s', *Journal of International Relations and Development 5/2*, pp.114–42.

Menéndez, A.J. (2002): 'Chartering Europe: Legal Status and Policy Implications of the Charter of Fundamental Rights of the European Union', *Journal of Common Market Studies 40/3*, pp.471–90.

Musil, R. (1996): *Der Mann ohne Eigenshaften* [The Man without Qualities, Volume 1: A Sort of Introduction and Pseudo-Reality Prevails], New York: Vintage Books, reprint.

Norman, P. (2003): *The Accidental Constitution. The Story of the EU Convention, Eurocomment*, Brussels.

Radaelli, C.M. (1999): *Technocracy in the European Union*, Harlow: Longman.

Risse, T. (2003): 'The Euro between National and European Identity', *Journal of European Public Policy* 10/4, pp.487–505.

Scharpf, F.W. (1997): 'Economic Integration, Democracy and the Welfare State', *Journal of European Public Policy* 4/1, pp.18–36.

Shaw, J., Magnette, P., Hoffmann, L. and Verges, A. (eds.) (2003): *Convention on the Future of Europe: Working Towards an EU Constitution*, Kogan Page, London.

Weiler, J.H.H. (1999): *The Constitution of Europe: 'Do the New Clothes have an Emperor?' and other Essays on European Integration*, Cambridge and New York: Cambridge University Press.

Constructing European Constitutional Discourse? Arguments for Common Values in the European Convention

DANIELA PIANA

INTRODUCTION

The European Convention for the future of Europe was a crucial event in terms of its political and institutional impact as well as its symbolic value. Strangely enough, though, as Sonia Lucarelli and Claudio Radaelli note in their introduction, few political scientists have analysed it in terms of process. The studies focusing on the Council of Nice remain the essential point of reference (Stubb 2002). For the time being, the majority of studies of the European Convention are framed within constitutional law (Bilancia 2002; Weiler 1999, 2002) or, more generally speaking, within the field of legal studies (Manzella 2002). This explains the existing emphasis on formal, procedural aspects (Lenaerts and Desormer 2002; Rosenfeld 2003). Apart from legal interpretations, there are also a wide range of theoretical and philosophical considerations, concerned above all with the justification of constitutional principles (Pernice 2002), the legitimization of European law and the historical origins of the European constitution – the latter being interpreted as the follow-up to a revision of the Treaties (de Witte 2002a, 2002b). The legal approaches tend to focus much more on an evaluation of the outcome of the Convention rather than on any explanation of the process. As a consequence, they fail to grasp some interesting aspects, mainly related to its symbolic, discursive and cognitive dimensions.

In this essay, I focus these dimensions in order to highlight the role played by ideas, knowledge and beliefs in the process of building a constitutional discourse inside the Convention. I use the concept of a deliberative arena as a heuristic tool to point out the creation and the construction of arguments used to compose the discourse about the European Constitution. Therefore, my insight into the Convention will select some aspects of the process – those related to 'arguing' activities (Elster 1993) – and will interpret it as a broad and multiple-voiced process of construction of collective, practical reasoning (Wright 1963). The analysis and the reconstruction of the underlying premises will provide evidence of the innovative capacity of the Convention concerning ideas, values and arguments. Hence, the analysis will not deal with the explanation of the whole outcome of the Convention. The purpose here is limited to the reconstruction of the main arguments proposed inside the Convention in order to argue for common constitutional values. This reconstruction, even though not fully comprehensive of the whole 'decisional process' of the Convention, can show that deliberation has represented in this case, a method of arguing and debating that is able to produce ideational innovation, both at the level of new interpretation of institutionalized principles and at the level of production of new normative arguments to support common values (Bacharach and Lawler 1984).

The organization of the essay is simple. I will first present the analytical framework of deliberative democracy and explain my research design, based on the analysis of the Convention as a deliberative arena. I will then examine empirical evidence across different ideational innovations and conclude with a note on the potential of argumentative-ideational explanations of the European Convention.

DELIBERATION: A THEORETICAL PERSPECTIVE FOR EUROPEAN DEMOCRATIC LIFE

Over the past two decades, political studies have seen a broad paradigm shift resulting from a widespread criticism of positivistic and rationalistic views. This shift includes what has been called the 'argumentative turn' (Fischer and Forester 1993). An increasing focus on the argumentative aspects of political behaviour and on the constructivist perspective within the theoretical paradigm used to interpret political and social phenomena has been accompanied by an increasingly strong emphasis in the social sciences on communicative and discursive interaction as factors capable of affecting the causal chain of social process (Berger and Luckmann 1966; Majone 1989).[1] Concepts such as 'communicative rationality' (Habermas 1969) and 'discursive democracy' (Dryzek, 1990) have led in the same direction, encouraging scholars to accept the commonly held belief that decision-making in social processes is more the outcome of the mutual adjustment of the different views and ideas introduced by social players than any sequential, objective chain of decisions (Pelletier *et al.* 1999).

One of the reasons why this view has found widespread support in the field of political theory and in the political sciences in general is the existence of certain phenomena that have rendered previously held theoretical views inadequate. One of these phenomena is the so-called 'postmodern state' (Habermas 1996, 2000). This state is characterized by forms of participation in decision-making and of governance of collective action that were not present in the classical modern state (Marks, Hooghe and Blanck 1996). An aspect of the postmodern state that has been the target of considerable attention is the discursive nature of its democratic life. Democracy in a post-national state (Shaw 1999) is more the result of deliberation and discursive interaction than of voting and representative election (Susskind and Cruikshank 1987). This view is in keeping with those studies based on the concept of deliberation as a kind of alternative approach to collective equilibrium and collective choice.

Some fundamental points raised by this literature have to be recalled in order to understand the meaning of deliberation in the EU context and, specifically, in this essay. Firstly, deliberation is conceived as a kind of collective process that goes far beyond bargaining and vote procedure. This is due to the fact that deliberation is grounded in common values and normative arguments, before and instead of being grounded in the strategic communication of specific and partisan interests (Elster 1998). Secondly, deliberation is strongly related to a supranational view of political life or, more generally speaking, to a non-nationally conceived view of democracy. This holds for every kind of public sphere where deliberation takes place. The main meaning of deliberation is, therefore, that civil society, as the body sharing common values and common normative arguments, is the true source of democratic rationality. Furthermore, national discourses are embedded in a wider discourse related to people that, equally and fairly, participate in the construction of a political discourse independently from their national identity. Finally, deliberation appears to be the *conditio sine qua non* of democratic debate in a public sphere because 'communicative rationality' anticipates strategic and instrumental rationality. Those aspects play a different role in a prescriptive use and a descriptive use of the deliberative theory. In the first case, the aspects listed before represent the conditions that have to be fulfilled in order to realize what deliberative theorists call a better model of democracy (Habermas 1998). In the second case, one looks at a political arena and assesses the extent to which it is deliberative. To what extent is deliberation the main method of decision-making? This is a typical question for the descriptive-empirical use of the theory.

What are the implications for the analysis of European arenas? Some European scholars have argued that the European Union (EU) is a special kind of political organization (Ham 2001). Some see it as a sort of postmodern or post-national state (Habermas 1998). According to them, democratic life in the EU would seem to be more easily understandable when seen in terms of 'deliberative democracy' – where 'deliberative' refers to the extensive participation of social and institutional players in European governance (Przeworski, Stokes and Manin 1999). In any case, it has been difficult to assess if the deliberative approach to EU decision-making really grasps the fundamental aspects that make the EU something substantially different from other political spaces. Is the extension of deliberative models of decision-making what makes the EU special? Or is the EU 'politics as usual'?

The jury is still out, but the European Convention and, more generally, the constitution-making processes present fertile terrain for this type of analysis. Once again, prescriptive and descriptive approaches have to be distinguished. Some legal scholars have pointed out that one of the most challenging weaknesses of the EU is the paucity and, at times, the total absence of any constitutional debate or 'constitutional discourse' (Weiler 1999; Ward 2001). Yet the Convention may represent a qualitative leap in the history of European integration. One, though, has to be precise about what this means. Indeed, the debate on new governance and the European Constitution has not focused on the constitutional dimension of democracy within the EU – that is, the constitutional constraints on the legitimate exercise of political power – but the participative aspects of the EU's decision-making processes (Garcia 1993). This dimension of participatory governance – the argument goes – is empowered by the adoption of a constitution. In fact, the constitution defines spaces and methods of participation. In turn, this may legitimize and justify the decisions taken: 'there will be no remedy for the legitimation deficit, however, without a European public sphere – a network that gives citizens of all member states an equal opportunity to take part in an encompassing process of focused political communication' (Habermas 2001: 17). The deliberative dimension of European policy-making has been acknowledged by some scholars (Follesdal 2000; Magnette 1999) as being one of the main features of the EU's constitutionally based decisional style. Seen from this perspective, the European Constitution can be built up through deliberation (Habermas 1995).

Here again, the empirical accuracy (as opposed to normative precision) of these statements is another matter. Many criticisms can be raised, for example, concerning the causal relationship implicit in the deliberative approach to constitution-making in the EU. There must be an assumption of some form of common values – which make deliberation effective. One can find them in the common identity of people participating in the debate. Therefore, in order to talk correctly about deliberation, it seems that the existence of a common identity should be previously verified (Scharpf 1997; Closa 1998).

One can see, then, that the empirical analysis of the Convention in terms of deliberative democracy raises some difficulties. This is the reason for which I have adopted the concept of the deliberative arena with the caveats mentioned above. To repeat: throughout this essay, deliberation is more a guide in the reconstruction of some of the main arguments used to defend a normative ground able to support a constitutional discourse about the European democracy, than a concept which supposedly explains how actors have achieved some common results at the end of their work inside the Convention.

THE EUROPEAN CONVENTION AS A DELIBERATIVE ARENA

When political scientists talk about deliberative arenas they usually refer to a highly diversified set of collective experiences which seem to share certain fundamental features (Bobbio 2002). Despite differences in the extension of participation, duration and method of working, the 'deliberative arena' concept can be used to identify a political public space with certain common properties. When these features occur, we are dealing with a deliberative arena.[2] Furthermore, these features:

- are created *ad hoc* in order to manage specific collective dilemmas;
- are highly structured and organized;
- are such that their output is not legally binding;
- are strongly inclusive[3] (Goodin 2000); and
- work through the mechanism of deliberation.

Deliberation means that voting and bargaining are embedded in a political discourse where the common ground is composed of shared values and common beliefs concerning what ought to be done in a certain public space of collective action. In this essay, the 'deliberative arena' concept is a tool to enquire into the premises that have been elaborated and proposed inside the Convention concerning what the EU should be and how it should work out in current policy-making. Hence, the European Convention is examined in terms of the problem-specificity of its mission, its method of working, and the rules working out the access of ideas and arguments to the fora of decision (Habermas 1989).

The Declaration of Laeken stated that the European Convention was designed to resolve a set of problems that the European Council had failed to solve (see also the introduction to this volume). These problems were all linked to the future of the European Union and concerned both its internal structure and its external action. Therefore, the European Convention was created as a specific arena with a specific mandate on the basis of the previous experience of the Convention of the Charter of Fundamental Rights. The Convention was asked to provide a collective answer to the problem of the reorganization of the EU. This reorganization involves both the institutional structures of the EU and the very constitutional principles underlying the process of European integration. From the point of view of the analysis presented here, the questions faced by the Convention can be summarized in three main orders of problem: 'who are we?' (Ham 2001) – our political and cultural identity; 'where are we going to?' (Wiener 2002) – the model of the EU that we would like to plan and to implement; and 'which instruments and which strategies do we have in order to achieve our goal?'[4]

The choice to create a specific arena where not only representatives of national institutional interests can get access to the debate, but where civil society, in the broadest sense of the word, can advance its own proposals, seems to be justified by common ideas. European constitutional discourse should be democratic and supranational – that is to say that is has to be justified and grounded on the basis of common ideas (Diez 1999). This choice, finally, created the opportunity for actors moving beyond the political arena and the institutional triangle of the EU to create ideas, exploit cognitive resources and mobilize arguments.[5] In terms of participation, the Convention represented a formidable opportunity to test the argument that civil society, more than institutional actors and national states, shares ideas and normative frames (Surel 2000; Christiansen, Jorgensen and Wiener 2001).

The main problems raised by the Declaration of Laeken were divided into a series of sub-problems, corresponding to the parts expected to be included in the Constitutional Treaty. Each sub-problem was considered to be a separate issue, and its analysis was delegated to a working group composed of members of the Convention and chosen experts. These groups included policy-makers, representatives taking part in the Convention and experts. Their mandate was to propose a draft formula to be integrated into the final text to be submitted by the Convention to the Intergovernmental Conference.[6] Some working groups started meeting once the European Convention had opened its session, while other additional groups were organized some months later (the 'External Action', 'Defence', 'Simplification' and 'Freedom, Security and Justice' groups). The 'Freedom, Security and Justice' group, whose job was to focus on the social aspects of Europe,[7] was in a sense one of the most active sub-arenas in terms of ideational innovation.

The main debate evolved during the plenary sessions of the Convention, while parallel working sessions were organized from one session to the other – in particular for those working groups focusing on the specific issues in question. The final result of the official debate and the informal consultation took the form of a document identifying policy solutions, institutional settings and constitutional principles. The degree of consensus and the reasons for dissent were specified for each proposal. Therefore, the working method and the access to the arena followed broadly the main principles of accountability and of open democracy stated in the Declaration of Laeken. These principles have been accepted and put in practice firstly by the members of the Praesidium (Cartabia 2002). This feature reflects the need for transparency and clarity of the procedures used within the European Convention – a specific feature of deliberative arenas. Not only were the actions and interaction of the official delegates to the European Convention regulated by a method, but public participation and consultation with civil society were placed in a specific parallel arena – that is, the Forum.[8] Clearly, the feeling was that representative mechanisms of legitimization necessitated an additional form of wider social legitimization.

The Convention worked in three stages – that is, 'listening and hearing', 'reflection' and 'making proposals' (see the introduction to this volume). Listening and reflective understanding are crucial to the deliberative nature of the arena (Weiler 1997). The vice-president of the Convention, Dehaene, stated at the very beginning that one of the most important aspects of the mission of the Praesidium was the ongoing consultation with civil society and public opinion in general. The ideas submitted in the Forum circulated among the members of the Convention. In such a way, more than one channel of communication would emerge – interconnecting the Praesidium with civil society (Dehaene 2002).

Formal rules of access to the Convention and the Presidium were as important as the routines established and fixed during the 15 months of work. First of all, participants to the Convention and participants to the Forum were crucially different. Their interactions were regulated inside the plenary sessions by the method of work and presentation of arguments/ positions, while outside the Convention, informal meetings occurred. The presence of actors coming from the Commission and the Parliament increased the importance of the topic of institutional reforms. In turn, this brought to the Convention more technical elements and legal questions.

As for the Forum, there were different categories of actors – as on the website of the Convention – political and public authorities, socio-economic organizations, academies and think tanks, non-governmental organizations, civil society schools of thought and others. The exchange of opinions between Forum and Convention took an informal shape, and became more or less routinized. In particular, the Economic and Social Committee and the Committee of the Regions (CoR) were granted access to the Praesidium with meetings with individual Praesidium members.

Having described how access to the Convention was regulated formally and informally, what about the quality of the arguments? It is to this question that I now turn, paying particular attention to values and normative concepts. In the remainder of the essay I will refer to the whole set of participants to the Forum, except the academies and the think tanks (see, however, Closa, this volume, on intellectuals and think tanks in Spain, as well as the country reports).

A NEW INTERPRETATION OF INSTITUTIONAL LEGACIES: THE MULTI-LEVEL STRUCTURE OF EUROPEAN GOVERNANCE

The main arguments proffered by those participating in the European Convention and the Forum seem to converge (unintentionally) towards certain common principles and values. The reference is, above all, to the principles of subsidiarity and participation. The first of these principles was introduced by the Maastricht Treaty (Art. 3b). The second was strongly stressed in the White Paper on Governance (European Commission 2001). In the Convention, the most interesting new item concerns the link between the idea of the EU working according to the subsidiarity principle and the idea of an open, broadly shared process of European policy-making. This constituted one of the most widely agreed answers to the problem raised in Laeken concerning the legitimacy and the effectiveness of the EU.[10]

During the Convention debate, two different conceptions of subsidiarity were advanced. The first one, which was employed in the legal texts, involves the relationship between levels of power: to be more precise, it concerns the relationship between the national and European decisional levels. The second one, which has been strongly defended by certain social and economic associations (Eurochambers and the European Economic and Social Committee [EESC]),[11] is more closely related to local action and the horizontal interpretation of the same principle. The debate over subsidiarity in the Treaty thus focused on this distinction. In a number of different documents, CoR and local associations have underlined the fact that one aspect of European integration is constituted by 'territorial cohesion' (Assembly of European Regions 2002; see also Keating, this issue).[12]

While the interpretation of the local authorities and CoR placed considerable importance on the multi-level organization of European governance, the socio-economic players' interpretation linked subsidiarity to the importance of social dialogue. Indeed, subsidiarity was interpreted in a horizontal sense. The argument was that local-level social cooperation and dialogue can render the policy-making process much more democratic and much more responsive to needs and problems as perceived by local communities (Eurochambers 2002). Obviously, particular importance was given to the concept of solving problems via interaction at the local level. Here, the collective interest revolves around the commercial activities of economic agents operating in the commercial field and owners of medium and small enterprises, where interests are linked to the good functioning of the local market system. This section of the economy perceives the EU as an organization that needs to be particularly aware of local capacity and of the freedom available to regulate locally-based activities.

The defence of the local level of governance has justified the defence of the subsidiarity principle. Throughout the Convention, subsidiarity emerged as a fully fledged political issue, rather than a purely legal/ technical issue. It was not related to the discussion on the structure of the EU – neither the Praesidium nor the working groups were concerned about the opportunity of giving formal and political power to regions – but to the substantive aspect of policy-making. This is confirmed not only by the views of the Regions (Assembly of European Regions, 2002), but also by the proposals made by citizens' associations and social movements (such as the Permanent Forum of Civil Society and ATTAC – *Association pour une Taxation des Transactions financières pour l'Aide aux Citoyens*). Here, great emphasis was placed on the idea that subsidiarity enhances democratic participation in local decision-making.

The interpretation of the subsidiarity principle that best summarizes these aspects is the concept of participatory democracy, usually perceived as grounded in a bottom-up form of democratic policy-making. The next step was from participatory democracy to social dialogue. Participation was linked to consultation with society and to the enhancement of social dialogue.[13] Therefore, the Convention as a discursive arena was instrumental in producing a sort of argumentative expansion. Subsidiarity merged with participation and social dialogue, thus creating the premises of a strong argument. This argument can be outlined as follows. Subsidiarity means making decisions as closely in keeping with the interests of stakeholders as possible. The implication is that the more this principle is applied, the more the decision-making process is participatory. Finally, the subsidiarity principle has to be made effective both through social dialogue and through local action.

At the end of the Convention as an argumentative process, the subsidiarity principle was charged with a normative value. Now it has acquired a sort of ethical meaning concerning the fairness and the legitimacy of European decision-making (Weick 1995). Contrast this with the narrower debate on the organizational structure of the EU in relation to subsidiarity, especially the so-called 'federalist debate' (a debate that cropped up in several of the countries reviewed by the other contributors to this volume, such as Spain and Greece). Civil society was less interested in this discussion on federalism. Only a few groups elaborated federal proposals for institutional design, mainly focusing on the role of the Parliament – as the institution that is supposed to represent the 'people of Europe' – and the Commission.

'SOCIAL EUROPE' AS A LOGICAL CONSEQUENCE OF ARGUING

Another crucial element of ideational innovation within the Convention was the social dimension of the EU. If we look at the debate, great emphasis seems to have been placed on the concept of 'social cohesion'. If one looks at outcome alone, the Convention seems to have somewhat missed the opportunity to define 'social Europe', which remains a hotly debated question (Kleinman 2002). However, the idea of 'social Europe' was debated at length in the Convention and its working groups.

There was an interesting convergence of ideas submitted by several different players. One of these is the EESC (CONV 513/03). It argued that one of the most important reasons for the weakness of the EU is the lack of 'social governance'. Such governance is called for in order to balance the economic and monetary dimensions of European integration. According to the EESC, social priorities should be strongly tied to the economic aspects of EU integration: 'economic and social cohesion is an essential factor in shaping European identity, particularly when an adequate redistribution of resources is taken into account, as a redistribution that is not the result of a bargaining among states' (CONV 513/03). Here, the emphasis is on the word 'social', a connotation of a European identity which has still to be clearly defined.

A significant part of the European Convention debate aimed to create a conceptual link between three concepts, all of which share the word 'social': 'social governance', 'social progress' (European Confederation of Workers Co-operatives, Social Co-operatives and Participative Enterprises – CECOP), 'European social model' (*Confédération Générale du Travail* – CGT; *Deutsche Gewerkschaftbund* – DGB, Federal German Trade Union). This link is of considerable interest as it forged a discursive arena with a network of players who recognize themselves as being part of European social governance. The question of the social dimension of European integration is one that is shared by trade unions, business associations and civil society. One of the commonly shared ideas within this network is that the EU itself ought to be an arena in which social demands are suitably addressed. Different justifications are given for this position. In the case of trade unions and business associations, the main argument is that there is a need to coordinate, at the trans-national level, the outcome of the collective bargaining of social-economic governance. Of course, trade unions also underline the importance of social justice, whereas entrepreneurial associations are more concerned with their role in European social policy.

From the point of view of civil society networks and associations, the justification for the social dimension of integration is based on the existence of a European policy – with social cohesion as one of the main objectives – which goes beyond the priorities of individual member states (Permanent Forum of Civil Society).[14] The definition of a 'social Europe' and the identification of an area where European objectives merge with social priorities were taken on board by the working group 'Social Europe'. Civil society has been urging for a stronger social dimension to the European Union, and has been lobbying both the working group and the Praesidium. Meetings with both institutions have taken place during the Convention's 15 months of work, while some representatives of civil society have drawn up a specific set of proposals designed to render the Union more responsive to the needs of society. The working group, in the end, recommended 'the inclusion in Article 3 ... of full employment, social justice, social peace, sustainable development, economic, social and territorial cohesion, social market economy, quality of labour, permanent learning, social inclusion, high level of social assurance, equal opportunities, rights of children, high level of public health, efficient social and public services' (CONV 516/1/03 REV 1, p. 2). However, no innovation like this followed in the Draft Constitutional Treaty. Therefore, argumentative innovation about aims and objectives does not imply necessarily innovation about the instruments and the means proposed to obtain those aims.

AN INNOVATIVE VIEW OF EUROPEAN DEMOCRACY

The stress placed on the subsidiarity principle, and the arguments in favour of the social aspects of European integration, should affect the activity of the EU at various levels of governance. They would suggest the statement of jointly defined and agreed guidelines, and call for policy embedded in the local areas where the beneficiaries of such social policy live and work – policies based on equal opportunities, the quality of employment and the concept of life-long learning. Regardless of the level at which such policy is to be implemented, the legitimacy of the decisions taken depends on the openness of participation. These two factors constitute the very basis of the Convention's European constitutional discourse, which consists of a set of premises – discussed below – formulated around a certain specific concept of democracy.

The first of these premises concerns the importance of the proximity of policy-making to stakeholders in enhancing – where possible – the social capital and the social heritage shared by members of local communities. Collective problems can be debated at the community level, but they also need to be solved through the active, crucially important involvement of local players. The second premise concerns the importance of participation and consultation in the policy-making process. When a decision is going to be taken, the participation of the largest possible section of society should be encouraged in order to ensure a more legitimate, justified decision. The third premise regards the importance of positive integration and collective aims rather than that of negative integration and collective rules. As it concerns social justice, sustainable development and social equity, it refers to common aims which ought to direct the decisions taken at all levels of the system of European governance. According to this view, a common social dimension of the EU can be identified, given the existence of shared values and a common identity (Scharpf 1997) that make collective deliberation possible. Only these conditions make it possible to discuss and agree on common aims shared by social partners and social players from within civil society.

These premises enable us to draw conclusions about the nature of democratic life within the EU. A surprising degree of commonality arises from a highly differentiated set of players, each defending their own values. The EU is conceived as an arena where opinions are voiced from all sections of the entire social system and may in fact merge (Hirschman 1970) at all levels of the European governance system. The dimension of participation has thus far received much more attention than representation. Moreover, the legitimacy of political power depends much more on the openness of participation than on the verifiability and the accountability of the outcome. Even if the Convention's mission, according to the Declaration of Laeken, includes both the democratic openness and the effectiveness of the European decision-making process, debate over the last 15 months has clearly placed greater emphasis on the former aspect. According to Scharpf, the legitimacy of European democracy is linked to input rather than output (Scharpf 1999). Given that participation in the decision-making process is more important than controlling and evaluating the outcome, the rights of citizens that the Constitution is expected to grant and to protect are far from being those negative rights postulated by a constitutional vision of democracy (Buchanan and Tullock 1962). Rights of citizenship are not only about the protection of citizens from public authorities (negative rights), but are particularly linked to the right – the *positive* right – to take part in decision-making and in the rule-defining process. The strong emphasis placed on participation in democracy, rather than on the control of democracy, is probably due to the fact that it is more difficult to control and to correct social processes once they have been started. This is because such processes become so complex and multilayered that local players have serious difficulty in controlling the results of decision-making (Bellamy 2001). Therefore, the new EU is to be based on those old values – solidarity, social cohesion, positive rights for citizens – that are already stated in the Charter of Fundamental Rights (Rossi 2001), together with new forms of participation in policy-making within certain protected areas defined by the Constitution itself.

CONCLUSION: DOES IDEATIONAL INNOVATION 'EXPLAIN' THE EUROPEAN CONVENTION?

The European Convention was broadly designed as a deliberative arena. This choice was justified by the idea that some common ground, concerning constitutional issues, does actually exist inside the EU. It is hard to assess to what extent the Convention worked by deliberation instead of being a complex process where deliberation and negotiation interacted. Indeed, this essay is not concerned with this question, as explained in the first two sections. Rather, this essay has sought to shed light on what kind of normative arguments have been produced by civil society and the organizations that have participated in the Forum. These arguments created a common semantic framework, one – I would argue – that gives sense to a specific and well-identified notion of democracy. Of course, the arguments proposed are not the result of an absolutely innovative cognitive action. The mobilization of cognitive resources which has characterized the Forum is embedded in institutionalized principles, legal legacies and previous examples. So, the deliberative aspects of the European Convention can be fully accounted for only if they are considered as a process embedded in the history of ideas and institutions of the EU. Thanks to this common history, a communicative action (Walker forthcoming) characterized by the adjustment and the incremental creation of a common discourse, has been able to take place and develop.

A final consideration is worth stating at this point. Talking about the European Convention from the point of view of deliberation theory allows us to point out the cognitive mobilization that has occurred once a public arena has been opened and regulated in a transparent and accountable way. Actors from civil society and bodies revolving around European institutions participated in the elaboration of ideas and proposals. This wide process – which is mainly cognitive and ideational – does not cover the whole meaning and political results of the Convention. Some cognitive innovations were not accepted as final proposals. In order to explain the whole 'politics of the Convention' and to measure to what extent deliberation and arguing have determined the outcome of the Convention, a more detailed analysis of the debate that took place on the amendments to the Treaty is required. In any case, the empirical study of the semantic and cognitive frames of the constitutional discourse about European democracy, represents a first step towards the overall understanding of what kind of political and institutional entity was produced by the Convention.

NOTES

1. Reference to the philosophy of action and the philosophy of language is, from this point of view, very important. One of the most quoted and highly considered authors is Toulmin (1958).
2. Given that this conclusion results from an inductive generalization, we can still hypothesize the existence of a deliberative arena that does not possess all of these properties.
3. This means that each social player who may be affected by the problem dealt with in the arena's debate has the chance to participate in that debate.
4. Such questions, their meaning, their rationality and their own relevance for the debate about the institutional structure and the fundamental principles of integration are far from being trivial points. Previously, similar questions would have been submitted and assessed in an official, formal manner, and European member states would have decided not to answer them or to answer them by shifting the decisional level (from the internal to the external) or by simply bypassing the problem.
5. This awareness does not appear to be a sufficient reason for claiming that if we look at the outcome of the Convention, we see a product that has been unaffected by side-payments and, more generally speaking, by national and interest-oriented positions.
6. For the follow-up to the working groups' procedure, see the website of the Convention: www.european-convention.eu.int.
7. The group was created in December 2002.
8. The Forum was established on the basis of a specific Article within the regulatory text of the Convention's method of working (Art.9) as a consequence of a proposal made by the vice-president J.-L. Dehaene, and was designed to stress the democratic, participative character of the Convention.
9. I am talking about groups, even if they are not groups in the voluntary, organizational sense of the world. This expression is useful when referring to the set of players that share certain common ideas about social Europe and/or participative democracy and that have contributed towards developing and forging those concepts in a new fashion.

10. The draft of the Constitutional Treaty proposed by Giscard d'Estaing in the autumn of 2002 included the principles of subsidiarity and of proportionality, in keeping with the legacy of the Treaties and of the pattern of European policy-making (Art.I-9.3).
11. All contributions to the Forum can be viewed on the following website: www.europa.eu.int/futurum/forum_convention/doc_en.htm.
12. This is quite a new concept in European discourse, and one that is interestingly included in the Treaty (Art.I-3.3).
13. This point is integrated in the Treaty (Art.I-46.3 and Art.I-47).
14. Parallel debates developed by academic research centres and universities have contributed towards raising interest in European social policy, which up until now has been considered by scholars to be one of the weakest areas of EU policy.

REFERENCES

Assembly of European Regions, 'Meeting with President Valery Giscard d'Estaing', Valencia, 7 March 2002, Contribution by the Assembly of the European Regions, www.european-convention.eu.int.
Bacharach, S.B. and E.J. Lawler (1984): *Bargaining Power. Power, Tactics and Outcomes*, San Francisco: Jossey-Bass Publishers.
Bellamy, R. (2001): 'The Right to have Rights: Citizenship Practice and the Political Constitution of the EU', in R. Bellamy and A. Warleigh (eds.), *Citizenship and Governance in the European Union*, London: Continuum, pp.41–70.
Bellamy, R. and D. Castiglione (2000): 'The Uses of Democracy: Reflexion on the European Democratic Deficit', in Eriksen and Fossum (eds.), *Democracy in the European Union*.
Berger, P.L. and T. Luckmann (1966): *The Social Construction of Reality*, Garden City and New York: Doubleday and Co, pp.65–84.
Bilancia, P. (ed.) (2002): *Il processo costituente europeo*, Milano: Giuffrè.
Bobbio, L. (2002). 'Le arene deliberative', in *Rivista italiana di politiche pubbliche* 3, pp.5–29.
Buchanan, J.M. and G. Tullock (1962): *The Calculus of Consent. Logical Foundations of Constitutional Democracy*, Ann Arbor, MI: Michigan University Press.
Cartabia, M. (2002): 'Riflessioni sulla Convenzione di Laeken: "come se" si trattasse di un metodo costituente', *Quaderni costituzionali* 3, pp.439–48.
Christiansen, T., K.E. Jorgensen and E. Wiener (eds.) (2001): *The Social Construction of Europe*, London: Sage.
Checkel, J.T. (2001): 'The Europeanization of Citizenship', in J. Caporaso, M. Cowles and T. Risse (eds.), *Transforming Europe: Europeanization and Domestic Change*, Ithaca, NY: Cornell University Press.
Checkel, J.T., J.Caporaso and J.Jupille (2003): 'Integrating Institutions: Rationalism, Constructivism and the Study of the European Union. Introduction', *Comparative Political Studies* 36/1–2, pp.7–40, special issue.
Closa, C. (1998): 'European Union Citizenship and Supranational Democracy', in A. Weale and M. Nentwich (eds.), *Political Theory and European Union*, London: Routledge.
de Witte, B. (2002a): 'Simplification and Reorganization of the European Treaties', *Common Market Law Review* 39/6, pp.1255–87.
de Witte, B. (2002b): 'The Closest Thing to a Constitutional Conversation in Europe: The Semi-Permanent Treaty Revision Process', in P. Beaumont, C. Lyons and N. Walker (eds.), *Convergence and Divergence in European Public Law*, Oxford: Hart, pp.39–57.
Dehaene, J.L. (2002): 'Note to the Convention: The Convention and the Forum', www.euconvention.be/contributions/detailsasp?ID = 68.
Diez, T. (1999): 'Speaking "Europe": The Politics of Integration Discourse', *Journal of European Public Policy* 6/4, pp.598–613.
Dryzek, J.S. (1990): *Discursive Democracy*, Cambridge: Cambridge University Press.

Elster, J. (1993): *Arguing and Bargaining in Two Constituent Assemblies*, New Haven, CO: Yale Law School.
Elster, J. (1998): *Deliberative Democracy*, Cambridge: Cambridge University Press.
Eriksen, E.O. and J.E. Fossum (eds.) (2000): *Democracy in the European Union. Integration through Deliberation?*, London: Routledge.
Eurochambres (2002), 'European Convention on the Future of Europe', June, www.european-convention.eu.int.
European Commission (2001): *European Governance: A White Paper*, COM(2001) 428.
Fischer, F. and J. Forester (eds.) (1993): *The Argumentative Turn in Policy Analysis and Planning*, Durham and London: Duke University Press.
Follesdal, A. (2000): 'Subsidiarity and Democratic Deliberation', in Eriksen and Fossum (eds.), *Democracy in the European Union*, pp.85–110.
Garcia, S. (1993): *European Identity and the Search for Legitimacy*, London and New York: Pinter.
Garrett, G. and B.R. Weingast (1993): 'Ideas, Interests and Institutions Constructing the European Community's Internal Market', in J. Goldstein and R. Keohane (eds.), *Ideas and Foreign Policy*, Ithaca, NY: Cornell University Press, pp.173–206.
Goodin, R. (2000): 'Democratic Deliberation Within', *Philosophy and Public Affairs* 29/2, pp.81–109.
Habermas, J. (1984): *The Theory of Communicative Action: Volume 2, Reason and the Rationalization of Society*, Cambridge: Policy Press.
Habermas, J. (1969): *Structural Transformation of the Public Sphere*, Cambridge, MA: MIT Press.
Habermas, J. (1995): *Justification and Application: Remarks on Discourse Ethics*, Cambridge: Polity Press.
Habermas, J. (1996): *Between Facts and Norms. Contribution to a Discourse Theory of Law and Democracy*, Cambridge, MA: The MIT Press.
Habermas, J. (1998): *Die Postnationale Konstellation. Politische Essays*, Frankfurt: Suhrkamp.
Habermas, J. (2000): 'Beyond the Nation-State? On Some Consequences of Economic Globalization', in Eriksen and Fossum (eds.), *Democracy in the European Union*, pp. 29–41.
Ham, P. (2001): *European Integration and Post-Modern Condition Governance, Democracy, Identity*, London: Routledge.
Hirschman, A. (1970): *Exit, Voice and Loyalty*, Cambridge: Cambridge University Press.
Kleinman, M. (2002): *A European Welfare State? European Union Social Policy in Context*, New York: Palgrave.
Lenaerts, K. and M. Desormer (2002): 'Brick for a Constitutional Treaty of the European Union: Values, Objectives and Means', *European Law Review* 27/4, pp.37–407.
Magnette, P. (1999): *La citoyenneté européenne*, Bruxelles: Editions de l'Université de Bruxelles.
Majone, G. (1989): *Evidence, Argument and Persuasion in the Policy Process*, New Haven, CO: Yale University Press.
Manzella, A. (2002): '*La Convenzione e le garanzie dell'allargamento*', *Quaderni costituzionali* 3, pp.463–8.
Marks, G., L. Hooghe and K.Blanck (1996): 'European Integration from the 1980's: State-Centric versus Multi-level Governance', *Journal of Common Market Studies* 34/3, pp.341–78.
Pelletier, D., *et al.* (1999): 'The Shaping of Collective Values through Deliberative Democracy: An Empirical Study from New York's North Country', *Policy Sciences* 32, pp.103–31.
Pernice, I. (2002). 'Multi-Level Constitutionalism in the European Union', in *European Law Review* 27, pp.511–29.

Przeworski, A., S.C. Stokes and B. Manin (1999): 'Elections and Representation', in A. Przeworski, S.C. Stokes and B. Manin (eds.), *Democracy, Accountability and Representation*, Cambridge: Cambridge University Press, pp.29–54.

Rosenfeld, M. (2003): 'The European Convention and Constitutional Making in Philadelphia', *International Journal of Constitutional Law* 1/2, pp.373–8.

Rossi, L.S. (2001): *Carta dei diritti fondamentali e costituzione dell'Unione europea*, Milan: Giuffrè.

Scharpf, F. (1997): *Games Real Actors Play: Actor-Centered Institutionalism in Policy Research*, Boulder, CO: Westview Press.

Scharpf, F. (1999): *Governing in Europe: Effective and Democratic?*, Oxford: Oxford University Press.

Shaw, J. (1999): 'Postnational Constitutionalism in the European Union', *Journal of European Public Policy* 6/4, pp.579–97.

Susskind, L. and J. Cruikshank (1987): *Breaking the Impasse. Consensual Approaches to Resolving Public Disputes*, New York: Basic Books.

Stubb, A. (2002): *Negotiating Flexibility in the European Union: Amsterdam, Nice and Beyond*, Basingstoke: Palgrave.

Surel, Y. (2000): 'L'integration européenne vue par l'approche cognitive et normative des politiques publiques', *Revue française de science politique* 50/4, pp.235–54.

Toulmin, S. (1958): *The Uses of the Argument*, Cambridge: Cambridge University Press.

Walker, N., (forthcoming): 'The Charter of Fundamental Rights of European Union: Legal, Symbolic and Constitutional Implications', in P.J. Cullen and Zervakis, P.A. (eds.): *The Post-Nice Process: Towards a European Constitution?* Bonn: Nomos, pp.119–128.

Ward, I. (2001): 'Beyond Constitutionalism: The Search for a European Political Imagination', *European Law Journal* 7/1, pp.24–40.

Weick, K.E. (1995): *Sensemaking in Organizations*, London: Sage.

Weiler, J. (1997): 'To be a European Citizen. Eros and Civilization', *Journal of European Public Policy* 4/4, pp.459–519.

Weiler, J. (1999): *The Constitution of Europe. Do the New Clothes Have an Emperor? And Other Essay on European Integraton*, London: Sage.

Weiler, J. (2002): 'Diritti umani, costituzionalismo ed integrazione: iconografia e feticismo', *Quaderni costituzionali* 3, pp.521–36.

Wiener, A. (2002). 'Finality vs Enlargement. Constitutive Practices and Opposing Rationale in the Reconstruction of Europe', in *Jean Monnet Working Papers* 8/2, www.jeanmonnetprogram.org/papers /02/020801.html, NYU School of Law.

Wright (von), G.H. (1963): *Norm and Action*, London: Routledge & Kegan Paul.

Italy: A Special Case and a Mixed Record

JESSE SCOTT and FILIPPO VERGARA CAFFARELLI

INTRODUCTION

From the beginning of the 'Future of Europe' process, Italy, as holder of the rotating Presidency of the European Council in the second half of 2003, had ambitions to host the intergovernmental conference (IGC) addressing the negotiation of the new European Treaty for which the European Convention was preparation.

That ambition, however, appeared far clearer than did Italy's attitude towards the Convention itself. On the one hand, Italy is one of the original six signatories of the Rome Treaty and has been a historic stalwart of 'ever closer union'. Both President Carlo Azeglio Ciampi and Prime Minister Silvio Berlusconi laid claim, therefore, to a special Italian moral obligation to lead the way forward to the new Europe of 'Rome II'. On the other hand, since becoming a net contributor to the European Union (EU) in 1996, Italy – like Spain – has begun to question the benefits of integration. The Berlusconi government (since June 2001) contains openly Euro-sceptic elements. Notably, in the build up to the Convention's launch in January 2002, and shortly after the internationally lamented resignation of Europhile Foreign Minister Renato Ruggiero in protest at the government's equivocation on Europe, Berlusconi told the *Financial Times* that Italy had abandoned her established approach. Italy, he said, would 'pursue limited shared sovereignty in the EU, an economy based on liberal free market principles and the country's national interest' ('Berlusconi says Italy will become EU broker', *Financial Times*, 17 January 2002, web edition). In short, it became clear that Italy's positions on, and its debate around, the future of Europe and the Convention would be important, but not straightforward.

This analysis is necessarily broad-brush and interim (up to date to mid April 2003). It outlines the structure, politics and scope of Italian

The authors would like to thank *Banca CR Firenze* for financial support to Convention Watch. The opinions expressed in this article are those of the authors alone.

government action and policies regarding the Convention, and the different facets of the public debate – including civil society participation, the press and e-democracy.

ITALIAN MEMBERSHIP AND GOVERNMENT ACTIVITY

Italians in the Convention

The catalogue of the Italians working in the Convention process merits detailed enumeration. Participating directly, as Convention members, alternate members, or observers, were fully 13 Italians, as follows.

- For the government: Gianfranco Fini, deputy prime minister (*Alleanza Nazionale*, www.alleanzanazionale.it/index-orig.html); *alternate*: Francesco Speroni (*Lega Nord*, www.leganord.org), Member of the European Parliament (MEP; not affiliated), chief of staff to the minister for institutional reforms and devolution;
- For the chamber of deputies: Marco Follini, leader of the *Unione dei Democratici Cristiani e Democratici di Centro* (www.udc-camera.it), member of the chamber of deputies committee on foreign affairs; *alternate*: Valdo Spini, leader of the *Democratici di Sinistra* (www.dsonline.it) group in the chamber of deputies committee on foreign affairs.
- For the senate: Lamberto Dini (*La Margherita*, www.margheritaonli-ne.it), vice-president of the senate, vice-president of the European Liberal Democrat and Reform Party, and a former prime minister; *alternate*: Filadelfio Basile (*Forza Italia*, www.forza-italia.it), member of the senate constitutional committee and secretary of the senate European affairs committee, and chairman of the Parliamentary Federalist Intergroup for the European Constitution.
- As vice-president of the Convention: Giuliano Amato (vice-president of the Party of European Socialists – PES), twice prime minister.
- From the Commission: as *alternate* to Antonio Vitorino: Paolo Ponzano, director of the Commission Task Force on the Future of the Union and Institutional Affairs.
- From the European Parliament (EP): Antonio Tajani, (*Forza Italia* and vice-president of the European Peoples Party – EPP), member of the European Parliament Committee on Constitutional Affairs; Cristiana Muscardini (*Alleanza Nazionale* and Union for a Europe of the Nations); as an *alternate*: Elena Paciotti (*Democratici di Sinistra* and Party of European Socialists, ex-president of the influential *Associazione Nazionale Magistrati*, www.associazione-magistrati.it).

- Finally, as observers: Claudio Martini, president of the region of Tuscany for the Committee of the Regions (CoR), and Emilio Gabaglio, secretary-general of the European Trade Union Confederation for the European Social Partners.

Moreover, European Commission President Romano Prodi was a powerful external player in the Convention debate, as was Giorgio Napolitano (PES), long-standing (since 1999) chairman of the European Parliament Committee on Constitutional Affairs.

Italy was thus represented in the Convention across most of the political spectrum, excluding the refounded communist left. Its representatives were senior political figures, whose individual voices – we will argue – were distinct both nationally and in the Convention. While only the six appointed delegates of the government and parliament actually represented Italy (in practice, alternates participated as full members), the presence of the additional seven Italian Convention members – and Prodi and Napolitano – made Italy a busy presence at the European level. Indeed, by this count there were more Italians in the Convention than there were nationals of any other participating country.

This observation, in itself perhaps trivial, highlights two points. First, it recalls the cleavages in Italian national politics on Europe that gave rise to the dispute that occurred just before the Convention opened, about whether vice-presidents Amato and Jean-Luc Dehaene should be considered as representatives of their respective countries – which was agreed at the Laeken summit. Had the negative view of this dispute won out, Italy and Belgium would not have been entitled to appoint additional government representatives. However, Berlusconi did not wish to be represented by Amato, his predecessor in office and a leader of the opposition, and Amato let it be known that he would resign from the Convention rather than be required to represent Berlusconi's government. After a stand-off, it was agreed that Amato and Dehaene (who had fewer national problems) should have the same independent status as Convention President Valéry Giscard d'Estaing.[1] Second, the observation that Italy and Italians had a high profile within the Brussels-based Convention stands in stark contrast to the low public profile of the Convention in the Italian national sphere. These two themes are the focus of the discussion below.

Structure of Government Activity

Governmental preparations for, and official tracking of, the Convention were organized into three dimensions: ministry committees, parliamentary and regional debates, and occasional/special events.

In the first category, Rocco Buttiglione, the minister of European Community policies (responsible for European Community (EC) matters, while the Foreign Ministry is responsible for EU matters), in February 2002 set up a Convention Observatory (*Osservatorio sulla Convenzione Europea*).[2] A junior, bipartisan and *ad hoc* committee-come-working-group, initially bringing together the assistants of the 13 Italians in the Convention – and increasingly diverse others from politics and civil society, the Observatory was conspicuous as the first official committee of its kind not to be constituted solely among officials and diplomats. As the centre of gravity of elite political engagement with the Convention, and coordinating Italian representation and producing a monthly bulletin on the progress of the Convention, the Observatory aimed 'to assist in the formulation of concrete responses to the Convention process and to promote consultation between the Italian members of the Convention and the many initiatives taken by national groups interested in its work'. It also considered itself 'the driving-belt between the Italian Convention members and civil society'. Perhaps noteworthy is the implied presumption of the term '*i costituenti*' (the constituents – as in constituent/constitutional assembly) – that the Observatory applied to the Convention members. This indicated that from the outset it preferred a bold interpretation of the Convention's task and character – such as was by no means fully typical of any big state's government positions in the first half of 2002. Opinions differ strongly, however, as to the success and importance of the Observatory.

The Foreign Ministry, where Berlusconi was 'temporarily' his own foreign minister for 11 months after Ruggiero's resignation, was far less visibly busy. In addition to a representative of the foreign minister sitting in the EC ministry observatory, a Foreign Ministry diplomatic working group acted as Fini's team. Its leading officials, heading the EU division and its legal and institutional affairs bureau, regularly contributed to academic and public discussions.[3] Among other foci, the Conference of Italian Ambassadors encompassed the Convention in its study of EU developments. It was expected that as the future of Europe debate moved into the IGC phase – and beyond the competence of the EC ministry – the Foreign Ministry would increasingly take a stronger lead within the government and on the broader political stage.

In the second category, in the Chamber of Deputies and the senate, the Treaty of Nice was ratified almost unopposed in March and May 2002 respectively, and in a similar way the pattern of debate around its successor-to-be was unheated. Since September 2001 the Convention prelude and process were monitored by means of special joint hearings (*Indagine conoscitiva sul futuro dell'unione europea*) of ministers,

Convention members and other experts by the senate's Committee III (Foreign Affairs) and *Giunta per gli affari delle Comunità europee* (EC Affairs) and the chamber's Committee III (Foreign Affairs) and Committee XIV (EU Policies). Among the experts heard were German ex-chancellor Helmut Kohl, the president of the Belgian federal senate, Armand de Decker, Amato, Napolitano, and (Italian) EP vice-presidents Renzo Imbeni and Guido Podestà. The accession chief negotiators from the Czech Republic, Hungary, Poland and Slovakia were heard in March 2002.

Beyond Rome, regional governments' approaches to the Convention varied. While Tuscany established an observatory of its own (to assist Martini), Friuli Venezia-Giulia ran a website (www.regione.fvg.it/fvg-europa/fvgeuropa.htm) carrying background information and referring citizens' participation to the EC ministry observatory, and Latium included its response to the Convention in its regular online EU news digest (www.lazioeuropa.it). Participating in the October 2002 Madeira *Conferenza delle Assemblee Legislative Regionali* (CALRE; the Conference of European Regional Legislative Assemblies) meeting on European governance, most Italian regions issued position documents on the Convention agenda - notably seeking that the effort to build links between the European and national parliaments should also incorporate the regional level. The EC ministry observatory encouraged the regions to organize a standing committee and public fora on the Convention, and hosted regional events – for instance, a round table in Bologna (*Osservatorio sulla Convenzione Europea 2002*). All Piedmont schools participated in a Convention programme, which was planned to conclude with a Youth Convention in May 2003.[4]

Thirdly, in the area of occasional/special events, there was little extraordinary to report. Giscard visited Rome (and the Vatican) to talk with Italian Convention members in October 2002. Ciampi made a series of speeches on the future of Europe. Less formally, Berlusconi and his centre-right allies hosted the Convention (majority) EPP's 'constitution project' meeting in Sardinia in September 2002.[5] It was at this meeting that Berlusconi first won support for a 'Rome II' treaty. A PES Convention seminar in Florence in January 2003, attended additionally by the national left-wing leadership and members of parliament, likewise worked towards common positions. Finally, in the footsteps of the Laeken Declaration's 'basic challenge' that young citizens be brought 'closer to the European design and the European institutions' and of the (messy and disappointing) July 2002 Youth Convention in Brussels, in January 2003 a government-organized Italian Youth Convention sought to develop this branch of debate among delegates aged 16–29 from schools, non-governmental organizations, church organizations, universities and political movements (*Osservatorio sulla Convenzione Europea 2003*). The content of these engagements is considered below.

ITALIAN POSITIONS

Government Positions

Italy's coalition government contains many party leaders. Their opening statements on the future of Europe followed a broad pattern of individual stances, which in part may have aimed to keep each leader in the headlines – and which, on Europe, may have disguised an underlying reality that Berlusconi alone has decided.[6]

In the January 2002 *Financial Times* interview cited above, Berlusconi extended his statement that Italy seeks a Europe of national interest by declaring a 'clear understanding' with Tony Blair, prime minister of the UK, and José María Aznar, the Spanish premier, on the future of Europe.[7] Labelled by the press the 'BAB' (Blair, Aznar, Berlusconi), this international identification of Italy as a leading player in the particular forum of the debate on the future of Europe did not, however, long outlast the Seville summit, being replaced by talk of an 'ABC' (Aznar, Blair, Chirac). While media reports of the ABC and the January 2003 renewal of the Franco-German 'motor' were centred on the vexed question of a longer term EU (Council) president, Berlusconi himself had yet to state where he stood in relation to the various competing options. With Aznar, Berlusconi agreed – although this was not communicated to the Convention – an EU legal personality, the European Charter of Fundamental Rights in the future constitution and qualified majority voting (QMV) for all issues – including the Common Foreign and Security Policy (CFSP).[8] Overall, nonetheless, Berlusconi's views were an enigma. His few utterances, however, were sufficiently dramatic that the contrasting silences were variously interpreted as a masterly waiting game, a decision not to pre-empt the IGC and Italy's role as a broker, or a symptom of inattention to the Convention phase. Most internationally reported were repeated statements that Russia should one day become part of an enormous EU – a story first picked up and spread by the largely Euro-sceptic online EU news resource *EU Observer*.[9] Berlusconi himself suggested that he kept his distance from the Convention in order to later (as IGC host) freely act as a mediator.[10]

The choice of the Italian government's Convention nominee was 'seen as an important signal of Italy's position on the future architecture of Europe' ('Fini to join convention on future of the EU', *Financial Times*, 23 January 2002). The appointment of Fini, nationalist and 'post-fascist',[11] to the Convention – indeed, as one of its highest-ranking members – was ill-received in much of Europe's media and interpreted as a personal bid for political respectability.[12]

Nonetheless, it is notable that Fini's line on many Convention issues was more carefully nuanced and Europhile than expected. On the one hand, in the context of new hardline legislation in Italy, Fini insisted that immigration law must remain within the national ambit. On the other hand, he said that Europe must become a leading protagonist in world politics (by operating a Common Foreign and Security Policy [CFSP]). He held back from joining the summer 2002 dispute regarding an elected EU president, proposed at an early stage that the Convention must aim for 'consensus', urged a balance of power between the Council and the Commission, and argued – somewhat obscurely – that Europe 'does not mean less nation, but less state'.[13] Fini also took care to assure the parliamentary hearing of the consensual functioning of the Italian delegation in the Convention, praising Dini in particular (*Indagine conoscitiva* 17 July 2002). In October 2002, however, the tone briefly changed. Fini informed a *BBC* interviewer that the Convention would not reach agreement on reform of the European institutions – its unfinished business must instead be tabled for the IGC.[14] The same month, he enthusiastically backed Prodi's 'courageous' October 2002 dismissal of the Stability Pact as 'stupid' and 'rigid'.[15]

In contrast, within Italy, Fini's government colleague Umberto Bossi of the Lega Nord was steadily provocative, describing the EU as 'a new fascism, which is removing the power of the citizens' and calling for the start of a 'civil resistance against the technocratic and corrupt European superstate'.[16] The Lega Nord's 'The Europe We Want' manifesto emphasized the urgent 'danger' to regional diversity and the safeguarding of a 'confederal Europe of the peoples' (Lega Nord 2002).

Another vocal contributor in the first months of governmental debate was Giulio Tremonti, treasury minister, who initially declared himself a convinced supporter of a European constitution: 'We achieved the Euro, now we have to build a European constitution'.[17] In August 2002, however, Tremonti launched a rearguard defence of IGC prerogative, inveighing against the growing ambitions of the Convention to propose a text rather than 'hypotheses'; his attack on the Convention (and Amato, see below) for working towards a 'byzantine' European superstate provoked a furore. Fini, indeed, publicly replied that intergovernmental-versus-communitarian analysis proposed a false dichotomy of comp-lementary approaches to integration. Interviewed by *La Stampa*, Follini urged 'Europe is an opportunity, not an enemy'.[18] Tremonti subsequently became noticeably quiet in public, although was most likely active behind the scenes.

Meanwhile, Buttiglione did not publicly venture much into this type of question. Rather, he addressed his ministerial remit, outlining to the parliamentary hearing that the principle of solidarity must not override that of subsidiarity: European coordination of social policy is necessary, but its substance must remain a national competence, while development is a European-level mandate (*Indagine conoscitiva* 18 October 2001).

The parliamentary debate and its progress towards policy positions are best illustrated by the controversial sovereignty issues: CFSP, the role of national parliaments and a longer term/elected EU president. Here Ruggiero (when foreign minister) tabled at an early stage the direct election of the Commission president. Paciotti (a MEP, having a national parliamentary voice because of her Convention role) later put forward to the hearing that a longer term Council president would change the nature of European politics, asking what would be the status of a president chosen by a majority of one political colour when – with electoral changes in the member states – that colour changed: such a president would answer neither to the EP (excluded from the choice under this system) nor to the Council. On CFSP, ex-chancellor Kohl testified that majority voting will arrive at some point in the future. As for the role of national parliaments in European decision-making, transparency and accountability, Buttiglione remarked to the hearing that this problem is not much discussed in Italy. He reported that the task of the Convention was to 'lessen the area of opacity' and reinforce the roles of both parliamentary levels (*Indagine conoscitiva* 18 and 31 October 2001, and 7 March, 30 May, 17 July and 26 November 2002). Overall, there was the impression that these hearings accommodated the monitoring of Convention debate and broad comment, but that the debate was only slowly warming-up and that the parliament was willing to await delivery from Brussels of the final technical package before sharpening national scrutiny.

However, on 6 March 2003 the first government report to the Chamber was accompanied by a lengthy and close debate. Here, Fini's opening was that the Convention was working towards a consensus (and would not vote). He strongly developed the themes (apposite to the concurrent international crisis and its EU repercussions) of CFSP and military capacity, arguing 'Europe must become a political protagonist'. He particularly noted that Eurobarometer results confirm the Europhilia of Italians, and took the double-legitimacy (national and commonly European) of the EU as a starting point for urging a combination of a longer term Council president and six-month rotation of either a vice-presidency or the presidencies of the various policy councils.

At the same time, however, Fini said that the Italian government found the idea of a single, merged EU president of Council and Commission 'fascinating' (*affascinante*) – a possible end goal for the EU, to which any currently feasible – weaker – solution would be but a halfway house. Citing Kissinger's infamous request for a single telephone number for Europe, he then gave support to the idea of a 'Mr CFSP' shared between the Council and Commission. The other Convention participants were also notably enthusiastic about developing the theme of strong European goals. Follini picked up on 'Mr CFSP': his view was that this would not answer Kissinger's need; rather, we must strive for a single European president – the idea might seem unrealistic, but courageous steps were required. Both Follini (from the centre-right) and Spini (from the left) urged federalism. Spini wanted social policy to be a shared competence. Moreover, on the model of Article 11 of the Italian Constitution, he proposed that the Convention should draft an article repudiating war 'as an instrument of offence against the liberty of other peoples and as a means of resolving international disputes' in strict observance of the United Nations (UN) Charter (*Informativa del Governo sui lavori della Convenzione europea 6 March 2003*). At the Senate's parallel report session, Dini made the case for both 'Rome II' and (Ciampi's) proposal for coordination among the original six signatories. Basile supported the federal idea, and submitted that the new treaty be put to a referendum.[19]

Last but not least, constitutionally Ciampi plays no direct part in Italian decision-making but has devoted many public opportunities to the future of Europe. Speaking at the European University Institute (in Florence), Ciampi laid out that CFSP requires 'an entirely new approach', allowing Europe to act as a 'single global interlocutor' and translate a 'history of civilised values and negotiating ability' into a fuller political credibility (Ciampi 2002b). To Italian business leaders, Ciampi elegantly proposed that 'the EU is like a moving train, with 15 cars, and an engine designed for six' – thus, more than upgrading will be needed for another ten cars (Ciampi 2002c). Internationally, he urged that the EU must not merely be a free trade area, and ought to be able to act in areas like the Middle East (Ciampi 2002a). To the University of Leiden, who heard that hesitation has damaged integration, he argued that courage has always paid-off: the Convention must advance a European identity for citizens through an effective constitution (Ciampi 2003).

Ciampi also obliquely addressed the thorny question (a question urged by the Vatican) of a mention of Christian values in a new constitution. This occasion provoked a press incident, when unfortunately phrased words were misquoted to the effect that Ciampi considered that immigrants to Europe should adopt its Christian heritage ('Ciampi: Citizens unclear about EU goals', *EU Observer*, 10 May 2002[20]). Subsequently, it must be added, other Italian leaders turned to this issue. At a January 2003 conference organized by the Pontifical Council for Justice and Peace, Fini urged 'a step forward' from the Charter's slender citation of 'spiritual and moral heritage', and Dini proposed 'specific reference to the role of the Church in the formation of Europe over the past 2000 years'.[21] Again, to the Chamber on 6 March 2003, Fini presented an amendment to Article 2 of the first draft 16 from the Convention Praesidium that would insert the phrase 'Judeo-Christian roots', while Follini, on the same occasion, preferred an ecumenical reference in the Preamble (*Informativa del Governo sui lavori della Convenzione europea 6 March 2003*).

We do not propose to venture a conclusion to this summary. More so than even in most EU and accession countries, few hard-and-fast Italian positions on the future were yet struck: the government's positions for the Convention remained in constant evolution.

Work at the Convention

Speeches and submissions ('contributions') to the Plenary Convention by its members provide the verbatim record of Italian participation in Brussels. Here, Dini undertook early to urge the Convention to examine the missions of integration. To the Convention plenary of 15–16 April 2002 he affirmed the centrality of subsidiarity and diversity, seeking clarity about objectives in the form of an allocatory catalogue of competences (on the current Italian devolution model, which defines the remit of higher levels of government while, by default, all other matters pertain to the lower level; Article 117 of the Constitution). At the 20–21 January 2003 plenary on institutional functioning – somewhat hijacked by the Franco-German proposal of a few days earlier – Dini (speaking English) was again among the first to take a position: two presidents would risk 'friction' and disrupt the institutional balance to the detriment of the Commission. Amato warned against hoping to move faster than politically possible at this moment, and focused on the need to restructure the legislative council and to have 'the courage' to create a 'Legislative Affairs Council'. 'In none of our countries', he said, do we accept legislation that derives exclusively from ministries in only one policy sector: 'we want legislation to be made in the presence of, and with the participation of, every aspect of the public interest'. Fini (who played down the Franco-German document's importance), Speroni and Follini also intervened: Speroni pointed out that a longer term EU presidency, in which member states could not guarantee that one of their nationals would regularly hold office, should be no more of a problem than a national Italian or German presidency, which regions or länder would not expect to rotate; Follini spoke out in favour of the 'two-hatted' presidency model. Predictably, Martini and Speroni throughout took a particular interest in the question of regions.[22] Basile, meanwhile, focussed on the role of national parliaments and the missions of the EU, arguing that 'the borderline between EU and national competence' should not be 'static', and that 'first of all' national parliaments should be able to effectively scrutinise their own government's actions.[23] That not all the Italians members sought to speak in each debate or to address every topic may support Fini's message of consensual cooperation.

Clearly, however, the bulk of the Convention's debate in its first year took place in its working groups (WGs) (for which only progress summaries have been published). In the 'first wave' of Convention WGs, Dini chose to join WGI on subsidiarity, while Fini, Martini and Paciotti opted for WGII on the Charter, and Amato chaired WGIII on legal personality – also attended by Muscardini and Tajani. Left-wingers Gabaglio and Spini (with Follini) participated in the contentious WGVI on economic governance, which had been expected to recommend positions on the so-called 'European social model' (later addressed by its own working group). In the 'second wave', Dini, Fini, Follini and Martini all selected WGVII on external action, seen as a priority issue by many government representatives, while Amato chaired the legally crucial, but low-key, WGIX on simplification (of instruments and procedures – namely of European legislative tools and the institutional balance of power) – seemingly not deemed important by many governments, but attended by Speroni.

Prodi, Amato and Napolitano

Neither Amato, leading the Convention, nor Prodi, institutionally leaning on the Convention, may be formally said to be part of the Italian case study. In the European context they are independent, of expert rather than party stature, and stand above and apart from national affiliations. It would, nonetheless, be difficult – and certainly artificial – to sketch the Italian picture without them. To say the least, both Prodi and Amato are leaders of the national opposition, and from autumn 2002 talk was rife of Prodi concluding his Commission term early (so that a new post-enlargement Commission could come into being) and returning to Italy to head the centre-left *Ulivo* alliance.

Much press comment compared Prodi's 'poor' performance at the Commission, and especially in the debate about the future of Europe, with his powerful reputation within Italian politics.[24] Judged tactical blunders, the Commission's aggressive efforts not to be sidelined in the Convention debate – especially its December 2002 'Penelope' feasibility study advocating Commission control of CFSP and a treaty 'declaration confirming the resolve of [a] people to continue to belong to the EU' – certainly did not represent Italian Convention positions.[25] By virtue of his office, Prodi did not formally speak in Italy on the debate about the future of Europe.

Amato's authority as a constitutional scholar gave him a special role. Despite the early dispute as to Amato's Italian status, in contrast to January 2002 both Berlusconi and Fini later strongly recommended Amato's abilities and the consequent benefit to the national interest in the fullest terms.[26] Demonstrating a similar (although hostile and, in this case, party-political) assessment of Amato's expert input, Tremonti's denunciation of the fervid speculation that circled the constitutional aspirations indicated in Giscard's Le Monde article[27] identified Amato as the author of this plan's alleged, elusively circulating, 'non-paper' blueprint.[28] Amato himself, however, prioritised clear-speaking and democratic communication, saying 'simplification is a complex issue', adding that, 'as a citizen', he would feel 'offended' if there were no exclusive competences of the EU in the constitution.[29]

Moreover, Amato's frequent 'letters from Europe' in Il Sole 24 Ore sought to stimulate national debate. Arguing for European majority decisions on war/peace – if we can accept majorities in the national context then this can work for the EU also, albeit the EU is far more 'fragile' than any nation; having an EU decision with which one might disagree is yet better than to fail in division – he proposed that Europe recall Garibaldi and Vittorio Emmanuelle II (despite their different aspirations) saw that they must work together to unite Italy.[30] He similarly reflected on Italy's possible strategies of influence in the last phase of the Convention: mediation, an anti-Franco-German alliance with the UK, or (better) joining and reinforcing the Franco-German axis – the original six route.[31] Interviewed in Corriere della Sera, Amato treated the religious clause question with a touch of provocation, recalling that – alarmingly – freemasonry falls within the existing Amsterdam provision for 'philosophical and non-confessional organizations', and suggesting that a role for the churches might be an added factor in the social dialogue.[32]

Napolitano, as chairman of the European Parliament Constitutional Affairs Committee, president of the Italian section of the European Movement, a former president of the Chamber of Deputies and former minister of the interior, is another influential contributor to the future process. Interviewed about a European constitution for the PES online newsletter in November 2002, Napolitano stressed the importance of transparency and the necessity of including the Charter in the constitution, but downplayed Berlusconi's *'extempore'* (*'sortite estemporanee'*) proposal that Russia might ever join the EU, arguing that it is simply too big. Asked whether the political dividing lines in the Convention have been between countries or between 'political families', he firmly replied that it is the latter.[33]

PRESS AND PUBLIC DEBATE

Press Coverage and Comment

The Convention defined the first phase of its work as 'listening: identification of the expectations and needs of the member states, their governments and parliaments, and those of European society'. The same task also rested on national governments. As numerous as Italian politicians were in the Convention, the future of Europe debate nonetheless began with faint resonance in the Italian press (strengthening in winter 2003) and public debate was conspicuous by its absence. Here, the Italian case, as other national- and European-level cases, demonstrates a fundamental failure (Scott 2002).

Many reasons may easily be guessed at to explain press apathy, not least a lack of expertise on the sometimes highly intricate subject matter of the Convention (hence the importance of politicians' interviews and articles). The Convention, though, ought to be extraordinary news: as Giscard argued, all our futures are being fashioned by its hands.[34] Italian reporting of the question of a European president (or two) was slight and bland in comparison to that in France and Germany, and frequently weaker even than UK coverage. When the Blair–Aznar proposal for the election of a five-year EU president hit the headlines in May 2002, *La Repubblica* minimally cited its apparent approval by Prodi, Giscard and Amato, and commented that this model would have the advantage of encouraging the development of a pan-European political constituency but would not cure the EU's congenital defect of tending towards technocracy rather than a democratic polity.[35] Later references to the Convention in the Communist daily, *Il Manifesto*, were linked to the national *'Articolo 18'* issue (about radically disputed change in employment rights) and the future fate of the Charter.[36] Beyond these issues, one frequent press topic was the place of Christian values.

Although the Convention's gathering pace brought an increase in press coverage, it is difficult to see how newspaper readers (by no means, it should be pointed out, the majority of Italian citizens) could assess the Brussels debate from such sources: a deficit of media attention contributed to the democratic deficit. A (rare) frustrated letter to *Corriere della Sera* complaining at the lack of interest in the future of Europe in Italy, thus criticised both politicians and citizens for their neglect of debate and observed that the press had largely reduced its comment on Convention proceedings to occasional footnotes in the context of other questions. The writer of the letter proposed that the Convention appeared to be a remote body, and that if it had been constituted among directly elected representatives it would have inspired greater interest.[37]

Of course, both television and radio (on the occasion of the signing of the enlargement treaties in Athens in April 2003, and frequently when Amato features in news reports) also mentioned the Convention. This again, however, was usually a matter of footnoting other stories, although there are exceptions to the rule. In February 2003, *Radio Radicale*, together with the *Fondazione Roma Europea*, broadcast a debate of over two hours involving Fini, Amato and some 17 other speakers.[38] Another such session (with the Aspen Institute) discussed 'America and the future of Europe' with Amato and Foreign Minister Franco Frattini, who was appointed in the middle of the Convention process.[39]

Public Initiatives and Debate

There was, then, no sense in which the Convention caught the Italian public imagination (unlike the great excitement of the Euro currency launch) (Giuliano Amato, various interviews with Jesse Scott, May 2002–April 2003). If the EC ministry observatory 'driving belt' laboured to mobilize discourse in civil society, this effort was directed at traditional channels and traditional projects (making information available, convening meetings, the Youth Convention). Other institutions acted in a similar fashion.

Italian interest groups issued bare statements on the Convention. Among the trade unions, the (Catholic ethos) *Confederazione italiana sindacati lavoratori* (CISL; Confederation of Workers' Union) predictably highlighted the role of the social partners in the European institutions, the inclusion of the Charter and the strengthening of the European Parliament (CISL, www.cisl.it). The left-wing *Confederazione generale italiana del lavoro* (CIGL; General Confederation of Labour; www.cgil.it/segretariatoeuropea) and *Unione italiana del lavoro* (UIL; Union of Italian Labour; www.uil.it/internazionale/convenzione_europea1.htm) unions adopted similar positions, with the latter headlining 'a Europe of solidarity, strengthened and more democratic'. At the November 2002 European Social Forum in Florence, the radical *Comitati di Base* (COBAS; Committees of the Base) and CGIL together held a session discussing the Convention, the Charter and the crisis of democratic deficit.[40] The Italian Confederation of Industry argued that the European decision-making process must be speeded-up, that QMV (Qualified Majority Voting) was necessary and that the division of competences between Europe and the member states must be clarified (Confindustria 2002). Public statements of these groups' positions did not – in the main – keep pace with the ever-changing Convention debate.

Examples of civil society initiatives regarding the Convention were to be found in the usual quarters. In academia, the Italian Institute for International Affairs in October 2001 presented the parliamentary hearing with a written contribution dealing with three issues: the role of the Convention, institutional reform and CFSP. At the same time, a special issue of the Institute for International Affairs journal, *The International Spectator*, contributed to the pan-EU Trans European Policy Studies Association (TEPSA) Europe Forum (Istituto Affari Internazionali 2001). Another academic network at the *Osservatorio sul Federalismo* [Observatory on Federalism] carried papers by and links to both Italian and other national debates (and a useful bibliography) on its excellent website (www.costituzioniregionali.it/federalismi/index.html). At La Sapienza University in Rome, a law and economics conference in November 2002 brought together pan-European academic networks and policy-makers to discuss 'The European Constitution in the Making' (Università di Roma La Sapienza 2002). Elsewhere, the Italian section of the European Movement was also heard by the parliamentary hearing (*Consiglio Italiano del Movimento Europeo*; www.eurplace.org/italy/index.html), the Giovanni Agnelli Foundation held a series of Convention seminars, and the ASTRID (*Associazione per gli Studi e le ricerche sulla Riforma delle Istituzioni Democratiche e sull'Innovazione nelle administrazione pubbliche*) group (the Italian section of the International Association for Reinventing Government, and part of the European Policy Network) – of which Amato is President – attentively commented on the progress of the Convention's proposals and the technical options involved (Astrid 2003). Similarly, the *Fondazione Basso* (with Paciotti as president) set up its own observatory, and combined forces with other groups for seminars on the Convention. Regionally, the *Euroforum Firenze* organized a series of local meetings on the theme 'Towards a European Constitution' with the University of Florence and the European University Institute; the *Fondazione Circolo Rosselli* (of which Spini is president) issued a journal volume on the European Constitution (*Circolo Rosselli 2002*); and the newly established, Rome-based *Thesmos* group of young researchers and professionals similarly dedicated its first volume of essays to the Convention (Federico 2002).

Meanwhile, the long-established Italian section of the Union of European Federalists (since 1943) took part in a pan-European 'Come and vote "yes" or "no" to a federal constitution' campaign, appealing to the Convention to hold a Europe-wide referendum on the future simultaneously with the June 2004 EP elections. A smaller experiment in November 2002 aimed to 'bring the Europe debate to the man-on-the-street' by holding a series of mini-referenda at street stalls in towns in France, Germany and Italy, asking passers by their opinion on a federal constitution.[41] Among the very few early polls undertaken in relation to the Convention debate, the Lombardy section of the *Gruppo Giovani Imprenditori* [Young Entrepreneurs of the Confederation of Industry] commissioned a national phone poll. This produced results in favour of European integration (the Euro currency, freedom of movement) and its impact upon market competition, large-scale privatization and public finance – and thus also for greater EU powers and a bold outcome from the Convention.[42]

At the Italian Youth Convention, a strong motion from right-wing and church groups in favour of a European constitution enshrining Christian values was defeated in the final vote. It was agreed that Europe should be committed to peace, that a federal EU should have a CFSP and have as its president the president of the Commission (www.avvenireuropa.it).

Demonstrating a strong response to the Convention in circles professionally committed to public policy discussion and analysis, and encouraging some broader fora, the impact of such initiatives beyond their authors' and the participants' immediate circles is, however, without evidence.

E-Democracy

An additional feature of the future of Europe debate is its aptitude to be a testing ground for the much-vaunted possibilities of e-democracy. Specifically, at the summer 2002 civil society and Youth Convention sessions in Brussels, Dehaene declared that the Internet – and the Convention website – were wondrously facilitating a crucial debate. This assertion, however, was not sustained by the Convention's official journal-type site, by Giscard's October 2002 web-chat, or in looking at the Commission's 'Futurum' site and its hollow discussion lists (European University Institute 2003).

In Italy, official dedicated websites echoed this limited model. The Foreign Ministry's EU-site posted Convention digests and

Berlusconi's and Ciampi's speeches.[43] The Chamber's *'Futuro dell' Europa'* and EC Ministry's observatory websites, likewise, posted short summaries of issues discussed in the Plenary Convention.[44] A catch-all portal at 'Avvenire Europa', maintained by the Observatory, provided links to these and other Italian sites (www.avvenireuropa.it). Through the Formez Institute, the 'EuroPA' section of the prime minister's Department of Public Functions site similarly supported links.[45] Perhaps unsurprisingly given this paucity, minutes of the parliamentary hearing were not fully easily accessible online. The 'Parlamenti Regionali' website comprehensively carried up-to-date documents relating to regional positions, but its debate forum was inactive (www.parlamentiregionali.it). As for political parties, the *Democratici di Sinistra Europe* site carried, at best, minimal bulletins,[46] and *Forza Italia* was almost less thorough (mainly posting the latest statements from Tajani). The online editions of Italian newspapers (*Il Sole 24 Ore* excepted), unlike many other European newspapers, did not set up special report pages on the Convention – and, in turn, were not often cited as press cuttings on non-media sites. Perhaps the best Italian site on the Convention was that of the Institute for International Affairs (www.europa2004.it). Thus, while this essay footnotes many websites as sources, this convenient information reference demonstrates a technical development which falls well short of e-democracy in the fuller sense of the use of the Internet as a new forum of debate and a hub of popular deliberation on political questions.

However, small experiments can be cited: *Il Sole24Ore* took up the challenge of an article by Amato about possible names for the new Europe to run an email vote, offering four options: 'United Europe', 'European Union', 'United States of Europe', and 'European Community' – of which 'European Union' (44 per cent) won.[47]

CONCLUSIONS

During spring 2003 the Italian government began to put pressure on the Convention to conclude its work on schedule, before the beginning of the Italian EU presidency. This would allow, Frattini said, for a 'cooling down period' between the Convention and the IGC.[48] Looking forward, therefore, to autumn 2003, it was clear that Italy's role regarding the Convention would be at its most visibly significant after that unique assembly had ceased to meet.

To this observation, two concluding points need to be added. First, in terms of government policy, it remained uncertain how far attitudes to a future Europe had crystallized since January 2002, when Giscard went so far as to reassure the international press that

'There could be no EU without Italy', and that the 'internal issues' of the country would not impact upon the work of the Convention.[49] Or, indeed, since October that year, when (on his official visit to Italy) he confidently affirmed that he found Italy 'the most European country in Europe' (Giscard d'Estaing 2002).

These unusual statements touch upon the essential analytic difficulties: any assessment of the pattern of Italian positions regarding the Convention requires both a judgement about the complex relationships among the various components of the national political configuration and about the relationship between this domestic politics and Italy's European role. Despite the 'Rome II' bid, the Convention generated conflicting conceptions (Tremonti's 'hypotheses' versus the EC ministry's '*i costituenti*') and intricate dynamics. Meanwhile, Italy's established Euro-experts, Prodi and Amato, are out of power in Italy but were at the centre of the European level of the political process on the future EU. At the time of writing, therefore, it appears probable that the final flavour of government attitudes to the new treaty – and the Convention's draft – may be partly contingent upon the progress of the IGC and Irish willingness (should the IGC continue into Spring 2004) that the treaty be signed in Rome. Possibly the only firm prediction to be made is that Berlusconi's focus on the Convention can be expected to tighten rapidly in the later months of the future of Europe process, and that his positions will be of some importance to the alignment of other European leaders.

Second, insofar as Fini's January 2003 announcement of a national referendum on the new treaty (not required by the Constitution and not necessarily binding) echoed the growing momentum of a range of calls to democratically legitimize the new treaty, the apathy of the public debate on the Convention is a looming challenge – not only, of course, in Italy. This referendum would risk embarrassment by low voter turn-out, and might fall victim to 'second-order' national or international issues (think of the continuing impact of the war with Iraq, against which vast demonstrations have assembled in Italian cities) – or might follow traditional patterns of pro-European sentiment. At the same time, however, a referendum would have the potential to animate debate and catalyze engagement with Europe. Whether this is a strategy pursued by Italy's leaders, and how such an opportunity would be taken up by its voters, will be among the most interesting aspects of the Italian picture to watch.

NOTES

1. 'Italy heads for new EU storm', *BBC*, 22 January 2002, web edition; 'Italy sparks row over composition of Convention', *EU Observer*, 31 December 2001; 'Berlusconi: I prefer Fini for the Convention', *EU Observer*, 25 January 2002b; 'Guiliano Amato threatens to resign from Convention on EU Reform', *Euractiv*, 17 January 2002; '*Berlusconi punta su Fini*', *RaiNet News*, 23 January 2002, web edition.
2. www.politichecomunitarie.it/Osservatorio/osservatorio1.htm.
3. They spoke, for example, at 'The Contribution of Italian Universities to the European Convention and to the Italian Presidency of the EU', University of Padua, 31 Jan. 2003, and 'Regions in Europe: The Competence and Role of the Regional Legislative Assemblies in the debate on the European Constitution', Regional Council of Lombardy, 30 Sept.–1 Oct. 2002.
4. www.provincia.torino.it/europa/infopoint/iniziative/convenzione/index.htm.
5. 'Conservative summit puts pressure on Convention', *EU Observer*, 9 September 2002; European People's Party 2002.
6. '*Il governo è europeista, Berlusconi il garante*', *Corriere della Sera*, 6 January 2002, web edition.
7. 'Berlusconi says Italy will become EU broker', *Financial Times*, 17 January 2002, web edition.
8. Conclusions of the 28 November 2002 bilateral summit at Rome, www.governo.it/GovernoInforma/Dossier/vertice_italo_spagnolo/conclusioni.html.
9. 'Berlusconi: Russia should form part of EU', *EU Observer*, 3 April 2002; see also '*Rom soll Moskau näher an Europa binden*', *Die Welt*, 27 January 2002.
10. '*Estendiamo il voto a maggioranza per non paralizzare la nuova Europa*', *Corriere della Sera*, 29 November 2002.
11. A label Fini himself strongly refutes, see '*Fini: Chiedo scusa per le leggi razziali*', *La Repubblica*, 13 September 2002, web edition.
12. 'Post-fascist Fini takes EU job', *BBC*, 24 January 2002, web edition; 'Berlusconi assures EU of support for convention', *Financial Times*, 11 January 2002; 'Fini to join convention on future of the EU', *Financial Times*, 23 January 2002.
13. '*Nessuno vuole un super Stato europeo*', *Corriere della Sera*, 27 August 2002, web edition; 'Fini: a third way for the future EU', *EU Observer*, 17 June 2002; 'A Federal Europe would mean byzantine conditions', *EU Observer*, 26 August 2002; *Indagine conoscitiva* 17 July 2002; '*Fini a Tremonti: Non ci sarà nessun super Stato europeo*', *La Repubblica*, 26 August 2002, web edition.
14. 'EU Foreign policy set for Greek boost', *BBC*, 17 December 2002, web edition.
15. 'Italy shows its discomfort in eurozone straightjacket', *The Times*, 22 October 2002, web edition.
16. 'Italian EU policy questioned after anti EU comment', *EU Observer*, 5 March 2002; 'Ruggiero blames Italy's Europhobes for his Resignation', *The Guardian*, 6 March 2002.
17. '*Ue: Tremonti, fatto l'euro ora serve la constituzione*', *Asca*, 17 January 2002, web edition.
18. '*Tremonti, il grande mistero della Costituzione europea*', *La Stampa*, 25 August 2002, web edition; '*L'Europa è un'occasione, non un nemico*', *La Stampa*, 26 August 2002, web edition; '*Nessuno vuole un super Stato europeo*', *Corriere della Sera*, 27 August 2002, web edition; 'A Federal Europe would mean byzantine conditions', *EU Observer*, 26 August 2002; '*Fini a Tremonti: Non ci sarà nessun super Stato europeo*', *La Repubblica*, 26 August 2002, web edition.
19. '*Discussione sulle communicazioni del Vice Presidente del Consiglio dei Ministri sull'attività della Convenzione europea e connesse mozioni*'

5 March 2003, www.senato.it/bgt/ShowDoc.asp?leg = 14&id = 00060382&tipodoc = Resaula&modo = PRODUZIONE&js = 1&offset = 205516&size = 200293.

20. Original Italian text of speech can be found at www.quirinale.it/Discorsi/ Discorso.asp?id = 17531. It reads (our translation): 'Europe can welcome new influxes of immigrant citizens, respecting their cultures of origin, but observing – in order to avoid destructive tensions – the rules of the welcoming States; [this is] in the spirit of unifying elements of the Christian and the humanistic roots of European civilisation.'.

21. 'Italian Leaders Back Recognition of Christianity in European Constitution Cross Section of Leaders Notes Religious Influence in Continent', *Zenit*, 28 January 2003.

22. See documents CONV 518/03, CONV 328/02, CONV 195/02 and CONV 494/03.

23. See documents CONV 94/02, CONV 239/02 and CONV 334/02.

24. 'The Two Romano Prodis', *Financial Times*, 23 December 2002, web edition.

25. 'Ue, il progetto di Prodi', *Il Sole24Ore*, 5 December 2002, web edition; 'La Commission européenne présente son projet de constitution', *Libération*, 5 Deecember 2002, web edition; 'Prodi under fire for federalist proposals', *Guardian*, 6 December 2002, web edition; Prodi 2002.

26. *Indagine conoscitiva* 30 May 2002; *Informativa del Governo sui lavori della Convenzione europea* 6 March 2003.

27. 'La dernière chance de l'Europe unie', *Le Monde*, 22 July 2002, web edition; www.ue.eu.int/pressdata/FR/conveur/71672.PDF.

28. 'Tremonti, il grande mistero della Costituzione europea', *La Stampa*, 25 August 2002, web edition.

29. 'Amato: simplification is a complex issue', *EU Observer*, 8 November 2002; 'Amato receives huge support for simplification plans', *EU Observer*, 6 December 2002 .

30. 'Unione, più delle visioni contano le scelte concrete', *Il Sole24Ore*, 16 March 2003, web edition.

31. 'Convenzione Ue, una strategia per Roma', *Il Sole24Ore*, 5 January 2003, web edition.

32. 'Solo un superpresidente può riunire la politica estera dell'Europa', *Corriere della Sera*, 6 February 2003, web edition.

33. 'Intervista a Giorgio Napolitano sulla Convenzione europea', *dsonline*, 14 November 2002, www.new.dsonline.it/stampa/documenti/dettaglio.asp?id_doc = 8457.

34. 'La dernière chance de l'Europe unie', *Le Monde*, 22 July 2002, web edition; www.ue.eu.int/pressdata/FR/conveur/71672.PDF.

35. 'L'Europa alla ricerca del leader della Provvidenza', *La Repubblica*, 18 May 2002, web edition.

36. 'Diritti in soffitta', *Il Manifesto*, 28 January 2002, web edition; 'Il referendum sull'art.18 parla europeo', *Il Manifesto*, 2 February 2002, web edition.

37. 'Una classe politica disinteressata all'Europa', *Corriere della Sera*, 13 May 2002, web edition.

38. 'Roma, la convenzione ed il futuro dell'Europa', *Radio Radicale*, 11 February 2003.

39. 'La questione americana nel futuro dell'Europa', *Radio Radicale*, 20 February 2003.

40. 'Le iniziative di interesse sindacale', *Rassenga.it*, 6 November 2002, www.rassegna.it /2002/attualita/articoli/social-forum-firenze/cgil2.htm.

41. 'Testing EU constitutional referenda on the streets', *EU Observer*, 7 November 2002.

42. www.giovaniimprenditori.com/incontri.htm.

43. www.esteri.it/polestera/ue/index.htm.

44. www.camera.it/_aveur and www.politichecomunitarie.it/Osservatorio.

45. www.europa.formez.it/politiche_istituzioni.html.

46. www.new.dsonline.it/europa/index.asp.

47. '*Scegliete il nome della nuova Europa*', *Il Sole24Ore*, 30 November 2002, web edition.
48. 'Finish Convention work by June, says Rome', *EU Observer*, 26 March 2002.
49. '*Berlusconi asegura que Italia es el país 'más europeísta' de la UE*', *El Mundo*, 11 January 2002, web edition; 'Giscard: No Europe without Italy', *EU Observer*, 11 January 2002; 'Berlusconi assures EU of support for convention', *Financial Times*, 11 January 2002.

REFERENCES

Astrid (2003): 'For the Constitution of the European Union: Convergences, Divergences, Possible Paths (and a Few Proposals)', *EPIN* 2, www.epin.org/pdf/AstridConst.pdf.
Arcelli, F. (ed.) (2002): *Appunti Europei, I quaderni di Thesmos I*, Cosenza: Rubbettino.
Ciampi, C.A. (2002a): '*Laudatio del Presidente della Repubblica Carlo Azeglio Ciampi alla cerimonia di conferimento all'eure del premio internazionale Carlo Magno, Aquisgrana*, 9 May 2002', www.quirinale.it/Discorsi/Discorso.asp?id = 17531.
Ciampi, C.A. (2002b): 'Speech of the President of the Republic at the European University Institute of Florence, European University Institute, 26 September 2002', www.iue.it/About/News/PdfFiles/SpeechCiampi_EN.pdf.
Ciampi, C.A. (2002c): '*Intervento del Presidente della Repubblica Carlo Azeglio Ciampi in occasione della consegna delle insegne dell'Ordine Al Merito del Lavoro ai Cavalieri del Lavoro nominati il 2 giugno 2001*, Rome, 29 November 2002', www.quirinale.it/Discorsi/Discorso.asp?id = 15949.
Ciampi, C.A. (2003): 'The Identity and Unity of Europe: Speech by the President of the Republic Carlo Azeglio Ciampi at Leiden University, Leiden, 5 March 2003' www.ueitalia2003.it/EN/LaPresidenzaInforma/Documenti/20030305_D_05mar01.htm
Circolo Rosselli (2002): *Quaderni del Circolo Rosselli* XXII/77, 2, Firenze: Alinea editrice.
Confindustria (2002): *Più Europa per competere: Manifesto di Confindustria per il Consiglio Europeo di Barcellona*, Brussels, 20 Feb., www.europa2004.it/IT/Parti_sociali.htm#Confindustria2002/02/20.
European People's Party (2002): 'European Leaders meet in Sardinia', Press Release, 9 September.
European University Institute (forthcoming): *Evaluation of the Use of New Technologies in order to facilitate Democracy in Europe*, European Parliament (STOA).
Giscard d'Estaing, V. (2002): '*Allocuzione del signor Valéry Giscard d'Estaing Presidente della convenzione europea alla Sala Zuccari, Rome*' 31 October.
'*Indagine conoscitiva sul futuro dell'unione europea, Commissioni riunite III (Affari esteri e comunitari), XIV (Politiche dell'unione europea) della Camera dei deputati e 3a (Affari esteri, emigrazione), Giunta per gli affari delle comunità europee del Senato della Repubblica (2002–2003)*' www.camera.it/chiosco.asp?content = /_dati/leg14/lavori/stencomm/0314c0314/indag/futuro_ unione_europea/elenco.htm.
Informativa del Governo sui lavori della Convenzione europea (2002–03); www.camera.it/_dati/leg14/lavori/stenografici/sed276/s280r.htm.
Istituto Affari Internazionali (2001): *The International Spectator* 36/4, Oct.–Dec.
Lega Nord (2002): '*L'Europa che vogliamo*', Press Release, 30 August, www.leganord.org/pdf/leggere_compr/Aff_Istituz/Europa_popoli.pdf.
Osservatorio sulla Convenzione Europea (2002): '*Comunicare la Convenzione Europea. 200 giorni di attività dell'Osservatorio: Tavola rotonda. Bologna*', 19 September, www.consiglio.regione.emilia-romagna.it/forum2004/tavola_rotonda_compa.pdf.
Osservatorio sulla Convenzione Europea (2003): '*Convenzione Italiana dei Giovani sull'avvenire dell'Europa: Documento finale. Rome, 10–12 January 2003*', www.avvenireuropa.it/UserFiles/66.pdf

Prodi, R. (2002): *The Foundations for the European Project: Speech to the Conference of Presidents*, European Parliament, 22 May.

Scott, J. (2002): Listening at the Convention on the Future of Europe, *German Law Journal* 3/9, www.germanlawjournal.com/past_issues.php?id = 193.

Università di Roma La Sapienza (2002): 'The European Constitution in the Making. Challenges and Possible Achievements of the Brussels Constitutional Convention', Conference of Università di Roma La Sapienza, 31 May–1 June.

The Spanish Case:
Who Was Mobilized and How?

MARGARITA LEÓN, MERCEDES MATEO DIAZ and COVADONGA MESEGUER

INTRODUCTION

Spain is a parliamentary monarchy with a territorial distribution consisting of 17 Autonomous Communities (AC), all of them with legislative power. The first democratic elections after Francoist rule were held in 1977; the Constitution was enacted in 1978. In 1982, the *Partido Socialista Obrero Español* (PSOE; Spanish Socialist Worker's Party) gained power, inaugurating a spell of socialist governments that extended for 14 years. From the very beginning, joining the European Community (EC) was a major objective of the socialist cabinet led by Felipe González. The EC was seen as the road to modernization and a way to put Spain back into the international context after years of isolation. Eventually, in 1986, and following controversial negotiations concerning the agricultural policy, this target was accomplished.

The PSOE was voted out of power in 1996 and replaced by the center-right *Partido Popular* (PP) [Popular Party] led by José María Aznar. During its first term, the PP ruled in coalition with the nationalist Catalan party, *Convergencia i Unio* (CiU; Convergency and Union). In the 2000 national elections, the PP won an absolute majority in parliament, which, at the time of writing, it still had.

During the first semester of 2002, Spain held the presidency of the European Union (EU) with an ambitious agenda that included the debate on the EU Convention (*El Mundo*, 17 January 2002). This essay analyses how the debate has evolved in the Spanish political, social and regional arenas. Despite the demands of certain social and political actors – the Spanish Constitution envisages the possibility of organizing a referendum – the public will not be consulted about the final constitutional text to be delivered after the 2004 intergovernmental conference (IGC). It is foreseen that its approval will be handled through a parliamentary ratification procedure.

The essay proceeds as follows. We start with a discussion of the debate on the Convention in the national political arena. We then review how the debate has proceeded at the regional level as opposed to the national one. Next, we look at the coverage that the media has given the Convention and the analysis of opinion polls. We then focus on civil society, non-governmental organizations (NGOs) and the main interest groups. The final section comprises our conclusions.

THE CONVENTION DEBATE IN THE SPANISH POLITICAL ARENA: NATIONAL PARLIAMENT, CENTRAL GOVERNMENT AND PARTIES

This section surveys the Spanish political debate around the four topics of the Declaration on the Future of Europe (annexed to the Nice Treaty). These four topics are 1) a more precise definition of the competencies of the EU; 2) the status of the Charter of Fundamental Rights; 3) the simplification of the Union treaties; and 4) the role of national parliaments in the European architecture. The debate on the constitutional process is also considered. In particular, this section aims to identify how governments and parties prepare for the Convention by exploring whether or not the future of Europe constitutes a relevant part of their political agendas. The position of the Spanish government with regard to the main issues at stake is also discussed and contrasted with that of the major political parties in opposition.[1]

Within the Convention, two members represent the Spanish parliament. These are Gabriel Cisneros of the PP and Josep Borrell of the PSOE.[2] In addition, one of the Spanish members of the European Parliament (EP), Iñigo Méndez, has been appointed as a representative of the Convention.[3]

The Spanish government launched the debate with the *ad hoc* creation of several forums for debate. First, a Joint Committee Senate/Congress for EU affairs was established in May 2000, headed by the Socialist deputy Josep Borrell, to discuss issues related with the Convention process. This committee has, in turn, created two new subcommittees: one to monitor the enlargement process and the other to monitor the 2004 IGC.[4] Public access to the plenary sessions of the Joint Committee provides a very valuable tool with which to survey the main parties' positions in several ongoing debates.[5] Generally speaking, the motions and initiatives put forward by this committee are concerned with the 'visibility' of the different views representing the range of political parties in parliament and sub-national levels of government.

Second, on the initiative of the Spanish prime minister, José Maria Aznar, the Council for the Debate on the Future of the EU was created in July 2001. The Council, which hosts prominent figures involved in Spanish social, political and economic life, has a mandate to promote and mobilize as many sectors of society as possible – its goal being to create public opinion on European issues by bringing all groups of Spanish society into the debate, encouraging initiatives and collecting suggestions. Its web page gives access to a considerable amount of background information on the debate about the future of Europe, including collected speeches, documents and declarations from politicians and intellectuals, and provides an open forum for debate.[6] Together with the *Ateneo de Madrid*, the Council has created the European Permanent Forum, which holds monthly discussions about the development of the EU. The Council further collaborates with other Spanish foundations and associations in the organization of seminars and meetings on the future of Europe.

Third, the future of Europe constituted – at least on paper – one of the main issues promoted by the Spanish presidency of the EU, and developed from the beginning of January to the end of June 2002. This promotion took on concrete form through its web page (www.ue2002.es/; www.ue2002.es/principal.asp?opcion = 5& subopcion = 2&idioma = espanol), which provided information on the state of the debate and set up links to other relevant EU sites dealing with the Convention.

All these sources are the basis for the analysis that follows, which deals with governmental and political parties' positions with regard to the four issues identified above and the debate on constitutionalization.[7]

First, with regard to a more precise definition of the distribution of competencies or the revision of the controversial concept of subsidiarity, the position taken by the Spanish government has been fundamentally cautious. In particular, the Spanish government has warned against the possibility that this debate served as an excuse to revive nationalistic claims and a 'repatriation' of competencies from the EU towards the member states, and from the latter to their regions without the control of the EU. The government argues that, rather than reopening this debate, emphasis should be placed on an improvement in the coordination between the Union and member states in the administration of policies.[8] However, in a decentralized state such as Spain, with ACs that hold legislative powers and that have been given a considerable (although varying) number of competencies, this debate is highly controversial. This debate, moreover, permeates a considerable part of the Spanish discussion on the future of the EU and has also greatly determined the debate on the would-be role of national parliaments (see the next section). The discussion sets a cautious central government against some regional governments, the latter arguing in favour of a revision of the competencies to be transferred to the Union and standing in favour of the political recognition of regions with legislative competencies at the EU level.[9]

Second, with regard to the inclusion of the entire Charter of Fundamental Rights in the Union treaties, there is a strong consensus in the political arena. In addition, there is also consensus in reinforcing the legitimization of citizens before the European Court of Justice. This would allow citizens living in a member country different from their own to enjoy all the political rights traditionally reserved for the nationals of that country.

Third, with regard to the issue of the simplification of the treaties, the Spanish government agrees that there is a wide margin for making the treaties more comprehensive. In this kind of potentially simplified Treaty, neither the current possibility of opting out nor the second and third pillars would make sense. This, the government holds, should be made compatible with the permanence of procedures and mechanisms adapted to different policies. Also according to the government, a prior step in this simplification should be to give the Union legal personality.

Furthermore, any simplification should respect the *acquis communitaire*, with its institutional equilibrium. There is no support on the part of the Spanish government for the proposal to divide the text of the treaties into two parts of different nature, depending on whether the proposals are of fundamental character or of a sectoral or other type. Rather than simplifying, this division would only create more complications and might affect the enhanced role that is envisaged for national parliaments.[10] The Spanish government considers that this reform would exceed the Nice mandate to leave the meaning of the treaties unaltered.

Note, however, that this cautious approach to the simplification of the treaties is in clear contrast with an important institutional initiative launched during the Spanish presidency of the EU: the election of the president of the European Council for a period running from two-and-a-half years to five. In addition, the appointment of a presidential team made up of five or six heads of government, following a rotation system, has also been suggested. This initiative would put an end to the current mechanism of six-month rotating presidencies, which is regarded as untenable from the perspective of an enlarged EU. Another suggestion is to give the Council co-legislative powers together with the Commission. This initiative, if accepted in the IGC 2004, will mean that the treaties will need to be modified.

There has also been a heated debate on how treaties and the relative powers of institutions can be modified to reduce the alleged democratic deficit of the EU. In this regard, the major point of discussion has focused on the role that will be given to the Council and the EP and its standing *vis-à-vis* the Commission. Interestingly, the proposal launched by the Spanish presidency has been regarded as a potential threat to the current status of the Commission by other Spanish political forces and, overall, as contradictory.

Fourth, with regard to the role of national parliaments in the European architecture, the debate has been wide, especially given its domestic implications. Overall, the Spanish government has been opposed to radical transformations.[11] It has instead been in favour of increasing the democratic legitimacy of the Union, suggesting the drafting of a binding charter on the intervention of national parliaments in EU matters. This hypothesized 'Charter of National Parliaments' would establish some minimum requirement of control by national parliaments, consistent with the adoption of new competencies by the EU that are not explicitly recognized in the treaties.[12] At home, parties in opposition have asked for the recognition of the fact that regional parliaments with legislative powers should also be involved in the decision process and be granted representation in the EP and other institutions of the Union.

Finally, the Spanish territorial distribution of power has also influenced the debate about a constitution and what kind is required for Europe. On these issues, the Spanish government has defended the *status quo* with more emphasis than other political parties. It has warned against a misuse of both the terms 'federalism' and 'constitution'. For some, the discussion is seen in terms of greater decentralization and a renewed appropriation of competencies for national states and regions. This is certainly the view of Spanish nationalist parties. For others, the idea of a constitution would entail a greater integration and a transfer of sovereignty to the Union. Viewed in this perspective, the position of the Spanish government is quite sceptical, recognizing that 1) nothing prevents a treaty from having a constitutional character and 2) that neither the objective conditions nor the characteristics of the integration process, based on complex equilibria and evolution, fit with the rigidity that the classical concept of a constitution entails.[13]

THE CONVENTION DEBATE IN THE SPANISH POLITICAL ARENA: AUTONOMOUS COMMUNITIES AND THE 'REGIONAL QUESTION'

The Joint Commission senate on the EU mentioned above has discussed the role of the regions, and in particular the role of nationalist and regional parties, in the Spanish path to the Convention process.[14] Nationalist and regional parties have urged the central government to establish channels of communication and coordination among the national and regional levels of government, fearing an under-representation of their views in what some of them see as a 'centralist position'. Furthermore, issues concerning the substantive nature of the role of regions in the future of Europe have also been discussed in this political forum. For example, during the seminar 'The Europe of citizens' held in Trieste, Eduardo Zaplana (PPE), then vice-president of the Committee of the Regions (CoR) and member of the Convention, said that 'when we, the regional leaders, ask for a bigger role for the regions in Europe, we are convinced that this is the best way to bring the European Union closer to the citizens' (*El Mundo*, 01 December 2002; see also the Venice Declaration of the Group of the European People's Party in CoR).

The central government has always claimed a unified and consensual self-positioning of Spain in the Convention process. Regional parties, and particularly nationalist parties, tend to see this affirmation with a certain degree of scepticism. The root of the disagreement is, in the end, that Europe is conceived very differently by central government and nationalist parties in terms of power distribution and territorial divisions. Nevertheless, the degree of involvement in the debate has been very uneven. Of all the 17 ACs, the most clearly active regions in the Convention debate have been the Basque Country and Catalonia. The two regional governments have established parallel 'conventions' linked to the debate on the EU Convention.

The *Convenció Catalana per al Debat sobre el Futur de la Unió Europea* [Catalan Convention for the Debate on the Future of the EU] was created in October 2001 by the Catalan government and managed by a group of experts through the independent body *Patronat Català Pro Europa*. The idea was to promote the participation of Catalan's citizens in the debate on the future of Europe. This forum provides a wide range of information – accessible through the web page (www.infoeuropa.org/convenciocatalana) and translated into Catalan – about the debates on the EU Convention at the EU, national and sub-national levels. The Convention is particularly concerned with issues of cultural pluralism in 'plurinational societies'.

The final report '80 proposals for a New Europe'[15] by the Catalan Convention, published in January 2003, summarized the outcome of the eight working groups (WGs).[16] Many of the proposals support the explicit political and constitutional recognition of regions with legislative power (all the Spanish ACs), especially those, such as Catalonia, considered to be stateless nations. The report is also in favour of the recognition of national, linguistic and cultural pluralism inside member states. As for institutional design, the Catalan Convention supports the development of a federal system with the direct representation of regions with legislative authority in the Council, the Commission and the EP. Other suggestions include the creation of a Regional Chamber, the right to bring actions before the Court of Justice and the strengthening of the subsidiarity principle.

Other regions have also engaged with the EU debates. Prior to the Laeken Declaration, the Basque government launched an official declaration entitled 'Declaration of the Basque Government in view of the next European Summit in Laeken'. The contents of the document refer mainly to the role of the regions in the future of Europe. Like the Catalan project, the text strongly advocates an active political role for 'nations without a state' and regions with legislative capacities in the construction of the EU and in the decision-making processes of the Union. A clearer process of decentralization through the use of the principles of subsidiarity and proportionality is also demanded, which would be strengthened through a redefinition of competencies among the different governmental levels. It is also in favour of giving a constitutional category to the legislative regions. The declaration is clearly pro-European. In particular, and probably as a way to overcome the national conflict, the text is strongly supportive of a single European identity and European constitution in a pluralistic environment.

Overall, and given the highly decentralized nature of the Spanish state, the regions – especially those with a strongly differentiated character – have great expectations of the EU arena. Regional governments have criticized the central state for many years for not developing any instrument to enable the regions to participate in the European Council of Ministers. Moreover, in the broader context, regions and 'nations without state' all over Europe share a number of demands concerning their role in the reformed and enlarged Europe foreseen for the future. The lack of power of CoR and the interpretation of the subsidiarity principle exclusively in terms of the EU-state level, are two important questions that have been addressed in the constitutional debate – which has also been enriched by a lively debate among some of the regions at the European level (Keating, M. 2003 'Nations and Regions' *Holyrood*, 25 Feb; Keating 2003).

VISIBILITY AND COVERAGE OF THE CONVENTION TOPIC IN THE MEDIA

The fact that the Convention was launched when Spain held the EU presidency probably explains why the event had such extensive coverage in the Spanish press and media. An important part of the international section of newspapers in this period was devoted to issues and discussions surrounding the Convention process. More specifically, the issue of enlargement was given particular attention. The articles and news treating the Convention focused on four figures in particular: the president of the Convention, Giscard D'Estaing; the president of the commission, Romano Prodi; the representative of the Spanish government in the Convention, Ana Palacio; and the head of the Joint Committee senate for EU affairs, Josep Borrell. Furthermore, some newspapers created discussion forums and surveys on their websites to gauge readers' opinions concerning the future of Europe. This was the case, for instance, with *El País*, which launched two surveys under the title 'La Nueva Europa'.

The debate on the Convention was widely covered in the regional sections of the national press and in regional newspapers, especially in the Basque Country and Catalonia. The fact that none of the four members representing Spain in the Convention WG were from the Catalan and Basque nationalist parties (two were members of the PP and two the PSOE) gave rise to a heated debate, well documented in the press, about the 'centralist intentions' of the Spanish government.

Intellectuals and academics also contributed to the debate through the press and other circles. Several seminars and conferences were organized in universities and research centres. Not surprisingly, political scientists and constitutional theorists have, for the most part, dominated the debate. Intellectuals and academics have also participated actively within the different committees and groups of experts appointed by the central and sub-national governments. Two of these are, for example, the autonomous *Consejo para el debate sobre el futuro de la Unió Europea* [Council for the debate on the future of the European Union], directed by an ex-president of the Constitutional Court, M. Alvaro Rodríguez and the *Comisió d'experts de la Convenció Catalana* [Experts Committee of the Catalan Convention], directed by Ferrán Requejo, Professor of Political Science at the Pompeu Fabra University[17] and the Scientific Experts' Working Group of the Basque Convention. It is worth noting, however, that women are under-represented in these selected groups. For example, only two out of ten members of the Council for the debate on the future of Europe are female. Similarly, just two of the 14 members of the Experts' Committee of the Catalan Convention are women.[18]

Opinion Polls and Surveys

Two questions concern us in this section: Is public opinion well-informed about the issues raised by the Convention and the work in progress? If so, what is its opinion?

Compared to the relatively low coverage observed until the end of the year 2002, the first few months of 2003 saw a salient rise in Convention-related issues in the media. One might argue, with reason, that a rise in media coverage will be reflected in increasing levels of awareness and knowledge in public opinion. This fact justifies the discussion addressed in the coming paragraphs concerning measurements made at different points in time. Eurobarometers and other national surveys should shed some light on this question.

To start with, and in terms of interest shown by the public in EU businesses, awareness, information and knowledge, the Spring 2002 Eurobarometer has had a particular focus on the attitudes of public opinion in the member states towards the European Union.[19] It is a bit worrying to notice that, whereas the process of the Convention represents a wide consultative and participatory exercise aimed at inclusion and dialogue, the awareness of the public is very small: only about 28 per cent of the European citizens interviewed have heard about the Convention on the future of the EU. In Spain, the percentage (about 40 per cent) is over the European average, but still 50 per cent of those surveyed admit they had not heard of the Convention before (Eurobarometer 57.1: 30).

Compared to the spring edition, the Autumn 2002 Eurobarometer shows the same figure for the European sample (28 per cent) and a somewhat higher level of awareness in Spain – that is, slightly over 40 per cent (see Eurobarometer 58 Report 2003: 98; *Informe español* Eurobarometer 58.1: 14). Finally, the spring 2003 Eurobarometer once again displays an increase in the percentage of people who had heard about the Convention on the future of Europe (see Eurobarometer 59 Report 2003: 69). The latter observations point towards the expectation mentioned above – that is, as media coverage intensifies, there should be a progressive increase in public awareness.

Some of the EU political questions and events have awoken public interest more than others. For example, 70 per cent of the Spanish citizens surveyed were aware that their country held the presidency during the first six months of the year 2002 (see Eurobarometer 57 Report 2002: 19). As concerns the enlargement, almost half of the Spanish population felt not very well informed about the process, which is about the same as the European percentage. Sixty four per cent of the population showed positive attitudes towards the enlargement, whereas 14 per cent expressed disapproval. However, opinions vary concerning the way in which this process should be made and the countries that should be part of it. A majority of those surveyed think that enlargement will mean an enrichment in terms of cultural diversity and an increasing important position for the Union in the world.

The *Centro de Investigaciones Sociológicas* (CIS; Centre for Sociological Research) runs surveys – or 'barometers' – every month. One can find in them several questions with which to measure the level of knowledge Spanish public opinion displays about the Union. In January 2001, people were asked to assess the role of the Spanish government during the Nice IGC. Almost a half of the respondents had no knowledge of this summit. Almost one year later, in the barometer of April 2002, people were asked to express their awareness of the European summit held in Barcelona during 15–16 March 2002. On this occasion, a little more than 70 per cent had heard of it. However, among those, only a quarter showed a particular interest in following the event. A slightly higher level of awareness was also observed in the barometer of June 2002, concerning the European summit of Sevilla (77.7 per cent of the respondents had heard about the summit). However, the interest showed was even lower. Finally, in the barometer of July 2002, around 48 per cent of the surveyed expressed some or a great deal of interest about the news concerning the EU; only about 17 per cent of the respondents expressed no interest at all.

The interest people show depends to a large extent on how important they believe EU institutions and decisions are to their own lives. Therefore, as a second aspect, together with awareness and knowledge, the question of the EU's importance to the public will be addressed here. As a preliminary question concerning this topic, EU citizens were asked to express their opinion about the importance of different institutions and bodies in the life of the EU, and among them the role of the Convention on the future of the Union. In total, 35 per cent of the EU citizens interviewed think that the Convention has an important role, against 16 per cent who think that it does not play an important role in the Union's life. In Spain, 38 per cent of the interviewed would not be able to tell whether or not the Convention plays an important role in the Union (*Informe español* Eurobarometer 57.1: 30).

The EU citizens were also asked to say whether the activities and decisions of the EU have a great effect, some effect or no effect on people like themselves. Thirty three per cent of the population interviewed in Spain said that these decisions have a great effect, 43 per cent said it has some effect, and 14 per cent think EU decisions have no effect.

How is the EU perceived by citizens and to what extent do they trust its institutions? The question of the democratic deficit of the EU has been largely referred to in official and opinion papers. It is to a large extent, though, inspiring the reform process and therefore, as a third point, knowing the levels of trust and support the public has in and for the EU institutions and the European project is fundamental to the understanding what is to be achieved – in terms of both the meaning and scope of reform. It is important to stress that the levels of support are related to subjective perceptions of knowledge, in the sense that 'the more people feel they know about the European Union, the more likely it is that they support it' (Eurobarometer 57 Report 2002: 12). Overall, the levels of self-perceived knowledge have slightly increased in Spain, and therefore one should expect also an increase in the levels of support. Indeed, support for EU membership has increased significantly in Spain (9 per cent) between autumn 2001 and spring 2002 (see Eurobarometer 57 Report 2002: 22). Sixty six per cent of the interviewed said that the membership is a good thing for Spain.

Overall, the EU today has a more positive image among its citizens than before. Fifty seven per cent of the Spanish population interviewed expressed positive views about the Union, 32 per cent were neutral, and only 5 per cent were negative about it (see Eurobarometer 57 Report 2002: 51). Just as for a majority of the citizens of other member states, Spaniards tend to see the EU as something basically meaning freedom to travel, study and work anywhere – with the Euro following as a corollary of this basic meaning. The Spring 2003 Eurobarometer reveals no significant differences in this regard (see Eurobarometer 59 Report 2003: 56). Spaniards tend to see the Union as economic prosperity to a larger extent than the mean view of EU citizens on this subject, followed by perceptions of the Union as a way of having a stronger say in the world and a larger cultural diversity (see Eurobarometer 57 Report 2002: 53; *Informe español* Eurobarometer 57.1: 17).

Finally, this fourth and last section of the report on public attitudes concentrates on the reform process itself: what does the public think about the reforms undertaken in different areas and the process and institutions rethinking the future of Europe? The following will address people's opinions on several of the issues at stake in the discussions and the reform process of the EU.

Overall, 63 per cent of European citizens surveyed expressed positive attitudes about having a constitution for the EU. In the Spring 2002 Eurobarometer, Spain belonged to the group of countries in which support for a constitution was below the average: 58 per cent of Spanish citizens interviewed were of the opinion that the EU should have a constitution, whereas only 9 per cent were against it (see Eurobarometer 57 Report 2002: 67). As of Autumn 2002, the percentage of Spaniards supporting an EU Constitution had increased substantially – to 64 per cent, and was just one per cent the percentage of support expressed throughout all member states (see *Informe español* Eurobarometer 58: 30). Six months later, the Eurobarometer released during spring 2003 shows Spain moving up into the cluster of countries displaying higher support for a constitution than the average for the 15 EU member states. It is important to mention, though, that whereas the level of support remained stable in Spain (around 64 per cent), the European average decreased by two points to 63 per cent (see Eurobarometer 59 Report 2003: 83).

One of the four objectives stated in the Declaration on the Future of Europe – supposed to guide the Convention's work – was a more precise definition of the EU competencies. In the Eurobarometer of spring 2002, the interviewed were asked to express their views about current actions and priorities of the EU. Among the questions, they were asked to say whether or not reforming the institutions of the EU and welcoming of new member countries should be top priorities. Whereas more than half of the citizens in the member states said that institutional reform ought to be a priority (53 per cent), only 27 per cent gave priority to enlargement (against 60 per cent who said it was not a priority). Overall, the top priorities for EU citizens seem to be the maintaining of peace and security in Europe, the fighting of terrorism and reduction of unemployment (all three are supported by 90 per cent of those interviewed). Furthermore, around 80 per cent of people think that the guaranteeing of the rights of the individual and respect for the principles of democracy in Europe should also be a priority issue, and 68 per cent think that it is important that the EU gets closer to European citizens – by, for example, giving then more information about the EU, its policies and its institutions (Eurobarometer 57 Report 2002: 73).

The May 2000 survey (CIS Study 2392) addressed the EU as special issue. The interviewed were asked to say whether the EU should have a real government, or if the governments of the member states should always have the last word when it comes to important decisions. A majority of those surveyed were of the opinion that national governments should have the last word, whereas 22 per cent of them wanted the Union to have an effective government. The same question was asked again two years later in the barometer of July 2002 (CIS Study 2463). The positions had barely experienced any change (the number of those who wanted a European government increased by only about three points – from 22 to 24.7 per cent, and the percentage of those who wanted the national governments to make the important decisions had slightly decreased – from 59.3 to 58.7 per cent).

As a final point, in the barometer of January 2002 (CIS Study 2444) people were asked to respond with what they felt were the key issues that the Spanish presidency should deal with. It was an open question, but respondents could not mention more than two issues. A majority of those surveyed mentioned fighting terrorism (62.3 per cent); this issue was followed in importance by the Euro (15.2 per cent), tackling unemployment (13 per cent), economic policies (9.6 per cent), the enlargement of the EU (9 per cent), immigration (6.8 per cent), agricultural policy (4.1 per cent) and the development of a common European foreign policy (3.2 per cent). Note that a majority of those issues are also identified as important by the public when it comes to domestic politics.

Summarizing, on the positive side, there is increasing support for an EU constitution among the Spaniards surveyed in the Eurobarometer between Spring 2002 and Spring 2003 (from 58 to 64 per cent). Another positive figure is a slight increase in public awareness of the Convention, which may be linked to an increase in media coverage as the end of the Convention works was approaching. Yet, increasing levels of awareness do not necessarily yield higher levels of public involvement and participation, which was one of the major objectives of the Convention – at least as stated in the declarations framing the reform process. A second remark concerns the still fairly poor interest people show in EU affairs as compared with domestic matters. The EU becomes an issue as far as people can feel that the national arena is directly touched. As an illustration of this, whereas the information Spaniards have about the discussions on the future of the Union is relatively low, the number of people informed about the national presidencies of the EU or the EU summits run in the country is significantly higher (around 70 per cent of people knew about Spain's presidency, as opposed to 40 per cent who had heard of the Convention). On the whole, one can say that not only do politicians tend to drag the Convention debates towards domestic issue targets – just as with European questions in general, but, as we have seen, public opinion also tends to see EU politics through the lenses of the most pressing domestic problems – such as, in the Spanish case, terrorism or unemployment.

CIVIL SOCIETY, NGOS AND MAIN INTEREST GROUPS

The groups that have been involved in the Convention debate are mostly groups that belong to a wider European network. This is the case, for instance, with the European Disability Forum (*Foro Europeo de Discapacidad*), the Association of Women of Southern Europe (AFEM), or the Network of European Citizens (*Red Ciudadanas de Europa*). The 'European link' gives these organizations the necessary information and space to express their views. Official Internet sites are the central gathering point for many.[20]

Perhaps motivated by the fact that 2003 will be the 'European Year of People with Disability', several European and national organizations for the disabled have raised a number of demands concerning the rights of this group and the Convention. The European Disability Forum, which comprises a total of 70 NGOs, the *Organización Nacional de Ciegos España* (ONCE; National Organization for the Blind) and the *Comité Español de Representantes de Minusválidos* (Spanish Committee of Handicapped Representatives) have common points of interest. First, they aim to integrate the Charter of Fundamental Rights with EU treaties. Second, they ask for constitutional guarantees of the non-discrimination principle and positive action instruments. Third, they are in favour of the 'social economy' and investment in social services of general interest.

Groups concerned with gender equality issues and women's rights – such as, for instance, the *Red Ciudadanas de Europa*, the above mentioned AFEM, the Association of Women Lawyers (EWLA), the Commission's Network of Legal Experts on Equality between Women and Men, and the European Women's Lobby (EWL) – have also raised a number of concerns. The main points put forward are the inclusion of a title on the 'equality of women and men' in the future treaty and related to the deficit of the representation of women in the debate on the Convention. The establishment of mechanisms to ensure gender mainstreaming is another issue that is often mentioned. In this respect, the Jean Monnet Project of the European Commission organized a conference in Brussels on 4 March 2003 concerning 'Gender Equality and Europe's Future', in which people from lobbies, NGOs, academia and other civil society representatives were invited to participate. Spanish attendance was significantly high.[21]

Through the intervention of the Spanish Pontifical Council, the church has also written and published a proposal for the Convention. In this proposal, it is urged – as the Pope and the European Pontifical Commission have done – that an explicit reference to the 'common Christian values of the European soul' is included in the final document. The issue has gained considerable salience after the presentation by the Praesidium of the 1st and 2nd preliminary drafts of the Constitutional Treaty,[22] in which, however, no explicit reference was made to 'Christian values'.

As for interest groups, the two main Spanish trade unions (CC.OO. and UGT) devote significant coverage in their international sections to the Convention and related topics. These organizations are also part of the European Trade Union Confederation (ETUC) and thus their views and opinions can be seen as part of the general position adopted by the European Confederation. Trade unions' documents on the Convention are primarily concerned with aspects regarding the European social model and the European Employment Strategy. The main Spanish employers' organization (CEOE) is also a member of the Union of Industrial and Employers' Confederation of Europe (UNICE). Thus, they are involved in those aspects of the Convention which refer to economic and labour policy and new forms of governance.

Finally, it is interesting to note the emphasis that the EU has placed on young people as compared to other traditionally organized interest groups. In Spain, youth organizations have been fairly active in the European debate. Just as an example, the *Foro Generación del 78*, an association of young professionals that has been active since 1999, aims at providing a meeting point for discussion about current political, economic and cultural issues. During 2001 and 2002, they organized a series of joint activities with the *Consejo para el Debate sobre el Futuro de la Unión Europea* around the topics of the Convention and the reform process of the EU (see *Foro Generación del 78* 2002a; 2002b).

CONCLUDING REMARKS

The Spanish debate on the future of the EU was decisively framed by the declared priorities of the Spanish EU presidency, which coincided with the opening of the Convention process. The debate on the Convention was always an important issue on the agenda of the Spanish EU presidency. However, this debate has, to a certain extent, been overshadowed by a host of many other important topics with a strong domestic impact. In particular, among the six declared priorities during the Spanish presidency of the EU (the effective establishment of the Euro; economic reforms; the enlargement process; the debate on the future of Europe; foreign policy; and the fight against terrorism), those that already have an important internal dimension were given priority on the agenda. It is obvious that detaching these issues from that of the future of Europe is artificial. Clearly, the greater role of the Union in issues such as immigration, foreign affairs or the fight against terrorism is connected with the discussion on the distribution of competencies, and the enlargement of the EU is one of the main thrusts behind the proposals to change some aspects of the European architecture. Still, it is worth pointing out the extent to which the debate on the future of Europe in Spain has been driven by some specific features, which might or might not be common to other EU countries.

First, the debate is strongly affected by the particular characteristics of the Spanish territorial distribution of power. The limits and/or potentialities of a 'plurinational' or decentralized state are still a major source of conflict between the central and regional administrations. The territorial organization of the state as drawn by the Spanish Constitution in 1978 is still subject to dispute in a far-from-finished political debate. The strongest Autonomous Communities, predominantly Catalonia and the Basque Country, ask for greater economic and political independence in what they consider as a legacy of the democratization process. The EU is in this respect seen as a 'window of opportunities' by all the parties involved. While the central government argues that 'more Europe' cannot mean greater territorial fragmentation, regions hope for a strong supranational power that will allow for the direct representation of regions with legislative powers and home nations, and a clear definition of the subsidiarity principle. Yet, and quite surprisingly, this internal debate is only to a very limited extent reflected in the official declarations and the proposals of the Spanish government, which redirect any question related to the voice of the ACs to the Committee of the Regions.

A second defining feature of the Convention debate in Spain is, as has been stated earlier, the attention given by politicians and the media to questions of particular relevance to domestic politics. Possibly as a strategy to catch the interest of public opinion or its support, the EU arena has often been used as a 'legitimizing factor' and a chance to push domestic politics and problems forward. The best example of this is the fight against terrorism since the events of 11 September 2001 have brought this right to the centre of the international political agenda. This has also been one of the Spanish domestic priorities during the last few decades, and one of the major concerns of Spanish public opinion. A specific focus on this question when engaging in European politics in the national arena probably allows political leaders to engage in a double-edged politics: on the one hand, they bring Europe into the national arena more easily, and, on the other, they legitimize their action at the European level by linking it to domestic issues.

In a similar vein, different actors (either governmental or non-governmental) have profited from the Convention debate to raise issues of their own concern that have not found any representation in the national political sphere. The case of groups for the disabled and women's rights are examples. Other organizations, trade unions and the employers' confederation, for instance, have been actively involved in the debate at the European level through their respective European federations ETUC and UNICE. Their sphere of action, in this case economic and labour market reforms and the European Social Model, is no longer limited to the nation state but now has a very robust transnational character. The defence of workers' rights or employers' interests takes place at the EU level as much as at the national level.

Thirdly, Spanish public opinion usually shows a pro-European character – and the debate on the Convention is no exception. However, the public's awareness in relation to the Convention is, generally speaking, low even though it is higher than the European average. This is worrying if we consider that the underlying aim of the debate is in principle to function as a consultative and participatory exercise.

Finally, and as a concluding remark, the debate on the Convention has addressed important substantive issues both for the country and for the future of Europe, but the mobilization of society in these areas has been noticeably weak. Perhaps this is because at the European level more generally, it is more of a top-down debate than a bottom-up one. In other words, only individuals (intellectuals and politicians) and groups with access to information and to the different networks have been able to fully participate in the debate, while the ordinary citizen, though approving, is generally not actively involved in this open forum. In the first months of the year 2003, the saliency of the Convention in the media increased significantly. With the final outcomes of the work of the Convention group approaching, the debate on the Convention gathered momentum. On the positive side, an intensification of the debate has resulted in increasing levels of awareness and knowledge in public opinion; however, this may well have not entailed any increase in public involvement.

NOTES

1. These are the PSOE, the CiU, the United Left (IU) and the Basque Nationalist Party (PNV). Other parties with representation in parliament are: Galician Nationalist Party (BNG), Canary Coalition (CC), Andalusian Party (PA), Eskerra Republicana of Catalonia (ER), Initiative for Catalonia-Greens (IC), *Eusko Alkartasuna* (EA) and Chunta Aragonesista (CA). All these parties, except for PP, PSOE and IU, are regional parties.
2. The substitutes are Alejandro Muñoz (PP) and Diego López (PSOE).
3. He has also taken part in the drafting of the Charter of Fundamental Rights.
4. See www.congreso.es, under Joint Commissions.
5. It also reveals a notable degree of discontent with the way the Commission has worked to date in terms of the quantity and quality of information from the government to the Commission.
6. www.futuroeuropa.es/consejo.html
7. The website www.europa.eu.int/futurum/congov_es.htm#spain, under the European Commission web page on the Convention, was also used; it contains documents by the Spanish government and parliament.
8. José Maria Aznar, speech delivered at the Institute for International Studies, Paris, 26 September 2000; José Maria Aznar, speech delivered at the Ceremony of the European Merit Award to Viviane Reding, Brussels, 9 October 2001.
9. This argument is forwarded with great frequency. See, for instance, CiU, 8 Oct. 2002; *Grupo Mixto*, 25 Oct. 2001, Joint Commission for the EU).

10. This is because everything that is not fundamental could be ratified by qualified majority of the Council, regardless of having been passed by the national parliaments.
11. Rudi Ubeda (2002). See, also, www.europa.eu.int/futurum/congov_es.htm#spain.
12. José Maria Aznar, speech delivered at the Ceremony of the European Merit Award to Viviane Reding, Brussels, 9 October 2001.
13. Working Paper of the MFA, Sept. 2001.
14. Diario de Sesiones Cortes Generales (2002) VII Legislatura n.90 Comisiones Mixtas para la Union Europea.
15. See www.infoeuropa.org/convenciocatalana/cas/spanish_80_propuestas.pdf.
16. These were: Simplification of the Treaties; Towards an European Constitution; Delimitation of Competencies; Institutional Design; Democracy: Participation, Transparency and Efficiency; Democracy and Cultural Pluralism; Democracy: Stateless Nations and European Regions; Democracy and Globalization.
17. See for instance, Requejo, F. 'La UE y la Convención Catalana' [The EU and the Catalan Convention], La Vanguardia, 18 March 2002.
18. No data was available for the members of the Basque Convention.
19. For a detailed description of the sampling and other technical specifications, see both the Spanish and the EU15 reports.
20. See www.futuroeuropa.es.
21. See www.europa.eu.int/comm/education/ajm/equality.
22. Plenary session on 28 Oct. 2002 (CONV 369/02), and 6 Feb. 2003 (CONV 528/03) respectively.

REFERENCES

Foro Generación del 78 (2002a): Introducción al 'Documento sobre el Futuro de la Unión Europea' [Introduction to the Document about the Future of the European Union], Madrid, June; www.europa.eu.int/futurum/forum_convention/documents/contrib/acad/0260_r_es.pdf, downloaded 12 June 2002.
Foro Generación del 78 (2002b): 'Documento sobre el Futuro de la Unión Europea' [Document about the Future of the European Union], www.europa.eu.int/futurum/forum_convention/documents/contrib/acad/0260_c_es.pdf, downloaded 12 June 2002.
Grupo del PPE (2002): 'Europa necesita a sus ciudadanos! Regiones y cuidades fuertes – los pilares de Europa' [Europe needs their care! Strong regions and cities – the pillars of Europe], Declaración de Venecia del Grupo del PPE en el CDR, 5 July 2002; www.cor.eu.int/convention/pdf/EPP_es.pdf, downloaded 12 June 2002.
Keating, M. (2003): 'The European Constitutional Convention. Debates within the European Regions', Paper for the Committee of the Regions, Jan.
Pique, J. (2002): 'Intervencion en el Seminario "Fazit: Europe"', Organizado por el periodico Frankfurter Allgemeine Zeitung y el Centre for Applied Policy Research [Intervention in the Seminar: Europe', Organized by the Frankfurter Allgemeine Zeitung newspaper and the Centre for Applied Policy Research], Berlin, 4 June, www.futuroeuropa.es/declar.html.
Rudi Ubeda, L.F. (2002): 'The Role of National Parliaments in the European Union', Paper prepared for the 'Conference of Speakers of the European Union', Madrid, 8–9 June; www.europa.eu.int/futurum/documents/contrib/cont080602_en.pdf, downloaded 12 June 2002.

Official Records

Office of the European Parliament in Spain, www.europarl.es/futuro/presentacion.htm, downloaded 12 March 2002.
The European Convention, www.european-convention.eu.int, downloaded 10/15/2002.
European Parliament website, www.europarl.telemak.com, downloaded 12 May 2002.

Consejo Español para el Debate sobre el futuro de la Unión Europea [Spanish Council for the Debate about the future of the European Union], www.futuroeuropa.es/, downloaded 22 November 2002.

Secretariat of the European Convention, 'Report on National Debate on the future of Europe: Spain', Brussels (CONV 136/02), 20 June 2002; www.register.consilium.eu.int/pdf/en/02/cv00/00136en2.pdf, downloaded 11 December 2002.

Delegación española del grupo parlamentario del partido socialista europeo [Spanish Delegation of the Parliamentary Group of the European Socialist Party], www.psoe-pe.org, downloaded 12 March 2002.

Parlamento Europeo Oficina en España [European Parliament Office in Spain], www.europarl.es/referencia.php?source = parlamento/presenta.phtm, downloaded 12 March 2002.

Congreso de los Diputados [Deputies' Congress], www.congreso.es.

Surveys

CIS [Centro de Investigaciones Sociológicas], *Barómetro de Julio 2002* (Estudio 2463), http://www.cis.es/baros/mar2463.htm (as of 12/02/2002).

CIS, *Barómetro de Abril 2002* (Estudio 2454), http://www.cis.es/baros/mar2454.htm (as of 12/02/2002).

CIS, *Barómetro de Junio 2002* (Estudio 2459), http://www.cis.es/baros/mar2459.htm (as of 12/02/2002).

CIS, *Barómetro de Enero 2002* (Estudio 2444), http://www.cis.es/baros/mar2444.htm (as of 12/02/2002).

CIS, *Barómetro de Enero 2001* (Estudio 2406), http://www.cis.es/baros/mar2406.htm (as of 12/02/2002).

CIS, *Barómetro de Mayo 2000* (Estudio 2392), www.cis.es/baros/mar2392.htm (as of 12/02/2002).

European Commission (Spring 2003), *Eurobarometer. Public Opinion in the European Union* (EB 59), European Commission: Brussels, (http://europa.eu.int/comm/public_opinion/archives/eb/eb59/EB59_Rapport_Final_FR.pdf, as of 30/09/2003).

European Opinion Research Group (Spring 2003), *Eurobarometer. Public Opinion in the European Union: National Report Spain* (EB 59), European Commission: Brussels, (http://europa.eu.int/comm/public_opinion/archives/eb/eb59/eb59.1_spain.pdf, as of 30/09/2003).

European Commission (Spring 2002), *Eurobarometer. Public Opinion in the European Union* (EB 57.1), European Commission: Brussels, (http://europa.eu.int/comm/public_opinion/archives/eb/eb57/eb57_en.pdf, as of 12/02/2002).

European Opinion Research Group (October 2002), *Eurobarómetro 57 – Informe estándar nacional* (EB57.1), Brussels, (http://europa.eu.int/comm/public_opinion/archives/eb/eb57/eb57_spain.pdf, as of 12/02/2002).

The Spanish Intellectual Debate on the Future of the EU: Who Was Mobilized and with What Effects?

CARLOS CLOSA MONTERO

INTRODUCTION

Intellectuals made their voice heard during the Convention and the preparatory stage more than at any former round of major European Union (EU) reforms. The accessibility and transparency of the Convention and its 'listening' to civil society stimulated some degrees of mobilization of educated elites. However, this should not be taken as meaning comprehensive participation. Groups normally associated with this social category (such as artists, writers, liberal professions, etc.) remained aloof from the debate. Mobilization was significant only at the level of certain classes of intellectuals: specifically, lawyers, political scientists and philosophers or, in other words, those associated broadly with the academic and research world. Why did this happen? The reform process involved, to a large extent, an intellectual exercise of definition, a scholarly exercise of discussion of conceptual categories rather than the classical exercise of aggregating specific choices performed by governmental negotiators. What is a constitution? What is a federation? How should competencies be distributed? These are the kind of issues normally dealt with by academics.

The debate had a transnational, European dimension, but, in most member states, it remained constrained within national frames of reference. This essay examines the mobilization of Spanish intellectuals. It seeks to measure the influence of intellectuals on the domestic political process triggered by the Convention and their possible influence in terms of shaping the perceptions of Spaniards at the Convention. It draws on newspaper articles as well as discourses and scholarly articles as its main sources. The first section refers to the political background of the debate and presents the organizational arenas for it, whilst the second describes the background of intellectuals and the main topics in the discussion. The conclusions point towards a mixed evaluation: the Convention as a process of mobilization (Lucarelli and Radaelli, this issue) produced a high degree of interaction between political actors and intellectuals, but there is plenty of evidence of the limited ability of intellectuals to influence policy-makers and to operate as a bridge to wider audiences.

BACKGROUND: POLITICAL ATTITUDES AND ORGANIZATIONAL DIMENSIONS

The general attitude of the Spanish government towards the reform process, the Convention and the debate can be characterized as aloof (see also León, Meseguer and Diaz, this issue). Two features marked the debate (both political and intellectual) before the opening of the Convention: a reactive focus and a defensive tone. Spanish debate, broadly speaking, reacted to proposals formulated by other European leaders and/or by EU institutions (that is, the Declarations of Nice and Laeken) (on the debate before the Convention, see, generally, Closa 2003). Spanish politicians and academics alike produced a comparatively reduced number of contributions to the debate.

The Convention acted as a catalyst and as a point of reference that supplied intellectuals with both inputs and a diffuse target for their proposals. It also justified the creation of organizational forums for intellectual debate. Two of these deserve a mention: the Council for the Debate on the Future of Europe and the initiatives around the *Real Instituto Elcano*.

The Council for the Debate on the Future of Europe

In order to implement the Declaration of Nice with the creation of a national debate, the government created the *Consejo para el debate sobre el futuro de la Unión Europea* (Council for the debate on the future of the European Union).[1] The decree establishing the Council certified its independent character. The Council would not represent the government, and its members would act in a personal capacity. The government named Alvaro Rodríguez-Bereijo, professor of fiscal law, a former chairman of the Constitutional Court and Spanish representative in the Convention on the Charter of Fundamental Rights, as president. He had full freedom to designate the members of the Council. He named 11 public figures with a political, socio-economic or academic profile. Just one of them, Iñigo Méndez de Vigo (a member of the Convention and its Praesidium as representative of the European Parliament (EP)), could be considered a specialist on European issues.

Evidence suggests, though, a certain degree of steering influence by the government. First, even though the Council was located physically within the *Ministerio de Asuntos Exteriores* (MAE; Ministry of Foreign Affairs), it depended organically on the general secretary of the presidency (that is, Aznar's immediate environment). Second, the Council's official remit was to enhance public debate and 'transcend' narrow circles. Yet the mandate, paradoxically, constrained the autonomy of the Council by stating that the debate would focus on the four issues singled out by the Nice Declaration, thus limiting the option of debating other questions. More significantly, the scarce material resources assigned to the Council (staff, offices, etc.) indicated the limited influence that the government wanted to grant to this body.

Partly as a result of these limitations, the role of the Council as galvanizer of the debate passed largely unnoticed. The Council worked through two types of activities: conferences/presentations and an Internet forum. Conferences largely targeted academic audiences. Academics were almost invariably organizers and participants – a sign of self-referential discourse. Whether this was a deliberate strategy of targeting an elite or simply evidence of how academics seized the opportunity, the result was that the debate extended geographically through Spain – something that should not be taken for granted in this type of exercise. However, the most important events took place in Madrid, where the Permanent Forum holds scheduled presentations.

The second activity was an Internet web page around which the Council sought to mobilize a wider discussion on the future of Europe. Prospective participants were divided into three different colleges: academic, personalities and civic (meaning civic society leaders), plus an open forum for the general public. Contributions were expected to follow a questionnaire with 59 questions divided into four topics: the construction and political configuration of Europe, competency I, competency II, and democracy, institutions and enlargement. The wording of some of the questions pre-judged the responses in line with the positions of the government. The results were deeply unsatisfactory. The web page opened to the general public attracted a total of eight responses per question (average) after a year of operation (March 2002– March 2003). No question received more than 70 answers. Average number of responses was three in the civic and personalities forum; while the academic forum received an average of six responses per question (total) in the whole 12 months. The latter benefited from active involvement of the department hosting the site (the University of Oviedo). A highly revealing fact was that no professor participating in any of the conferences contributed to the Forum.

The Council activated an existing but practically empty institution, the *Instituto de España* (Institute of Spain), as a second forum for intellectual debate. This is the body, or, better, the 'label', under which the Royal Academies (arts, languages, political and moral sciences, etc.) gather. The idea was to reconvert this institute into a forum. The name has some nationalistic connotations. Arguably, this was an attempt to invest the process with solemnity.

The Real Instituto Elcano

The *Real Instituto Elcano de Estudios Internacionales y Estratégicos* (RIE), a new think tank (established in 2002) filled the vacuum created by the lack of mobilization of the Council. Under the leadership of sociologist Emilio Lamo de Espinosa and senior researcher Charles Powell, the RIE directed three types of initiatives. First, it provided the most important forum (and almost the only one) for the interplay between academics and practitioners. The RIE created, in collaboration with the *Instituto de Estudios Europeos-Universidad San Pablo* (CEU), a group of experts (the Group of Reflection) that gathered together on a monthly basis from December 2002 the Spaniards at the Convention (Palacio, Méndez de Vigo, Borrell, Carnero, etc.) with officials from the Ministry of Foreign Affairs and academics (by invitation). Both institutions also held a meeting of the European Constitutional Law Network. Second, the RIE acceded to the European Policy Institutes Network (EPIN), an initiative led by the Brussels-based Centre for European Policy Studies. Staff shortages, though, complicated a full and active participation in EPIN. Third, the RIE tried to stimulate a broader public debate through the four open sessions held in collaboration with the *Fundación Carlos de Amberes* (an institution that aims to maintain a relationship with the former Spanish low countries).

Apart from these forums, Autonomous Communities (ACs) organized their own debates and councils that provided an alternative organizational base for intellectuals. Thus, the Catalan Convention involved regional agents, and its Committee of Experts – made up of academics – drafted the proposals. Additionally, once again in Catalonia, the *Instituto de Estudis Autonomics* and the *Fundación Pi i Sunyer* organized a Standing Forum of Reflection in which mainly (but not exclusively) Catalan politicians, practitioners and academics met to discuss the European integration process. Similarly, the Basque debate created a Table for Reflection specifically for academics (alongside the political one), and the *Junta de Andalucía* has stimulated a similar initiative.

Intellectual Channels and Public Opinion

Academic conferences, newspaper articles and pieces in specialized journals became the main channels for intellectual debate. The daily newspapers included articles focusing on the most popular topics, such as religion, European values and the relationship (and differences with) the USA. Specialized journals, such as *Política Exterior*, consistently published essays by leading scholars and practitioners, whilst two journals with a large circulation among Spanish cultural elites – the *Revista de Occidente*[2] and *Papeles de Economía Española* – published monographic issues. The later focused broadly on the EU whilst the former analyzed 'The European federal debate' (the issue in question was coordinated by Areilza and featured essays by Weiler, Dehousse and Poiares Maduro). The scholarly oriented *Revista de Estudios Políticos* also published a large issue on the debate,[3] examining both the issues and the national debates on them. *Dossiers La Vanguardia*, a tri-monthly publication by the leading Catalan newspaper, published a monographic issue on the broader topic of *¿Qué quiere ser Europa?* (What does Europe want to be?).[4]

Intellectuals, though, failed to capture the attention of citizens or even the media. Public opinion and, broadly speaking, the mass media remained somewhat aloof (see details on public opinion in León, Meseguer, and Diaz, this issue). In this, there was no change since the Treaty of Maastricht, when domestic debate was very poor and ill informed. The Amsterdam Treaty passed largely unnoticed, and the Treaty of Nice attracted media attention only because of the 'battle for votes in EU institutions'. Interaction between intellectuals and society remained limited and the debate turned eminently self-referential.

THE ROLE OF INTELLECTUALS

Professional Profile

With very few exceptions, academics with a specialization in EU affairs captured the intellectual debate; the presence of other kinds of educated elites (writers, journalists, artists etc.) was merely anecdotal. Within the category of academics, lawyers featured prominently, with some input from political scientists. Lawyers prevailed thanks to their overall strength, expertise and a solid 'corporatist-networking' organization. Add to this the reticence of the Spanish legal community towards interdisciplinary work. Thus, public international lawyers, administrative lawyers and constitutional lawyers were the main players in the debate. This explains why intellectuals, as a whole, wanted the Convention to deliver a draft constitution. There was less interest in the process itself (as argued by Lucarelli and Radaelli, this issue).

Intellectual discussions revolved around two basic positions concerning the outcome of the Convention: the functional and the sceptical view. Constitutional lawyers upheld the sceptical or negative view of the 'EU constitution'. For them, it makes sense to speak of a constitution only in the presence of a state. It is worth noting here that most constitutional lawyers in Spain (with significant exceptions) have been, until relatively recently, unconcerned with the EU. Furthermore, rulings by Spanish constitutional law have conclusively established the infra-constitutional status of EC law. The Spanish Constitution has therefore gained a prominent political role, with highly positive symbolic connotations. Sometimes the Constitution is seen as an icon. For example, when it was reformed to adopt the Treaty of Maastricht, the changes were limited to just one additional word. In summary, from this standpoint, the notion of constitution applied to the EU does not fit easily with Spanish constitutional legal constructs.

The legal scholars arguing for the 'functional position' (such as Rodríguez Iglesias, Areilza or Díez Picazo) are more exposed to the influences of scholars such as Joseph Weiler, and they used in the debate on the Convention the same notions generated elsewhere in the domain of EU law – such as Weiler's notion of 'constitution tolerance'. The influence of these intellectuals should not be played down. Whilst in 2000 and 2001, Aznar argued that the very issue of an EU constitution was not real, he addressed the convention in 2002 with the following 'functional' position: 'The European political future must be a *plural constitution* that respects the multiple legal orders of Member States. [The political future] is the development of Law, Community law that the Laeken Declaration describes as the path towards *a constitution* for the European citizens' (Aznar 2003).

Attitudes in the Intellectual Debate

The initial stages of the debate reflected the defensive attitude adopted by the government. Most commentators, either explicitly or implicitly, argued that the Convention was nothing more than a German concern and possibly a 'minefield' for Spanish interests within the Union. Apart from criticism on specific issues, almost all commentators and politicians saw the whole exercise as compensation to Germany for the Nice outcomes:

> Despite its Europeanist rhetoric, Germany aims rather at weakening the Community system without replacing it by a federal system as the one established by the Fundamental Law. Chancellor Schröder pretends to call 'Constitution' what so far have been called Treaties and 'Federation' the Union, even though seriously limiting

its competencies for expenditure and regulation of the internal market (Areilza 2002b).

Generally speaking, almost all commentators subscribed to the view that German proposals focused exclusively on their own short-term interests and priorities (Areilza 2002a). This was the opinion behind the criticisms of concrete proposals on 'federalism' and the 'distribution of competences'. Aznar himself, reportedly, had grave doubts on the wisdom of seeking to impose Germany's constitutional model on the EU (Powell 2001). Even media traditionally critical of *Partido Popular* (PP) policies such as the daily *El País*, blamed Germany – in a ferociously critical article – for the failures of the EU over the past few years, emphasizing the shortcomings of the Treaty of Amsterdam, the crisis of the Santer Commission and the 'repatriation' interpretation of subsidiarity. The article portrayed Schröder's EU policy as 'abuse':

> (Berlin) frustrated the Treaty of Amsterdam, its principal group in the EP provoked the major crisis in the history of the EU by unjustifiably knocking down the Santer Commission and (Berlin) has insisted on an interpretation of subsidiarity that implies re-nationalization in favour of the Länder.

> The use of leadership has turned occasionally into abuse ... Schröder unsuccessfully struggled for the re-nationalization of the CAP [Common Agricultural Policy] ... and the reduction of structural or regional solidarity [sic] policy arguing that there is an excessive financial contribution – following a 'Margaret Thatcher' style. Recently, he obtained a German 'exception' to the Stability Pact (imposed by his predecessor) and he avoided a warning on his deficit. This is a double standard (with respect to the treatment of Ireland). He has exerted an enormous pressure against the decision of the competition Commissioner directed towards German firms ... ('La Europa alemana' [The German Europe], *El País*, 1 May 2002).

General and specific fears explain this Spanish reaction. Generally, Spain feared a clash between pro-constitutionalist and non-constitutionalist member states (Areilza 2001). More worryingly, most feared a turn towards re-nationalization behind German proposals and, in order to prevent it, Spanish discourses emphasized the defence of the *acquis* (see Areilza 2002b).

Beyond the specific issue of German dominance, the general involvement of intellectuals in the debate grew significantly with the commencement of the Convention. This provided items and a constant flow of issues on which timely scholarly opinion was welcomed. In Spain, though, perhaps more than in most other European countries, the Iraq war 'spilled over' and acted as a catalyst for the debate. This indirectly affected the way the Convention topics were framed in public discourse. The crisis served, first, as the referential point on which European (and American) intellectuals (such as J. Habermas, J.H.H. Weiler, A. Glucksmann, U. Beck, T. Garton Ash, R. Dahrendorf and Predarg Matvejevic) reflected on issues touching upon the European construction and European identity. The Spanish public, through the Iraq war, entered into contact with a wider and more international range of intellectual opinions. Furthermore, the crisis also prompted a heated debate on the repositioning of Spain's European and foreign policy, now clearly aligned with the USA and in opposition to France and Germany (traditional Spanish allies). All of this occurred at a critical moment in which the European constitutional future was discussed.

Non-contentious Issues: The Charter of Fundamental Rights, the Simplification of the Treaties and the Role of National Parliaments

The Charter of Fundamental Rights captured the attention of academics, who largely endorsed the incorporation of the Charter into the treaties (with significant exceptions in terms of those with a sceptical view, such as Rubio Llorente). This echoed the official Spanish position. As Rodríguez Bereijo, the Spanish government representative in the Charter Convention and chairman of the Council for the Debate on the Future of Europe, put it, the incorporation of the Charter reinforces the material constitution of the EU (Rodríguez Bereijo 2002).

Positions on a European Constitution

Paradoxically in a country with an integrationist pedigree, the issue of the EU constitution in Spain did not raise any great enthusiasm at the beginning of the process. The left-wing parties, intellectuals and media accepted the idea. In this vein, *El País* titled one of its leading articles 'A *por la Constitución*' (Let's get a Constitution) (*El País*, 9 September 2002), arguing that Europe needs a constitution in order to clarify and renew the principles behind its creation, to rejuvenate its basic objectives and to improve its institutions. Neither did right-wing politicians (and academics in this camp) approach the issue of a constitution with enthusiasm. Rodríguez Bereijo argued that the constitutionalization process was not a primordial issue since the EU 'already has a functional constitution'. The important issue – he went on – is to consolidate the European project. What is at stake is the construction of a political model and a model of European civilization (Rodríguez Bereijo 2002). Within this frame, intellectuals rallied around the two main positions briefly described above: the functional view and the more sceptical approach.

The functional view: A statement by Rodríguez Iglesias, the current Spanish president of the European Court of Justice (ECJ) and professor of Public International Law, summarizes the standard view on the Constitution: 'When the Court designates the treaties as a constitution (or Constitutional Charter), it characterizes them by analogy. They mean that the treaties function as a constitution in the juridical system of the Union,' (Rodriguez Iglesias, *'Una constitución para Europa?'* [A Constitution for Europe], *El País*, 1 March 2002). Spanish lawyers largely share this view, although they like to point towards two substantial limitations of the 'full' constitutional status of the treaties:

- Legitimacy must remain indirect, channelled by member states; and
- The future adoption of a text called a constitution will not change the fact that it will be based on a treaty agreed by member states (Rodríguez Bereijo 2002).

This academic view seems to have influenced the views of politicians. Referring to the result of the reform exercise, Aznar pragmatically accepted that nothing prevents a text that is formally a treaty from containing constitutional provisions. For him, this was an attractive approach with considerable scope to accommodate ideas for the simplification, access to legislation, and consolidation of the existing treaties (Aznar 2000). 'Constitutionalization' would entail the creation of a single legal personality for the European Union, clarifying its representation and profile on the international scene, while allowing the Community institutions to function in a more homogenous and coherent manner (Aznar 2001). In his address to the opening of the Convention, Aznar endorsed the key idea of European neo-constitutionalism; that is, the model of European constitutionalism defended and presented by scholars such as I. Pernice, J. Shaw, M. Maduro, etc., which apprehends the Constitution as a system of law that respects the legal systems of member states. He explicitly called it 'the pluralistic notion of constitutionalism' (Aznar 2003). In a similar vein, Areilza endorsed the principle of constitutional tolerance (adopted from Joseph Weiler) that avoids deciding in a definitive form what authority, national or European, must be the supreme one (Areilza 2001). Foreign Affairs minister Palacio commented on the draft of the Convention that the document – although formally an international treaty – would have both a constitutional nature and contents. In this way, citizens would perceive it as a truly European constitution (Palacio 2003). In a sense, academics seem to have played a clear role in making the concept palatable for politicians.

The sceptical academic camp: As mentioned above, the enormous symbolic importance of the Spanish Constitution as an instrument for democratic reconstruction and its almost iconic character may play a role in this sceptical approach. Some referred to the notion of 'constitution' as a trap-concept (Ortega 2001), whilst others argued that the utilization of the name 'constitution' instead of 'treaty' is a cosmetic or even misleading step (Areilza 2001: 116). Rubio Llorente, a former chairman of the Constitutional Court and leading constitutionalist argued that the proposal to equip the EU with a constitution is constructed as an incomprehensible discourse because of the inadequacy of language or the confusion of ideas. For him, it is not easy to identify the material contents of the proposed constitution, the new things it will bring and the reason to call an international treaty a 'constitution'. The mere simplification and systematization of the treaties is not enough to justify the change of name. From a highly sceptical view, he identified two problems: firstly, the judicial construction of a possible EU constitution is unstable. It lacks solid grounding in national constitutions. More importantly, discussion on the constitution may serve as a screen to elude discussion of real problems. It may also signal a trend towards looking for nominal solutions to real problems: 'Not only may discussion on the Constitution serve as a smokescreen to elude dealing with real problems, it is mainly a symptom of a dangerous tendency to look for merely nominal solutions and to fall into the "fetishism" of words' (F. Rubio Llorente, '*Un eurogalimatías europeo*', *El País*, 2 February 2002).

Distribution of Competencies

Most of the Spanish intellectual discussion of competencies adopted a defensive discourse against perceived attempts at re-nationalization of the Community *acquis*. One common view was that re-nationalization was, in fact, the priority objective of Germany in the European Convention. Almost all Spanish contributors shared this view (for instance, Beneyto, 2002; Elorza, 2001; Ortega 2002; Areilza passim; Rodriguez Iglesias, '*Una constitución para Europa?*' [A Constitution for Europe], *El País*, 1 March 2002).

The Spanish interpretation can be extracted from the arguments put forward by the current president of the ECJ, Rodríguez Iglesias. He maintains that departing from an erroneous perception that, in his opinion, seems to be common in Germany would mislead the whole issue.

The misperception is that Community competencies are badly defined and there is a tendency towards their uncontrolled expansion. In reality, the current system is based on a functionalist – or teleological – model (that is, competencies are used to attain Union objectives). This may lead to some unavoidable confusion because the EU has a cooperative constitutional order in which most competencies are, necessarily, shared. According to him, although it is difficult to disentangle them, the principles of attribution and subsidiarity provide clear limits (Rodríguez Iglesias, '*Una constitución para Europa?*' [A Constitution for Europe], *El País*, 1 March 2002).

This frames Spanish evaluations of system reform of distribution of competencies. First, no Spanish contribution to the debate accepted the proposal of drafting a list of competencies. Authors almost unanimously agreed on the unsuitability of this mechanism (which was viewed as a German priority and an obsession of the German Länder) for the following reasons. On the one hand, the catalogue model is seen as a mechanical translation of German federalism at the EU level (Areilza 2001; 2002b; Elorza 2002). This model, moreover, is alien to the constitutional tradition of many member states with widely diverse territorial traditions; Europe – the argument concludes – has highly centralized states, semi-centralized states, one state of autonomous regions (Spain) and various federal states.

Second, a list would become obsolete very soon (as federal practice itself shows) because of technological and socio-economic change, the interconnectedness of areas of activity, the pull of integration dynamics, or the teleological character of the Union. Worse, a definitive distribution of competencies by means of a list would freeze integration at the stage currently reached. This system might therefore prevent the Union from acquiring powers in areas where its intervention was needed, such as those agreed in Lisbon and Tampere (Areilza 2001; 2002b; Aznar passim; Ortega 2002; Benyeto 2002).

Most Spanish contributions to the competencies debate sought to spell out the conditions that have to be satisfied by an eventual reform:

- The delimitation of competencies may not be used as an alibi in order to reduce Community power and/or to re-nationalize the Community *acquis*. In particular, those policies that provide the juridical and instrumental foundation of the process of integration (CAP, competition, and cohesion) and which coincide with the ones targeted by Germany for their re-nationalization exercise, should be preserved.
- Equally, the reform of the principle of subsidiarity is acceptable, as long as it does not imply a re-nationalization of policies.

- Finally, the Union and its member states coordinate their activity in order to ensure the effective execution and administration of Community powers, rather than spending too much time on the distribution of powers as such.

The issue of the distribution of competencies produced a side effect in Spain – a sort of mirror image of the German debate: it percolated down to the ongoing domestic negotiations with the Autonomous Communities and the unsettled Spanish debates on federalism and asymmetry. Aznar forcefully argued that the EU debate should be confined to the best manner of sharing power between the Union and its member states, and that any attempt to widen debate to other areas (that is, to the regions in general and specifically the autonomous regions of Spain) would jeopardize the EU entirely. Foreign Affairs minister Piqué noted that the internal distribution of competencies is a constitutional issue. In coherence with this line, the government did not sign the Declaration on Subsidiarity of the Nice Treaty (that extended this principle to the regions) and did not grant any mechanism for AC participation in the debate whatsoever (see León, Meseguer and Diaz, this issue).

The Debate on Institutions

The debate on institutions did not feature prominently in Spain until the end of the Convention and the beginning of the IGC. One of the reasons was that Aznar felt satisfied with the current *status quo* negotiated at Nice, hence the defence of the *status quo* became a central objective. The government did not engage with the issue of institutions until the Franco-German proposal was published in February 2003. Spain reacted with a Spanish–British institutional proposal, the main elements of which were the election of the president of the European Council, the reform of the system of rotational presidencies and the creation of team presidencies. Curiously, the Spanish proposal did not attract the attention of Spanish intellectuals or the media: even in Spain, they passed largely unnoticed with few exceptions (Powell 2003).

The submission in April of the draft containing the first recommendations on the EU institutions prompted a strong reaction from the representatives of the Spanish government. Both in written amendments (Palacio) and in speech (Dastis), the representatives threatened with a veto the Convention results if the Nice agreements were to be modified and objected to the new Article 17 that defined the new system for qualified majority voting (double majority of states and share of population). Even though it did not greatly affect Spain in absolute terms, it did substantially reduce its coalition options. Again, not much debate arose around this issue, even though some commentators criticized this standpoint by arguing that Spain should support the new proposal because of the criteria of realism and fairness (Torreblanca 2003). Some, though, endorsed the standpoint of the government and argued in favour of restoring the equilibrium of Nice because it would avoid an excessive use of power by the big four (Areilza 2003). Once the Convention was over and the process entered into intergovernmental negotiations, the Spanish government became the stumbling block for the Constitutional settlement. Then, the issue of qualified majority in the council, the distribution of votes and the 'power' of Spain became the most debated issue of the whole exercise.

Religion and the Turkish Issue

Religion was a hot topic throughout the Convention. Journalists, philosophers (Rubert de Ventós, '*Sobre si Europa es cristiana*' [On whether Europe is Christian or not], *El País*, 5 March 2003), and occasionally theologians (C. Floristán, '*Las raíces cristianas de Europa*' [The Christian Roots of Europe], *El País*, 29 May 2003) argued about the issue. The more conservative ones voiced their opinions supporting a reference to Christianity and Christian roots in conservative media such as the daily *ABC* (for instance; C. Seco Serrano, '*Las raíces cristianas de Europa*' [The Christian Races of Europe], *ABC*, 2 June 2003). They also echoed the Pope's lobby. Pope John Paul II asked Aznar to support the idea that the Constitution should have a reference to the Christian roots of Europe (February 2003), and he repeated this plea in his visit to Spain when he called for the defence of the 'Christian roots' of Europe in the constitution of the enlarged Union (May 2003). On the opposite side of the debate, progressive authors argued that the European constitution did not require an explicit mention of the contribution of the Christian faith. Rather, what is required is the recognition of values of the Christian tradition that modernity has fully incorporated (C. Floristán, '*Las raíces cristianas de Europa*' [The Christian Roots of Europe], *El País*, 29 May 2003), mainly the separation, dissociation and autonomy between religious and civil arenas (F. Savater, '*Nuestras raíces cristianas*' [Our Christian Roots], *El País*, 4 July 2003).

The religious issue touched marginally upon the question of Turkey's EU membership. In general, Spanish politicians and intellectuals alike support the Turkish application. Some reflected on the question of opportunity, though, making references to the geopolitical situation of Turkey, its demographic size, and the possible relegation of the Spanish role in the EU (E. Lamo de Espinosa, '*Estar en Europa, ser europeos*' [To be in Europe, To be Europeans], *El País*, 31 December 2001;

Lamo de Espinosa 2003). Although the Sunday edition of the leading newspaper *El País* dedicated a report on the question 'Are we Turks Europeans?' (*¿Somos europeos los turcos?*, *El País Semanal*, 19 January 2003), the issue features as an alibi used in order to reopen a debate on European identity set in an ontological and transcendental context (often related to the vindication of Christian roots). In this line, a leading journalist wrote:

> this debate should not be resolved through the archaeological introspection of searching for common religious and cultural elements that are then thrown mercilessly in the face of the Islamic world. Rather, this debate should be resolved through an identity based on democratic values and voluntary commitments on the future and agreement on the tasks that we want to carry out together' (X. Vidal-Foch, '*La segunda refundación de Europa, una oportunidad*' [The second reformation of Europe, An Opportunity], *El País*, 11 December 2002).

CONCLUDING REMARKS

The Convention stimulated the participation of specialized intellectuals in the process of constitutional reform. They made their voices heard in a number of forums and activities, and interacted with the broader European debate (even though this happened to a limited extent) and tried to engage public opinion in a broad debate on the future of the EU. They did not achieve much, however, in terms of mobilizing society: civil society and public opinion remained largely at the margins of the process. Academics did contribute to shaping the perceptions of politicians engaged in the Convention, although not to a major extent. Spanish intellectuals contributed to frame debates within concepts and arguments broadly discussed throughout the EU.

NOTES

1. *Real Decreto 779/2001 de 5 Julio 2001*
2. See n.249 in the February 2002 issue.
3. See issue No.119 (2003).
4. See Dossier 6, April/June 2003.

REFERENCES

Areilza Carvajal, J.M. (2001): 'La reforma de Niza ¿hacia qué Unión Europea?', *Política Exterior* 79, pp.104–119.

Areilza Carvajal, J.M. (2002a): 'La Unión Europea y la piedra filosofal', *Política Exterior* 85, pp.57–68.

Areilza Carvajal, J.M. (2002b): 'España en el debate federal europeo', *Revista de Occidente* 249, pp.5–11.

Areilza Carvajal, J.M. (2003): 'Balance de la Convención Europea', *Política Exterior*, June.

Aznar, J.M. (2000): 'Hearing of the President of Government to inform on the Nice Summit', *DSCG Pleno y Diputación Permanente Año 2000 VII Legislatura No.52*, 20 Dec.

Aznar, J.M. (2001): Speech at the award ceremony presenting the European Merit Foundation prize to Viviane Reding, Brussels, 9 October, www.lamoneloa.es/inter/presi/p0910010.htm.

Aznar, J.M. (2003): 'Address to the opening meeting of the Convention on the Future of Europe', www.european-convention.eu.int/docs/speeches/196.pdf.

Barbé, E. (2001): '*La política europea de España 1999–2000*' [The European Politics of Spain], IUEE (Instituto Universitario de Estudios Europeos) Working Papers 1/2001, www.selene.uab.es/_cs_iuee/catala/obs/m_presentacion.html

Beneyto, J.M. (2002): *Tesis para la discusión sobre el reparto de competencias en la Unión Europea*, Seminario Hispano Alemán, 21–22 Feb., www.futuroeuropa.es/declaracad.html.

Closa, C. (2003) 'The Finality Debate in Spain: Explaining Absences, Revealing Presences', in S. Serfaty, (ed.), The Finality Debate and its Transatlantic Dimension (CSIS, Washington) 180–210.

Elorza, J. (2001): '*La UE después de Niza*', *Política Exterior* 79, 84–103.

Lamo de Espinosa, E. (2003): '*El test turco*' [The Turkish Test], www.realinstitutoelcano.org/publicaciones/46.asp.

Ortega, M. (2001): '*¡Viva la Constitución!*', *Política Exterior* 82, 87–98.

Palacio, A. (2003): 'La Convención europea, un gran avance', *Política Exterior* 91, [The European Convention: A Great Advance] Jan–Feb.

Powell, Ch. (2001): 'Fifteen Years On: Spanish Membership of the European Union Revisited', Paper presented at the conference 'From Isolation to Integration: 15 Years of Spanish and Portuguese Membership in Europe', Minda de Gunzburg Centre for European Studies, Harvard University, 2–3 Nov.

Powell, Ch. (2002): '*El debate español sobre el futuro de la Unión Europea*' [The Spanish Debate about the Future of the European Union], *Análisis del RIE*, www.realinstitutoelcano.org/analisis/216.asp?tipo = 1&num = 216&zona = 1&version = 1&publicado = Falso.

Powell, Ch. (2003): '*La propuesta franco-alemana y el debate sobre el futuro de la Unión Europea*' [The Franco-German Proposal and the Debate about the Future of the European Union] www.realinstitutoelcano.org/analisis/224.asp?tipo = 1&num = 224&zona = 1&version = 1&publicado = Verdadero.

PSOE (2001): '*El futuro de Europa*' [The Future of Europe], www.psoe.es/NuevasPoliticas-NuevosTiempos/NuestrasPoliticas/PoliticaGeneral/EL_FUTURO_DE_EUROPA.htm.

Rodríguez Bereijo, A. (2002): '*Intervención del Presidente del Consejo para el Debate sobre el Futuro de la Unión Europea*' [Intervention of the President of the Council in the Debate about the Future of the European Union], *La inauguración del Foro Permanente Europeo* [The Inauguration of the Permanent European Council], Ateneo de Madrid, 30 Jan., www.futuroeuropa.es/declaracad.html.

Torreblanca, J.I. (2003): '*¿Quién teme a la Convención?*', *Análisis del RIE*, 26 May 2003, www.realinstitutoelcano.org/analisis/292.asp.

What 'Europe'? Portugal's Reactive Adaptation to European Institutional Changes

FRANCISCO TORRES and ANA FRAGA

INTRODUCTION

A constant feature of the politics of European integration in Portugal has been the reactive position of negotiators (the administration in general, including cabinet members with a lower political profile), which has been supported by reactive political parties that resist any substantial institutional change until the important decisions are taken at the top political level (see Torres 2000). Chief negotiators (in general the prime ministers) and reactive politicians then generally adapt quite quickly to the new rules, silencing the voicing of the customary discomfort (resistance to change) within the administration at large in the name of national interest. The fear of being left out of the European integration process or, more recently, of being out of its political core is generally sufficient to trigger a change in attitudes.

Most of the time, public opinion is either receptive or indifferent to such changes (and in any case not well informed), which helps the politicians at the top to accept those proposed changes. We find that this model of behaviour also applied to the European Convention.

Only in particular moments, namely during the European exchange rate crisis-cum-recession of 1992–93 and at the time of the referenda of the Maastricht Treaty, has such resistance to change been politically explored. In fact, in the early 1990s, one particular party (*Centro Democrático Social – Partido Popular* – CDS-PP; Christian Democratic Party), seized by its youth, became an anti-European party. That anti-European stance had substantial backing from the written press (that is, opinion-makers and journalists) and the media as a whole, and was evident across all the other parties and, eventually, public opinion.

The authors would like to acknowledge that they benefited from many useful comments by Sonia Lucarelli, Claudio Radaelli and an anonymous referee on previous drafts of this contribution, and from discussions with Annette Bongardt. The usual disclaimer applies.

Such moments apart, there has been no strong political cleavage on European Union (EU) affairs in Portugal. Most of the time public opinion has no strong views on Europe and accepts many of the proposed institutional changes most feared by national politicians and the administration at large: the European Convention was a case in point. Public opinion consistently regards the 'Europeanization' of politics as positive. In fact, in Portugal, as in Italy and Greece, people tend to trust the EU more than the UN and national governments; in all other EU countries the UN, or the national government, are trusted more than the EU (Eurobarometer 57, 4).

Therefore, while politicians in Portugal fear EU institutional change and the deepening of the European integration process, public opinion is in general much more relaxed about it. Notwithstanding the contradiction, Portuguese public opinion may then react more than the Portuguese polity to the implementation of specific EU policies (Torres, 2002a). In fact, while Italy, Greece and Spain also score above average (at the top of the scale) concerning both the average level of support for EU decision-making (for 26 policy areas) and the number of policy areas where EU decision-making is more popular than national decision-making, the same is not true for Portugal (Eurobarometer 56, 4.1).

In the next section we analyze briefly, illustrated by examples, the recurrent features of the Portuguese stance on European institutional changes, summarizing the positions of the main political parties with respect to Europe and the Convention. The following section focuses on the Portuguese political debate on the future of Europe, namely on the parliamentary debate in the aftermath of the Nice Treaty and on the parliament's and government's preparations for the Convention. We then analyze the evolution of these two main actors' positions throughout the Convention. The final sections look at the role of other actors in the Convention, the promotion of public debate in the Convention amongst civil society in general and youth in particular, and the scarce coverage of the Convention in the media, together with the evolution of public opinion. Finally, we present our conclusions.

PORTUGAL'S STANCE ON EUROPEAN INTEGRATION SINCE ACCESSION

In an initial phase of European integration, from 1986 to 1991, the Portuguese administration concentrated on structural funds and on transition periods and derogations. With the country's first EU presidency in the first semester of 1992, the Portuguese government understood the importance of being part of the political core of Europe, and joined the exchange rate mechanism of the European Monetary System (EMS) in April 1992.

Experience suggests that the European integration process – and, in particular, the need to perform sufficiently well to be part of the inner political core, especially at the time of each country's presidency – provides member countries with a good incentive to leap forward and embark on a more proactive policy stance. This is especially the case for countries for which European integration is at the centre of their development strategy. In this context, the Portuguese EU presidencies (1992 and 2000) are illustrative, the most striking example being the so-called 'Lisbon process' agreed at the Lisbon summit in March 2000.

Yet, in between presidencies the Portuguese polity seemed to lose any interest in what the EU should become, turning to fierce national resistance of any European institutional changes to which it may adapt in the wake of the eventually established EU consensus. This is exactly what happened with the compromise achieved at the end of the European Convention.

However, even during the entire macroeconomic convergence phase of Economic and Monetary Union (EMU) in the 1990s, few politicians presented it as a desirable political reform instead of an external constraint (see Jones et al. 1998). For a long time, most politicians, bureaucrats and even economists just referred to it, initially, as an objective rather unlikely to be realised and, later on, as an unavoidable development within the EU.[1] In many instances, the EMU project was regarded as an unavoidable external constraint that went together with an exogenous political objective on which their political leaders had converged (Torres 2002a).

The issue of reinforced cooperation is also a good example. It was initially strongly rejected by Portuguese negotiators but, after discussions at the highest political level (heads of state and government), it was first accepted during the 1996 intergovernmental conference (IGC), and later even endorsed and presented as the Portuguese presidency's contribution to the 1999 IGC by the very same government (and negotiators).

The sudden change with respect to the endorsement of the convention method for the next IGC provides yet another example. Just a few months before the formal beginning of the Convention, the parliamentary standing committee on EU affairs had almost unanimously rejected mentioning even the possibility of the adoption of the convention method for the following IGC. Only when it was obvious that their European party families would fully endorse it did the two main political parties and their respective members of parliament (MPs) defend the convention method. In fact, with EMU, the new European co-decision process, the enlargement process and the prospect of a closer political union for a limited number of countries within the EU, it became more difficult – or politically much less attractive – for EU countries in general, and cohesion countries in particular, to postpone any decisions on the future of common European institutions and policies and thereby risk not to be part of the EU core.

The above examples illustrate that Portugal tends to fall in line with the core countries without much input or strategy. Public opinion has been essentially accommodating.

The Main Political Parties and their Overall Position on European Integration

Since 1975 there have been four main political parties with parliamentary seats: (from left to right) the *Partido Comunista Português* (PCP; Communist Party) – integrated within the Communist and Allies Group of the European Parliament, the *Partido Socialista* (PS; Socialist Party) – integrated within the Socialist Group of the European Parliament, the *Partido Social Democrata* (PSD; Social Democratic Party) – integrated within the European People's Party (EPP) of the European Parliament (EP), and the CDS-PP – part of the Union for Europe of the EP. At present, there are also two small parties in the national parliament: the Block of the Left (BE) and the *Partido Ecologista os Verdes* (PEV; Ecologist and Greens); neither of these two parties has any representatives elected to the EP.

The PSD joined the EPP in only the late 1990s, starting to work, as it had never done before, very closely with its Spanish counterpart. It won the last elections held in March 2002 with a simple majority and formed a coalition with CDS-PP. Since the fall of the executive at the beginning of 2002, the PS is perceived to have turned to the left but has basically maintained its European stance. Neither the PSD nor the PS were active as such throughout the Convention.

The four smaller parties were left out of the Convention. The CDS-PP had been expelled from the EPP in 1993 after an anti-European (Maastricht) campaign strongly opposed European integration on the grounds of national sovereignty. It has modified its stance over the last couple of years, especially since it became the junior partner of the PSD in Government in 2002. The PCP has come to accept Portugal's integration in the EU but it remains, as always, firmly opposed to any further deepening; the party repeatedly complained about not being involved in the Convention but did not present any alternatives to the reactive stance of the two main parties and the government throughout the Convention. The BE is not represented in the standing committee on European affairs and foreign policy and has affirmed itself during the Convention – not without some internal opposition – to be a 'critical' pro-European party, following the social movements against 'neo-liberal European integration'. The PEV is the junior member of an electoral coalition with the PCP and is not perceived as an autonomous party.

The two main parties – PS and PSD – claim to be in favour of further European integration and have identical programmes with respect to it. In each party there are several tendencies in their position towards European integration, but without specific and clear-cut positions. Therefore, no disruptions in the Convention were to be expected nor, indeed, materialized, neither at the time of the transition between governments – which was very smooth – nor at the level of parliament representatives.

THE POLITICAL DEBATE IN THE RUN-UP TO THE CONVENTION

The Political Debate on the Future of Europe in the Aftermath of the Nice Treaty

The parliamentary debate on the future of Europe started during the ratification of the Nice Treaty. The parliamentary standing committee on European affairs[2] followed closely the IGC negotiations on the Nice Treaty and decided to deal not only with the Treaty itself, but also with the debate on the future of Europe – a process established through the Nice Treaty. Immediately after the signature of the Nice Treaty, the committee held two meetings with the minister of foreign affairs and with the Secretary of State for European Affairs (SSEA) and another meeting with Portuguese MEPs to discuss the Méndez de Vigo and Seguro EP report.

In March 2001, the committee decided to draw up a list of questions and issues on the future of Europe with a view to finding out about the opinions and positions of several universities, social partners and non-governmental organizations (NGOs). Throughout the rest of the year, the committee remained active on the question of the future of Europe. It organized a round table and invited the current and all ex-ministers of foreign affairs since the accession and all the ex-chairpersons of the committee on European affairs. The Committee held meetings with other European members of government and parliament; it received opinions from several different law and social sciences schools and also contributions from local associations, NGOs and individual citizens (all the opinions and contributions were put on the parliament's website); and it organized a public hearing at which some academic papers were discussed. Last but not least, the committee also held regular meetings with representatives, members of government and ambassadors of all accession countries.

As pointed out above, the sudden preference for the convention method in the PSD and the PS came after strong opposition from both parties. Just some months before the beginning of the Convention, the parliamentary standing committee on EU affairs had rejected almost unanimously (only one independent MP defended it) to even mention the possibility of the adoption of the convention method for the following IGC. Only once it, was obvious that their European party families would fully endorse it, did both parties converge on that line of thought, adopting – as in many other aspects of the European integration process – a totally reactive stance. MPs followed party discipline – and the two main parties only initiated a more substantial internal debate on the Convention in May 2003, that is, shortly before it drew to a close.[3]

As the Convention started, it became almost obligatory (politically correct) to defend its method as a good thing, stressing the need to overcome the bad impression left by the power-focused negotiations of Nice – especially in parliament. In spite of this rhetoric, however, during the Convention, the government and its representatives defended the Nice results against the Praesidium's proposed institutional changes; parliamentary representatives did not voice any discomfort concerning that position.

Before the Maastricht Treaty the Portuguese parliament had felt that MPs should be informed about all European draft documents, as shown by the adoption of Law 28/87. However, there have been several problems with the implementation of the laws on parliamentary review and evaluation of EU affairs, either on the part of the parliament or the government.

The main problems of effective parliamentary intervention in EU affairs are related to the time factor (the parliamentary procedure for scrutiny of EU questions does not keep pace with the European rhythm of decision-making); complexity (the European legislation is by and large very technical and the parliament often fails to understand the political implications for the country, whereas the government, through its administration, enjoys a huge informational advantage over parliament); legitimacy (if the parliament relies only on the information given by the government what is its added value?)[4] and specialization (European legislation is not an external affairs question but should be dealt with as an integral part of the national legal system, requiring the involvement of the entire parliament – namely, of all the standing committees).

In Portugal, moreover, the lack of a long-established parliamentary tradition and the predominance of the executive, the consensus on the EU between almost all the main parties and public opinion, the existence of an absolute majority for most of the first ten years of EC membership, the scarce technical parliamentary resources and the low visibility of parliamentary activity related to EU affairs contributed to a very soft parliamentary intervention (see Fraga 2001 and Magone 2000).

Furthermore, from the parliament's perspective, the institutional and procedural mechanisms required for strong intervention – EU affairs are technical, complex and time-consuming – represent for MPs a very high cost compared to a very low benefit, given that parliamentary intervention has no immediate results or might have no results at all, media coverage is very low and EU affairs win no votes in national elections. Consequently, the Portuguese parliament and its members have few reasons to have a strong and clear position in this debate or even to pay attention to European developments. This was clearly demonstrated throughout the Convention, as discussed below.

The Run-Up to the Convention

In the run-up to the Convention, little attention was given to its preparation due to the special conditions of government transition. At the time when the first representative of the Portuguese government was appointed to the Convention, the PS was still in government and national elections were scheduled for 17 March 2002. The director-general of European affairs at the Ministry of Foreign Affairs (MFA), a former ambassador to Ireland, was nominated with the agreement of the then main opposition party, PSD. At that time, the ambassador could count on the SSEA for back-up for his dual function of director-general at the MFA and of government representative at the European Convention.

The new government was inaugurated on 6 April 2002. On 22 May, the new prime minister informed President Giscard d'Estaing that he had appointed Professor Ernâni Lopes (a former finance minister of the PS/PSD grand coalition in 1983–85 and chief negotiator of Portugal's entry into the European Community) as the new government representative and the deputy director-general of European affairs as his alternate.

The new government representative at the Convention was given an office in the premises of the SSEA, with the initial idea of establishing a task force comprising three advisors – two from the cabinet of the SSEA and one from parliament – who were to coordinate the work of both government and parliament representatives. However, the idea was not put into practice due to the reorganization of the SSEA. No special task force or advisory bodies were created, neither was a new member of cabinet. Instead, different departments of the secretary of state coordinated by the alternate member in the Convention provided support for the work of the government representative. This lack of formal support is indeed quite characteristic of Portuguese organization with respect to European affairs that draws on informal networking among the few people working in the field.[5]

While the socialist government, due to the imminent elections, was not especially concerned with the Convention at the time when the latter took up its work, there were nevertheless already some general guidelines stemming from the negotiations of the Nice Treaty. However, those guidelines were not taken as proposals for the Convention; the same is true for the first months of the new PSD-CDS/PP government.

THE MAIN ACTORS' POSITIONS THROUGHOUT THE CONVENTION

The Position of the Government and its Representatives

Only on 18 June 2002 did the minister of foreign affairs (the SSEA works within the MFA) present the basic government guidelines for the Convention to the new parliamentary standing committee on EU affairs and foreign policy. He stated that the government would prefer the work of the Convention to result in an open text with different options instead of a final (constitution-type) text. The minister put forward five principles to be defended by the Portuguese government:

- The principle of equality among member states;
- The principle of economic and social cohesion;
- The preservation of the current inter-institutional balance with the safeguarding of the community method and the refusal of any kind of directorates;
- A gradualist approach to deeper integration so that public opinion could understand a closer union; and
- The promotion of trust between member states that had been negatively affected by the Nice results.

The minister also argued that the IGC should only start its work in 2004 in order to allow for a six-month reflection period after the end of the Convention.

Portugal and other cohesion countries usually uphold the principle of social cohesion at the time of discussions on institutional changes or policy reforms such as EMU, Agenda 2000 and Common Agricultural Policy (CAP) reform. This is a precautionary stance on the part of these countries in order to safeguard their immediate financial interests, but it may also reflect their vision of a cohesive Europe. The other four principles are merely reactive and do not represent any particular vision of Europe or model of institutional reform. Rather, they simply represent the defence of the *status quo* and the lack of any long-term strategy concerning how the EU (and Portugal) should develop. This fear of any future developments has been a recurrent feature of the Portuguese position on European institutional reform and of the entire European integration process.

The day following the minister of foreign affairs' presentation of key principles, the government representative at the Convention went to the same parliamentary committee to present basically the same guidelines in his own wording – with the exception of the need for a gradualist approach to a deeper integration. He, moreover, pointed out that Portugal should have a role to play with respect to the coordination between the EU and the Africa–Brazil axis. While the reference to this axis is the traditional 'universal vocation' argument constantly advanced by most Portuguese politicians and diplomats when discussing the process of European integration, it was not really a point on the agenda of the Convention and was not, therefore, referred to again.

Besides the traditional solidarity argument (the principle of economic and social cohesion), the other main principles reinforced the idea of a very reactive position as a starting point to any potential institutional changes proposed at the Convention. As far as public debate was concerned, the government representative at the Convention explained that he intended to work on the promotion of the public debate on Convention matters mainly through press conferences after each plenary session, and meetings with social partners, political parties and civil society.

After these first meetings with the parliamentary committee, there were four more meetings: one with the minister and the SSEA (22 October 2002) and another three with the government representative in the Convention (20 November 2002, 12 May 2003 and 30 June 2003). From these meetings, as well as several interventions made in the Convention, interviews with newspapers and public conferences, it emerged that the government's position – as expressed by its representative – was quite consistent; it became more detailed, but its main principles did not change throughout the entire Convention.

Nevertheless, as the Convention working groups were approving their reports, the need arose to accept or refuse some proposals. One can divide the Portuguese positions into four main categories:

Defence:
1. Reinforcement of the Commission's role, provided that it maintained one commissioner per member state;

Acceptance:
1. Of an explicit recognition of the legal personality of the Union;
2. Of the simplification of decision procedures, taking into account the specificities of the Common Foreign Security Policy (CFSP) and of the Common Foreign Defence Policy (CFDP);
3. Of reducing the number of legal acts and clarifying their hierarchy;
4. Of the reinforcement of the role of national parliaments through the ex-ante control of their own governments, the renovation of the *Conférence des Organes Spécialisées aux Affaires Communautaires* (COSAC; Conference of European Affairs Committees of the EU), and the 'early-warning mechanism' for the control of subsidiarity, but some reservations in regard to the idea of creating a congress of the European people;
5. Of the insertion of the Charter of Fundamental Rights in the treaty and of EU accession to the European Convention of Human Rights;
6. Of the election of the European Commission president by the EP from a list put forward by the Council; and
7. Of the merger of treaties, without a significant modification of the inter-institutional balance;

Maintenance:
1. Preference for the maintenance of the current articles on monetary policy and for the coordination of economic policies;
2. Preference for the maintenance of the social policy articles and defence of the inclusion in the Treaty of the Union's aim of modernizing the European social model;
3. Preference for the preservation of the name 'European Union' and of the expression 'ever closer Union'; and
4. Preference for the maintenance of Article 308 (formerly Article 235) as it stood;

Rejection of:
1. A catalogue or list of competencies of the Union;
2. The abolition of the rotating presidencies of the Council;

3. An elected president of the Council (*'never ever'*); and
4. Any other model than the maintenance of one commissioner per member state.

Throughout the Convention, the government representative stuck to his position, being one of the main promoters of the position of the so-called 'Group of 16'. This group consisted of all small countries[6] with the exception of Benelux (traditionally at the centre of European institutional reform and integration) and Greece (the country with the EU presidency during the most important six months of the Convention); six EU members – namely Austria, Denmark, Finland, Ireland, Portugal, Sweden; and ten candidate countries – namely Bulgaria, Czech Republic, Cyprus, Estonia, Hungary, Latvia, Lithuania, Malta, Slovakia and Slovenia. The Group of 16 presented its opposition to an elected president of the Council several times and to the reduction of the number of commissioners. The government's representative also struck out alone against an explicit catalogue of competencies of the Union, based on methodological grounds only. He also presented two proposals for new articles: one on tourism and the other on sports. Neither was accepted.[7]

Note that all of Portugal's strong positions (see *'Rejection'*, above) – basically, the rejection of a catalogue or list of competencies of the Union, the preservation of the rotating presidencies of the Council and rejection of an elected president of the Council and the maintenance of one commissioner per member state – were rebuffed in the Convention's final draft treaty, which established a constitution for Europe.

In addition, the government, after having stated at the beginning of the Convention that trust between member states was negatively affected by the Nice Summit, ended up defending the Nice results as a way of avoiding the institutional changes proposed by the Praesidium. Moreover, the foreign affairs minister who argued that the IGC should only start its work in 2004, in order to allow for a six-month reflection period after the end of the Convention, accepted the *fait accompli* of starting it in October 2003.

In the process, the Portuguese government (especially the prime minister and the SSEA) appeared much more conciliatory than the Portuguese representatives at the Convention. The government left the tough positions to its formal representatives, accepting in the end all the proposals of the Praesidium and even qualifying them as a good starting point for the IGC. It was to be expected, moreover that the country's polity, as on many other occasions in the past, would initially adopt a reactive stance but in the end would adapt to the decisions taken by the core. The comparatively more pragmatic views of the prime minister during the Convention with respect to most Portuguese members of the Convention, namely on the Franco-German proposals before the Iraqi crisis had erupted, already pointed to that possible development. Shortly after the Convention was over, the prime minister even defended, in Berlin, that the then forthcoming IGC should not reopen the entire Convention final draft treaty establishing a constitution for Europe but just improve some points regarding the functions of the future president of the council.

Parliament's Representatives at the Convention

The two representatives of the parliament were appointed by the conference of parliamentary groups and not by the then committee on European affairs. With national elections scheduled for March 2002, the committee could not take that decision as it was limited to day-to-day matters. The conference of parliamentary groups appointed two members from the two main parties, PS and PSD, and two alternates from the same parties.[8] There was no representation of any of the smaller parties. PCP and the small BE criticized this approach to the Convention on the grounds that the PSD and PS do not differentiate themselves with respect to their positions on EU affairs.

During 2002–03, as mentioned above, there were four meetings of the parliamentary standing committee on European affairs and foreign policy with the government representatives at the Convention. The committee also held monthly meetings in which the parliamentary members of the Convention described their activities. However, the attendance at these meetings was extremely low, with numbers of present MPs, besides the members of the Convention and its chairman, ranging from one to ten. There were also two plenary debates on 26 June 2002 and 12 June 2003.

The amendments to the Praesidium proposals by the parliamentary members of the Convention were not very different from the ones presented by the government. There was no resolution expressing the parliament's views on the issues discussed in the Convention. The contributions to the reports of the Convention's working groups and the interventions of the Portuguese members of the Convention in its plenary sessions did not bind the Portuguese parliament and were made on a purely individual basis.

With respect to the amendments, the Portuguese MPs behaved in various ways: for the amendments of articles 1–16 the four MPs subscribed to the same proposals, while for all the other amendments the government, the PSD and the PS each presented a proposal. Only for the amendments of the articles on institutions and external action (which included commercial policy, cooperation and CFDP) did the PSD endorse the proposal of the representative of its own government; the PS presented its own text. In terms of proposals, parliamentary representatives only presented two for new articles: one on the Open Method of Coordination (OMC) by the PS, drawing on its former government's legacy and subscribed to by the PSD and the government representatives; the other, presented only by the PSD's alternate member, on the role of national parliaments following the CFSP.

All parliamentary representatives, though, agreed (following the government's general position on agriculture) on the principle that the CAP should clearly be an 'exclusive competency'.[9] The government representative maintained his objection to any 'exclusive competencies', explaining that it was based on methodological grounds only.

The Portuguese representatives at the Convention defended, on the one hand, definite positions on formal issues, such as maintaining the six-month rotating presidency and the current procedure for the election of the president of the European Commission by the European Council with the approval by the EP, and upholding the principle of one commissioner per member state. On the other hand, they were either quite open on some substantive issues, such as external representation by the Commission, co-decision, qualified majority voting (QMV) in community affairs, justice and home affairs and security, or rather undecided/ambiguous with respect to some other substantive matters, such as European Commission accountability and enhanced cooperation.

No divisions appeared in or proposals came from parliament, whose representatives merely fulfilled their obligations – participating in the Convention's plenary sessions and working groups and reporting their work to a parliament not at all mobilized by the Convention. Still, it was to be expected that both the government and the two main political parties, and all the parliament representatives, would come to accept – as they did at the end of the Convention, along the lines of other issues in the past – the end of the rotating presidency, changes in the current procedure of the election of the Commission's president and the end of the principle of one commissioner per member state.[10]

THE ROLE OF OTHER ACTORS

Main Interest Groups and NGOs

In Portugal there is no strong associative mentality. Therefore, the role of interest groups and NGOs is negligible with a view to European institutional reform. There were only a few exceptions, such as gender associations, that showed some interest in the Convention.

The academic discourse was not very rich either, chiefly because law schools show very little interest in EU affairs and because there are very few modern schools of political science in the country, which are mostly, moreover, very much absent from the European debate. Furthermore, there are very few political and other social scientists participating in the European academic debate (although some increase is occurring). Economists are, in general, much more internationalized in comparison (publishing in scientific journals and participating in academic conferences), but have not shown a strong interest in the debate on the future of Europe nor in EU issues. The few existing exceptions are not understood by and/or do not interact much with most opinion-makers. This may explain why an issue such as the question of which tasks should be centralized at the EU level and which should be left to the national or regional level, which is of much concern to Portuguese public opinion and to the academic debate in Europe among economists and political scientists (see, for example, Berglöf *et al.* 2003), passed unnoticed in the Portuguese public debate.

Contrary to what happened in other EU or accession countries (especially in Poland), the religious debate about the Convention was practically non-existent in Portugal. All parliamentary representatives agreed on the principle that no religious mention should be included in the treaty, as already defended in the discussions about the Charter of Fundamental Rights. Although some members of the Catholic Church raised the issue, obliging the prime minister to agree with the principle of having a religious mention included in the treaty, the church hierarchy was not perceived to be pushing much for any more specific positions in the Convention.

One MEP, José Pacheco Pereira (PSD and EPP), who was very critical of the entire Convention and of European politics in general, also defended through his skill as an opinion-maker (and one can say for the sake of controversy and of challenging political correctness and not really representing any religious interests) the inclusion of a religious mention in the treaty. In any event, there was no real debate about this particular issue, and the representatives at the Convention seemed happy (or deliberately chose to ignore the debate in spite of their different religious backgrounds) with the text agreed in the preamble of the draft treaty. This fact shows once more how little attention public opinion paid to the Convention: not even the more religious Portuguese representatives at the Convention bothered to raise or even discuss an issue that would have commanded some support among Portugal's large Catholic population. Later on, already at the time of the IGC, the religious question – being discussed at the intergovernmental level – was brought by public opinion into the national political debate that mirrored the European debate.

Regions and Sub-national Politics

Despite being a unitary/centralized state, Portugal has two autonomous regions – Madeira and the Azores – that possess their own legislative assemblies and executives, albeit with limited power. The committee on European affairs and foreign policy held a debate with representatives of Madeira and Azores on 11 February 2003, at which it became clear that the main questions of interest to these two regions regarded the implementation of the ultra-peripheral regions statute.

The main issue, though, was the introduction in the EU Treaty of the expression 'territorial cohesion', changing the principle of economic and social cohesion into the principle of economic, social and territorial cohesion. All Portuguese representatives, following the customary pressure by these regions' respective party sections on their party leaderships and the usual practice of defending what is consensually identified as national or sub-national interests, expressed that view in the plenary session of 6–7 February. Ultimately, the principle of territorial cohesion was established in the Convention's draft constitutional text (Article I-3° § 3).

Local municipalities also exerted some pressure – reflected only in the representatives' plenary speeches (no papers were presented) – with a view to increasing the role of CoR and to preserving structural funds, but without any success.

Other Portuguese Representatives at the Convention

Besides the representatives of the government and parliament, there were other Portuguese in the Convention (most of them former members of government): the European Commissioner for justice and home affairs (a prominent member of the PS), three MEPs (PS, PSD and CDS-PP) and an observer from the European Social Partners who also happened to be a national MP. Commissioner António Vitorino, although representing the European Commission at the Convention, was often referred to in the press as one of the Convention's Portuguese representatives – and sometimes the Portuguese representative with the most influence; he was also very active in national debates.

THE PUBLIC DEBATE ABOUT THE CONVENTION

*The Promotion of the Public Debate on the Convention
and the Future of Europe*

The promotion of the public debate was of concern to all Portuguese representatives at the Convention who participated in all kinds of conferences and seminars promoted by universities, trade unions, confederations, different organizations and the media. The principle for organizing debates was partnership, meaning that the representatives of the EP, the European Commission, the SSEA and the Portuguese parliament got together with different institutions and the specialized media to organize debates in different places – in general, universities – throughout the country. In practice, and from October 2002 onwards, one can say that there were regular seminars or conferences, sometimes several per week, mainly at universities.

A number of main initiatives may be illustrative in this context. The representatives in Portugal of the EP and the European Commission, through the Institute for International and Strategic Studies (IEEI) and with the support of most Portuguese universities, were involved in an initiative called 'The National Debate on the Future of Europe'. The initiative took off at the Institute for European Studies of *Universidade Católica* in Lisbon, the oldest of its kind in Portugal, in October 2002 and included several debates at the most important universities and institutes distributed all over the country, followed by the presentation of the theses that emerged on the future of Europe at a final two-day congress in Lisbon in the beginning of March 2003. The Institute also organized an international conference entitled the 'Future of Europe: Views from the Outside', and its reflection group on enlargement and institutional reform held periodical meetings, constituting a discussion platform for the major current issues on the European agenda.

The representation in Portugal of the EP implemented a series of debates on the future of Europe (one of them called 'Let's Talk about the Convention?') together with one national newspaper and one national radio station, and organized a series of debates at the regional level with the participation of local authorities and MEPs. The SSEA, with the support of both EP and Commission representatives and the European Information Centre Jacques Delors, also organized seminars and debates in various universities.

The Portuguese president showed some interest in these matters, too, and, with the support of the representatives of the European Commission and the EP and of the European Information Centre Jacques Delors, organized several debates. Moreover, the president's cabinet also organized seminars with the presidents of Italy, Slovenia, Hungary and Ireland and the vice-president of the Convention, Jean-Luc Dehaene. Since his re-election, the president has followed the examples of other European statesmen and decided to put forward his views on the future of Europe independently of the government or his own party.[11] The Ministry of Education led the 'Spring of Europe Initiative' and was keen that the event be a success. It held several meetings in conjunction with institutions/agencies linked to European affairs, culminating in a national ceremony to publicize it. Nevertheless, the initiative was not very visible in the media.

Universities, public and private institutions, political groups, economic agents, journalists and civil society were represented in the initiatives outlined above, but they drew only on a small group of people. The aim of discussing proposals with the Portuguese government, the national parliament and the political parties never materialized.

Moreover, notwithstanding all the information on the Convention (speeches, reports, etc.) that was made available on the parliament's website via a forum for citizens (although, it must be said, very few people knew about its existence, and it was allegedly not user-friendly), not a single contribution arrived at the site. Contrary to previous experience, namely the debate on the future of Europe in 2000 and 2001, the committee did not receive a single contribution from local associations, NGOs or individual citizens. As for the government, there was neither a dedicated website on the future of the EU nor any information on the Convention on the government's website.

Summing up, although there were many initiatives to promote the debate on the future of Europe, this does not mean that the debate trickled down and came to involve civil society in Portugal. The different actors behind the initiatives were sometimes just competing for some media attention, and, in general, there was no follow-up of individual initiatives. The result was that they did not manage to mobilize civil society and public opinion and, with the exception of some references in the specialized press, were basically ignored by the media.

The Mobilization of Youth

The mobilization of youth may be another way of assessing whether the debate was addressing substantive issues and mobilized society or if it ended up as symbolic politics that lacked real substance.

In spite of the fact that there has been a problem of motivation for and comprehension of the EU by its citizens, some events showed an interesting level of mobilization amongst youth. On the initiative of the European Convention, in its hearings phase, a European Youth Convention was convened in July 2002 with the aim of producing a contribution to the debate on the future of Europe. What came across at this Convention, which gathered 210 young people in the EP in Brussels, was that youth was aware of the European project, even if it was still distant and complex, and, more importantly, that they not only had specific concerns (education, employment, culture, etc.) but that they were willing to participate actively as far as decisions in these domains were concerned.

In Portugal, the representatives in the European Youth Convention took up the challenge launched by the Convention proper and convened a Portuguese youth convention that took place in the Portuguese parliament on 28–29 November 2002. This event got started with a tour made by the eight Portuguese that had been present at the European Youth Convention to every region in Portugal in order to share their experiences and call for candidates for the Portuguese convention. Through this process, the Portuguese youth convention attracted 63 young 'conventioneers' – three from each Portuguese region and three from the Portuguese communities abroad.

Whereas it is difficult to assess whether the debate mobilized citizens in general or whether it was effectively a cosmetic operation, it is possible to affirm that such a debate was important, especially among Portuguese youth: participants seemed to have understood the debate to be an opportunity for bringing the EU closer to its citizens in general, and to youth in particular. This is illustrated by the fact that the Portuguese youth convention was followed-up at different levels. It had a snowball effect which spread to several universities and districts that organized their own regional conventions, with the support of local schools and the EP.

Coverage of the Convention in the Written Press and the Media

The so-called 'civil society' is known to be quite weak in Portugal, in the sense that it is dominated by the government and political parties (which are active only on very specific issues). Generally, though, public opinion displayed a rather open attitude in regard to institutional reform leading to a European constitution.[12]

The Convention was first seen in Portugal as a political forum that was preparing a text with several options, a type of 'expert committee' to pave the way for an IGC. Media coverage was initially very scarce, although by the end of 2002 attention seemed to have increased thanks to the importance of the ongoing debate on institutional reform. With the statements by President Giscard d'Estaing on the need for a European constitution, the Portuguese media focused their attention on the positions of the governments of the bigger member states. After Giscard's presentation of the draft constitutional text and after several countries had nominated as their government representatives their ministers for EU or foreign affairs, media coverage became more focused on the development of the Convention. Coverage occurred essentially in the written press: television and radio stations basically ignored the Convention. Two main daily national newspapers (*Diário de Notícias* and *Público*) had journalists covering the work of the Convention and analyzing each plenary session. Some Portuguese members of the Convention also wrote about it in newspapers.

The main discourse that surfaced in the press (from journalists and people from opposition parties) concerned the lack of a clear Portuguese position on institutional reform ('lack of debate, lack of ideas'). There was a general criticism of Portugal's reactive attitude – a small country with no ideas that would accept whatever the others (the big countries) were willing to offer. The emerging discourse was more one of 'being against' some proposals, as in the case of the Franco-German memorandum, than of putting forward new ideas and proposals.

Opinion-makers or elites (composed mainly of academics, former politicians and journalists dealing with EU affairs) have been rather sceptical and/or critical about European integration in general. As far as the Convention was concerned, they were divided between those attacking the idea of a federal Europe (and the Franco-German stance more than the Franco-German proposals) – as often before – and those attacking the government, the main political parties and the parliament for not having a single idea on the future of Europe or at least a strategy for the Convention.

More specific topics were also addressed, notably: the composition of the European Commission (where changes led to the eventual loss of the Portuguese commissioner); the external representation of the Union; Mr 'double-hat' – CFSP/CFDP; social cohesion and the principle of solidarity; the coordination of economic policies, the budget deficit and the stability and growth pact; the loss of structural funds; the reform of the common agricultural policy and fisheries; and, especially, concern over a directorate of the big member states in one way or another.

'Equality' of member states remained the catchword in the public debate regarding the Convention. Note, however, that apart from that, the public debate was not centred on the Convention but rather on other contemporary issues such as the war against Iraq, the emerging cases of paedophilia and corruption in the country, and the economic crisis (more specifically, the budgetary situation and the danger of economic recession).

Public Reaction: Opinion Polls and Surveys

Throughout the Convention, Portuguese public opinion was not critical of further EU integration, although it maintained its concerns over the extension of EU decision-making. The intellectual debate and its critical positions on the lack of ambition and reactive attitudes of the politicians seemed not to influence public opinion, nor did it really encompass the debate on EU decision-making. There was, then, a clear separation between the discourse of the elites (opinion-makers, journalists) and the citizens.

Generally speaking, Portuguese public opinion is in favour of EU integration. This is not only because structural funds have contributed to the country's economic growth (although there have been some serious distributional imbalances and sustainability problems with the sudden enrichment of parts of the population derived from structural funds/lower euro interest rates) but also because of the idea that Portugal gained a voice in an international framework that gathers big European countries. As forwarded by Alesina and Tavares (2003: 103), such a capacity to design the rules of the game and influence policy is one of the main reasons why small countries joined the EU. This is especially important if one takes into account the geo-strategic shift towards Europe that Portugal made after losing its colonies in 1975.

Furthermore, while the Portuguese mistrust their political class somewhat, people tend to bear in mind the role of EC accession in the consolidation of Portuguese democracy (see Bandeira 1998) and economic growth. Accession took place on 1 January 1986 shortly after the PSD had won the elections. Following this victory, the PSD then governed alone for a period of ten years (1985–95) – which coincided with political stability and economic prosperity in the country, with the exception of the period 1992–95; this particular period was marked by a rather anti-European (anti-Maastricht) attitude of the opinion-makers.

For all these reasons, the Portuguese look at European integration positively, accommodating most European integration efforts. Comparative Eurobarometer data on support for the EU, perceived benefits from membership and the EU as a guarantee of democracy is illustrative in this context: large percentages of people support European membership and think that Portugal has benefited from its membership – always above 60 per cent in all Eurobarometers, and a high share (68 per cent in Eurobarometer 58) of Portuguese think that the EU is fairly or very effective in guaranteeing the principles of democracy in Europe.

The consensus in favour of a stronger EU and stronger EU intervention in most areas is not explained by the distrust of national politicians alone, but derives mainly from the self-proclaimed pro-European stance of the main political parties paired with a lack of information. It is striking that Portugal, since 1999 when this question was first stated, has always been one of the countries with a strongly pronounced sense that it lacks information about the EU (84 per cent against an EU average of 77 per cent; Eurobarometer 58). The initiatives to promote public debate in the context of the Convention referred to above, apparently did not change that picture.

As far as institutional reform is concerned, it has attracted comparatively large attention from the Portuguese – with 71 per cent maintaining that it should be an EU priority (19 points more than the EU average; Eurobarometer 59). However, the feeling of information lacking about the EU is also reflected in questions that address knowledge of the Convention. Low percentages of respondents actually knew what the Convention was: only 33 per cent stated that the Convention was working on proposals to reform the EU; 36 per cent knew that the government was represented in the Convention; 27 per cent knew that the parliament was also represented; 20 per cent knew that the governments of the new member states were represented; and 19 per cent knew that the Convention was to complete its work in 2003 (Eurobarometer 59).

Notwithstanding the lack of information, according to Eurobarometer 59, more than 60 per cent of the population support the idea of a European constitution and believe that decisions in a great number of policy areas should be taken jointly within the EU, instead of by the national government alone. Public opinion here goes further than national policy-makers: between 55 per cent and 62 per cent think that there should be a commissioner for every member state (although Portugal has the lowest percentage in favour of this principle) and 43 per cent think that the presidency of the European Council should be extended beyond its current six-month period.

In sum, Portuguese public opinion seems to fundamentally approve all institutional changes proposed by the Praesidium and/or the EU core countries, thereby ignoring all the major concerns and strong positions of the Portuguese representatives in the Convention. The only issue over which public opinion seemed to have strong reservations (only 26 per cent in favour, according to Eurobarometer 59) was the possibility of a member state giving up its veto rights or limiting this possibility to very few essential areas; public opinion was, therefore, against more decisions being taken by QMV.[13] Interestingly, the government, the Portuguese representatives and the main political parties were rather open (in community affairs, justice and home affairs and security) or rather undecided/ambiguous on the issue of extended QMV.

CONCLUSION

The Convention has confirmed again that Portugal eventually falls in line with the core countries of the European integration process without much input or strategy on how it should proceed or where it should lead. Throughout the Convention, Portuguese public opinion was either receptive or indifferent to most of the core's proposed changes coming from the Praesidium and/or from Franco-German quarters. Its generally favourable attitude towards the European integration process (as a substitute for the lack of trust in national institutions) accommodates most of the institutional changes necessary for its progress. Having lost their obsession with structural funds for physical (road) infrastructures that characterized the first years of integration, the government and the two major political parties seem to have lost any points of reference in the discussions about the future of Europe. The Nice Treaty was a first instance where Portugal appeared to defend the position of the smaller countries against the perceived danger of directorates from the bigger countries, which contrasted markedly with the prime minister's supranational stance during most of the Portuguese presidency six months earlier.

It seems that the Portuguese polity is out of tune with its public opinion, disregarding its major fears concerning the extension of EU decision-making and artificially amplifying its own fears of a directorate of the larger countries. Therefore, despite siding with the other non-core smaller countries (the Group of 16) throughout the Convention, Portugal eventually reverted to old patterns and, at the very end of the Convention, fell in line with the European core. As was to be expected, those rather rhetorical issues came to the forefront of the European political debate on the future of Europe at the time of the next IGC. The Portuguese position at the IGC was however very discreet – the prime minister emphasizing that Portugal could not risk to perceived as out of the EU core. Without a political debate on more substantive issues (so far politically neglected), such as which tasks should be centralized at the EU level and which should be left to the national or regional level and – more importantly – what kind of Europe (in terms of a model of society) Portugal wants to live in, the Portuguese adaptation to European institutional changes looks set to follow the same reactive pattern.

NOTES

1. Depending on the perspective, EMU was referred to as the only way of tying Germany into the European Union, of achieving more political integration or, simply, of maintaining access to EU structural funds.
2. At that time, the committee on European affairs and the committee on foreign affairs were still independent committees. They were only merged in the current legislature, allegedly for cost reasons.
3. Some agreed afterwards with the independent MP (one of the authors of this contribution) that they were just avoiding conflicting views with their respective government or party.
4. The only way to link the national parliament to European issues at the table of the Council of Ministers was by establishing a specific relation with the government.

With the co-decision procedure, however, national parliaments have found other channels to participate in the process. See Torres (2002b) for a discussion and several examples.

5. Professor Lopes was nominated chairman of Portugal Telecom in February 2003, and continued to serve as the government representative in the Convention. That situation contrasted with the nomination from Germany and France of their foreign affairs ministers as government representatives in the Convention.

6. See Král et al. (2003) for a detailed account of the position of the small countries throughout the Convention.

7. These proposals passed unnoticed in the press, with the exception of a sports daily.

8. The parliamentary representatives were: Alberto Costa (PS), at the time chairman of the European affairs committee, and Eduarda Azevedo (PSD), PSD spokeswoman at the committee; António Nazaré Pereira (PSD) and Guilherme d'Oliveira Martins (PS) were alternate members.

9. With respect to the CAP, the Portuguese government (and the two main political parties) have consistently complained about its inadequacy in the light of Portuguese interests and the situation in Portugal. Yet, when it comes to the adoption of possible changes to such an unsustainable (and harmful) policy, the Portuguese government becomes extremely conservative and resistant, sticking to the defence of the *status quo* (as it did again at the end of both the Convention and the Greek presidency). In this case, there is no convergence to the reform because such reform is blocked from the outset.

10. For an analysis of these formal and more substantive issues in regard to the Convention – and therefore as far as EU leadership is concerned in terms of its effectiveness, democratic quality and institutional balance, see Coussens and Crum (2003). Their analysis provides a link between these two types of issues that may help to explain the Portuguese expected – and, indeed, realized – convergence as the Convention proceeded.

11. See, for example, his speech delivered to the Alumni of the European University Institute in Florence, widely discussed in the Portuguese press and covered by the media (namely because of its critiques of the stability and growth pact) on 4 October 2002.

12. The Portuguese weekly newspaper *Expresso* published a survey on 1 November 2002 in which 51 per cent of Portuguese were in favour of a European constitution (32 per cent were against) and 69 per cent were in favour of an elected president of the EU (only 13 per cent were against). These results came as a surprise and contrasted markedly with the strong and consensual cross-party resistance to the institutional changes under discussion at the time.

13. This attitude is consistent with previous polls on EU decision-making already referred to in the introduction.

REFERENCES

Alesina, A. and J. Tavares (2003): 'Remarks on Macedo and Cunha and Abreu', in F. Monteiro, J. Tavares, M. Glatzen and A. Candoso (eds.) *Portugal: Strategic Options in a European Context*, Lexington: Lanham, pp.99–103.

Berglöf, E., B. Eichengreen, G. Roland, G. Tabellini and C. Wyplosz (2003): *Built to Last: A Political Architecture for Europe*, London: Centre for Economic Policy Research.

Bandeira, C. Leston (1998): 'Relationship between Parliament and Government in Portugal: an Expression of the Maturation of the Portuguese Parliament', in P. Norton (ed.), *Parliaments and Governments in Western Europe*, London: Frank Cass, pp.142–66.

Coussens, W. and B. Crum (2003): 'Towards Effective and Accountable Leadership of the Union. Options and Guidelines for Reform', European Policy Institutes Network working paper No.3, Brussels: Centre for European Policy Studies.

Fraga, A. (2001): 'The Parliament of Portugal: Loyal Scrutiny and Informal Influence', in A. Maurer and W. Wessels (eds.), *National Parliaments on their Ways to Europe: Losers or Latecomers?* Baden-Baden: Nomos Verlagsgesellschaft, pp.359–75.

Jones, E., J. Frieden and F. Torres (eds.) (1998): *Joining Europe's Monetary Club: The Challenges for Smaller Member States*, New York: St. Martin's Press.

D. Král, I. Brinar, J. Almer (2003). 'The Position of Small Countries Towards Institutional Reform: From Tyranny of the Small to *Directoire of the Big?*' European Policy Institutes Network Working Paper No.6, Brussels: Centre for European Policy Studies.

Magone, J. (2000): 'The Transformation of the Portuguese Political System: European Regional Policy and Democratization in a Small EU Member State', *South European Society & Politics* 5/2, (autumn).

Torres, F. (2000): 'Lessons from Portugal's Long Transition to Economic and Monetary Union', in A. Vasconcelos (ed.), *Portugal: A European Story*, Cascais: Principia, pp.99–130.

Torres, F., (2002a): 'On the Democratic Quality of Governance in the European Union: The Examples of EMU and of Environmental Policies and the Role of the European Parliament' Unpublished dissertation in International Affairs School of Advanced International Studies, Johns Hopkins University.

Torres, F. (2002b): 'How Efficient is Joint Decision-Making in the EU? Environmental Policies and the Co-Decision Procedure', *Intereconomics* 38/6, pp.312–22.

Greece: On New, European Tracks?

NICOS YANNIS

INTRODUCTION

The participation of Greece in the debate on the constitutional future and the political organization of Europe held during 2002 under the framework of the European Convention was characterized by endogenous and exogenous features.

One of the exogenous features was the progress of the Convention itself: in general terms, the Convention did not become a source of controversies and thus did not attract much interest, either from the public or from political parties. On the other hand, there is a series of intervening variables to be taken into account: the military intervention in Iraq – to which the overwhelming majority of the Greek public was opposed (the official Greek government and presidential position was against any military intervention without prior UN Security Council approval), developments in the Middle East – including the renewal of violence, and the Greek–Turkish and Europe–Turkish relations during a critical period – particularly because of the progress of Cyprus's accession to the European Union (EU) and the efforts for a settlement of the Cyprus issue. All these factors contributed to an extensive agreement in Greece regarding a common attitude on external relations and defence policy in Europe, leading in turn to the need to deepen the political dimension of European integration.

The unconditional accession of Cyprus to the EU, agreed upon at the Copenhagen summit, was one of the major endogenous features, since it was considered vitally important by all political forces in Greece at the Convention – in particular during the second semester of 2002. During the first semester of the same year, an issue of major public salience was the introduction of the euro. As far as EU issues are concerned, these were the two that attracted public attention in Greece, with the Convention ranking third. It should be noted that as political forces agreed upon the country's policy on Europe – and this consensus eliminated any political conflict on the domestic political agenda – these issues did not attract the public's attention, while Europeanization during the last eight years has indeed accelerated. It seems, therefore, that the Convention was not a real magnet of attraction for the public during 2002, although it reinforced a rather positive attitude towards Europe.

Despite the fact that a federalist structure of the EU appears to be a demand that all political forces in Greece share (with the exception of the *Komunistiko Koma Elladas* [KKE; Communist Party]), it is not accompanied by an equally intense internalization of the federal option: decentralization, local and regional government organization and fiscal federalism (Bird *et al.* 2002: 407–575), the modernization and transparency of public administration, rights and minority protection (McGarry 2002: 416) (as opposed to the unitary statist option (Chopin 2003)), federal-leaning conceptualization of the neighbouring geopolitical space, as well as of a global government (Sutter 2002) – all amount to a deeper consolidation of the federal concept of unity within diversity.

This essay focuses on various aspects of Greece's participation in the European Convention. In particular, we start by examining the official participation of Greece in the European Convention's deliberations, move on to the non-state channels of participation, investigate the Convention's agenda from the Greek point of view and end by drawing some critical conclusions.

GREEK OFFICIAL PARTICIPATION IN THE CONVENTION

The Government in the Convention

The Greek government was initially represented in the Convention by George Katiforis, Member of the European Parliament (MEP), and later substituted by Minister for Foreign Affairs, Georges Papandreou. The Ministry of Foreign Affairs (MFA), under the deputy minister in charge of European affairs, An. Yanitsis, was the official policy-making body regarding government positions and decisions on the Convention.

A consultative committee of eight experts, mainly academics, assisted the government in its tasks. As far as the government research unit is concerned, the issue of the European Convention was undertaken and promoted by the Hellenic Centre for European Studies (EKEM) in Athens.[1] The president of the Centre, Professor P.K. Ioakimidis, was the deputy delegate of the Greek government to the Convention. The Greek Permanent Representation in Brussels, comprising some 150 civil servants (20 of whom are diplomats), coordinated European affairs too, although it was and indeed is at times confronted by the bureaucratic attitude of the MFA – which has a leading role in EU policy.

The Convention sessions and the general debate on the future of Europe necessitated the updating of all participants or all members interested in the EU integration process – as is clearly indicated by the publication of a tailor-made web newsletter by EKEM. This newsletter includes all activities under the framework of the Convention, focusing especially on Greece's participation in this ongoing process.[2]

Prime Ministerial Statements and Official Government Positions

In an address to the College of Europe in Bruges on 31 January 2002 on the future of Europe and social cohesion, the Greek prime minister, Kostas Simitis, called for the enlarged EU to 'evolve into a fully-fledged Political Union', adding, 'however, we should continue to apply the Community model and method of integration, although the latter must be renewed and reinvigorated. Decentralized federalism based on the Community model constitutes for us the answer to the challenges the European Union faces as it forges ahead with enlargement.' Simitis, moreover, called for a 'clear, simple and understandable' constitution 'to strengthen the economic union' (when dealing with taxation and fiscal policy), adding that 'we must progressively develop the CFDP into a collective defence system, starting with the extension of the so-called "Petersburg tasks", without undermining, however, the role of NATO in any way'. He feels that 'the European project requires the transformation of the Union's institutional system into a democratically structured system of governance' where 'the European Commission and the European Parliament must continue to occupy a central place.' Simitis placed great emphasis on the Union being 'a delicate system of solidarity and cohesion' and stressed that the 'economic and social cohesion must remain, therefore, one of the prime objectives of European integration'.[3]

However, Simitis, speaking at a seminar organized by EKEM on 'the Future of Europe and Greece' a year before the Laeken summit, had pleaded in favour of the EU moving along the lines of a political union, possibly of federalist inspiration.[4] According to the Greek prime minister, therefore, in the future we should design a system capable of 'evolving flexibly, respecting the dynamics of societies … respecting those who want to move ahead in a certain sector, but also those who are hesitant or not yet able to do so'. According to him, this means: 1) a Europe with a 'differentiated system of integration' in which everyone would participate fully in the 'basic integration mechanisms' but allowing those who are ready to 'concede a larger share of the sovereign choices to the integration project, to proceed to more advanced stages of deepened integration', and 2) movement towards a political union. At this point, Simitis states that the appropriate model for the final transformation of the EU is the federal one based on the Community system. According to him, this system 'permits the constructing of a European sovereignty in order to regain collectively parts of the sovereignty that we are individually losing', considering that 'the coalition of those who can and want a federal model can be the answer to the need for a strong political driving force for the future of Europe'.

More specifically, Simitis believes that: 1) the Council of Ministers could develop along the lines of a second legislative chamber 'articulating the interest of the Member States', whereas the European Council 'must remain the supreme political body of the EU'; 2) the role of the European Parliament (EP) and the status of European political parties must be strengthened, as well as the possibility of national parliaments influencing the European integration process; 3) the development of policies and competencies of the EU calls for 'the clear definition of principles for exercising them', but 'it would be a serious mistake to attempt to draw up a list of competencies as a means of delimiting them.' The Union must remain a flexible system of 'sharing powers', Simitis argued, fearing that a strict distribution of competencies would lead to the re-nationalization of policies or even to 'the freezing of the integration process'; 4) in order to make citizens 'active parties to the process of integration, … Europe needs a Constitution'. Simitis pleaded in favour of the inclusion of the Charter of Fundamental Rights in the Union's institutional texts – as a legally binding text.

According to the (initial) official position of the Greek government,[5] Greece 1) supports the federal model based on the Community system and the Community method of integration; 2) considers the simplification of the treaties indispensable; 3) considers that the role of national parliaments can be reinforced, although new institutions should not be created; 4) opposes the re-nationalization of policies that would lead to the weakening of economic and social coherence; and 5) looks forward to elaborating the rules of a common course on the basis of flexibility that would allow different levels of integration.

In addition, Greece, although a country that appears to be an enthusiast of a federal Europe, still entrusts the MFA with European issues and their negotiation to diplomats. This dissonance is further aggravated as the Convention itself presupposes 1) broader participation in the constitutional treaty building process, and 2) reducing the significance attributed to national sovereignty. Establishing a ministry for EC/EU affairs has been discussed since 1981 but has not yet materialized due to sharp competition for competencies between the ministers involved. Therefore, coordination in integration issues has been shared in principle between the MFA and the Ministry for National Economy, both having alternate ministers or under-secretaries in charge of European affairs.

Political Activity in Parliament

On behalf of the Greek parliament, the regular representatives to the Convention were two Members of Parliament (MPs) who were also former MEPs: P. Avgerinos from the governing party *Panhellenion Sosialistiko Kenema* (PASOK; Panhellenic Socialist Movement), and M. Giannakou from *Nea Demokratia* (ND; the New Democracy party); while E. Stylianidis (ND) and N. Constantopoulos from *Synaspismos* (SYN; the Coalition of the Left) participate as deputy representatives. The KKE was not represented. However, Constantopoulos, objecting to this allocation of membership, did not participate in any of the meetings.

The Standing Committee for European Affairs does not meet on a regular basis.[6] Its competencies include the examination of institutional issues arising from EU membership, cooperation between the national parliament and the EP as well as with the other EU national parliaments, the incorporation of European legislation, and EU issues arising from other national parliamentary committees. The government should submit every year a general report on its activities on European issues to the Greek Chamber of Deputies. Ministers are supposed to brief the Committee and should be regularly available for questions – the commonly used parliamentary instruments of control.

Effective scrutiny by the Committee for European Affairs was not intense, although ministers and other government officials are always called upon to defend or explain the government's European positions. Hearings are usually a mere formality, even though the members of the Committee with an active role in parliamentary control thus gain awareness. European issues with special significance for the general public are dealt with in the ordinary plenary sessions as these are media-attracting events. The Chamber demands wider dissemination of information and involvement in European matters but is not adequately treated by the government. In addition, prime minister's question time is normally used by the opposition parties for government criticism instead of posing fundamental questions on EU issues. In fact, EU issues are largely neglected due to their complicated technical nature, rendering them rather unsuitable for party confrontations. Decision-makers at the governmental level with regard to European affairs seem to prefer traditional management rather than negotiations through parliamentary deliberation; it is thus ensured that positions prone to public or media criticism are avoided.

Turning to the Convention, in 2002 there were neither special nor dedicated plenary sessions in the Chamber of Deputies. There have been 12 meetings of the Committee for European Affairs, nine of which dealt with issues related to the Convention. These meetings took place once a month, with the exception of the summer period (see Appendix II). The agenda of the Committee included issues arising from the Convention workings of the same period. As expected, special emphasis was placed on the role of the national parliaments in the EU. This Committee had adopted specific positions towards the intergovernmental conferences (IGCs) leading to the Treaties of Maastricht, Amsterdam and Nice; however, this was not the case with the Convention. No public hearings took place, although the issue of initiative-taking by aiming at wider public debate had been discussed in the Greek parliament, and the will to do so was evident. This is due to the structural inadequacies of the parliamentary and administrative mechanism as well as to the widespread lack of interest and sensitivity for this specific issue. Other parliamentary activities have scarcely incorporated the Convention in their fields of interest.

The Views of the Greek Political Parties

PASOK, the governing party, emphasized that the EU can only exist – and continue to exist – as a union of states and people if it is based on democracy and respects human rights and the common cultural heritage.[7] Its future structure can be ensured, moreover, if a balance is struck between convergence procedures. PASOK supported the development of institutional instruments, the reduction of Community red tape, and the enhancement of cooperation between national parliaments and the EP. The European Constitution should ensure all the above elements, at the heart of which stands the European citizen. The views of Prime Minister Simitis, president of PASOK, were reiterated by him in the Party of European Socialists. In this capacity he stated that the Convention should aim to 1) draft a constitution and 2) create a European area of equal opportunities for all citizens, regardless of their nationality. He also added that the Union must assert its identity at the world level and develop into a legitimate centre of power.

The main opposition party, ND, presented its views on the Convention through the speeches of its president, K. Karamanlis. As was often stressed, ND believes in a federal evolution of the EU and supports a federation based on the solidarity of its members, promoting their cohesion while at the same time ensuring their distinct vital interests.

ND is in favour of a European constitution that ensures transparency and balance for European institutions and provides for specific competence allocation (at European, national and regional levels) while at the same time does not exclude small states. ND also believes that a charter of fundamental rights should be incorporated into the European Constitution and that the European Commission should be reinforced through the immediate election of its members by all European citizens and the upgrading of the national parliaments. Furthermore, under the light of enlargement, ND considers it necessary for a first group of states to proceed to deeper integration. These states can only be the states of the Eurozone, which should also acquire political characteristics.

It was only on 16 January 2003 that ND organized the first event on the Convention and the European Constitution.[8] President K. Karamanlis stated at this conference that there should be two keywords for the European Constitution: autonomy and participation.

The Coalition of the Left party (SYN), one of the parliamentary parties of the Left, agrees with various views put forth either by PASOK or ND. According to SYN, the EU should proceed to its political unification in such a way that democracy is assured and all member states waive the same degree of sovereignty in favour of common European interests which, at the same time, will preserve the uniqueness of each member state in terms of culture, history and society. According to President Constantopoulos, the EU should move towards a federal union characterized by democracy and transparency.[9] European citizens and their concerns about unemployment, social matters, education and public health should be given top priority. SYN criticizes liberal and social-democratic governments for being hesitant and making weak-minded choices, thus making the EU an issue to be dealt with at the intergovernmental level. SYN believes that the EU has to bring the decision-making processes on EU issues closer to European citizens. As far as foreign policy is concerned, the EU should assume a more active stance so as to control the role that the United States monopolizes. Ultimately, SYN believes the EU is the only power in the world that can guarantee democracy, provided it is a political union.

Finally, the KKE opposes European integration and Greece's European choice (the decision to enter and deepen the EU), considering it a manifestation of the capitalist and imperialist character of the member states. Consequently, the Convention is considered by KKE as an attempt to reinforce this aspect of Europe and adapt it to emerging conditions. According to KKE's secretary general, Aleka Papariga, the Convention would have a negative impact on the sovereignty rights of the member states and would endanger people's rights. The common foreign policy was portrayed as deeply reactionary and inequitable.

The Role of Regions and Sub-National Politics

Greece is not a federal state and, although during the last decade local government has been reinforced, its competencies are not decisively affected by the redistribution of authority between member states and the EU. Besides, there is no culture of participation of local government in the treaty reform procedures and re-identification of the institutional equilibrium within the EU. Therefore, it is not surprising that so far there has been a limited participation by Greek local government in the debate on the future of Europe. The initiative of the MFA to organize a public debate on the issues covered by the Convention in 2002 under the framework of the municipalities was not successful, although it has materialized in four cases at the prefecture level during 2003 – that is, with a serious time lag. Ten conferences in total were organized on the Convention in regional towns, four of which took place following an initiative by the EP.

THE NON-STATE ACTORS' PARTICIPATION IN THE CONVENTION (PARTICIPATORY DEMOCRACY)

Main Interest Groups

The *Syndesmos Ellinikon Viomihanion* (SEV; Greek Industries Association), among others, submitted its views along with the views of its EU umbrella organization, the Union of industrial and employer's confederations of Europe (UNICE), regarding the general topics dealt with by the Convention as well as issues of special interest for industry in a document entitled 'An Enlarged and Efficiently Functioning Union. The Future of Europe', which was included in the 'Position Paper of the Greek Business Community for the Greek Presidency 2003'. The positions of the Greek Chambers of Commerce were presented through the intervention of Georges Kasimatis, the deputy president of Eurochambres, at the Eurochambres Board meeting on 20 June 2002. The General Confederation of Greek Workers did not submit any views.

Non-Governmental Organizations and Think Tanks

While the participation of civil society and citizens themselves in the discussions regarding the Single European Act in 1985–87 was almost non-existent, the European Union treaty became the topic of heated debates. This was especially the case after the adoption of the Maastricht Treaty and, more specifically, after its ratification by the Greek parliament and, moreover, in view of the Amsterdam Treaty. The Amsterdam Treaty has been vividly discussed, particularly during the consultation period that preceded the opening of the IGC. The Nice Treaty itself, although not an issue of major importance for the Greeks – mainly because the means for Greece to fulfil the criteria of joining the Economic and Monetary Union (EMU) on schedule was at stake at the time, attracted the interest of certain parts of civil society and several think tanks as well. The only non-governmental organization (NGO) fully participating in the consultation with civil society at European level regarding the elaboration and adoption of the Charter of Fundamental Rights was a national one, *Evropaiki Ekfrassi* (European Expression).

Thus, the involvement of Greek civil society in the debate about the future of Europe during 2001 and in the broad consultation on the Convention with civil society during 2002 can be characterized as weak and lacking intensity. Nevertheless, the NGOs formulated claims of considerable diversity, based on their particular field of action, and contributed ideas and suggestions. At least seven national NGOs dealt with the Convention on their own: the association European Expression, the Citizen's Movement Against Racism, the Citizen's Union '*Paremvassi*', the Citizen's Movement for an Open Society, the Marangopoulos Foundation for Human Rights, the Research Institute for European and American Studies (RIEAS) and the Young Researchers Association for European Studies (ENEES). Among the Greek antennas and representations of European and international NGOs, at least four produced written proposals: Amnesty International – Greek Section, the European Women's Lobby, the Greek Association for Atlantic and European Cooperation and the Human Rights Defence Centre.

Of notable significance was the fact that some Greek sections of NGOs at least communicated the views and positions of their mother European organizations, in this way informing the Greek public about their activities. Thus, these NGOs contribute to the dissemination of information, the transparency and the fuelling of questioning, and to limiting the range of a 'government-restricted area' where the negotiation of statutory texts remains obscure.

Within this context, we should also note the exceptional presence of the *Association des Femmes de l'Europe Meridionale* [Association of Southern European Women], the representative (S.Spiliotopoulou) of which was the only Greek voice heard at the special meeting of the Convention with civil society on 24–25 June 2002 in Brussels.

The Convention issues were discussed in at least thirty public meetings organized by various organizations and bodies (during the period March 2002 to April 2003). It should be noted at this point that we owe half of these meetings to an initiative of the MFA and the EP office in Greece. Under this framework, Nikitas Lionarakis, an advisor to the minister of foreign affairs and president of the governmental committee on NGOs, played a critical role. He supported the debate on the future of Europe with civil society as well as the contacts of Greek NGOs with the Convention through the means and communication channels of the Ministry. It was under his initiative that an 'ad hoc Committee of Greek NGOs for the European Convention' was set up. The Committee held four meetings and several consultations with Greek representatives to the Convention and Greek political parties, and also organized a large-scale meeting with the participation of the Convention vice-president, J.-L. Dehaene.

Rather characteristic of the participation of NGOs and think tanks is that of EKEM[10] and the Greek Centre of European Studies and Research (EKEME),[11] which contributed to a more theoretical processing of the issues and triggered a wider exchange of ideas. Almost all Greek members of the European Convention have participated in the two conferences organized by these centres, along with many academics experts and some journalists and NGO activists. The European Centre of Public Law, another Athens-based think tank, set-up an international Convention monitoring committee with the participation of numerous academics from various member states.

Two further conferences on the Convention and the future of Europe were organized in Athens by the Hellenic Committee for the EU on 9 May 2002 and 20 February 2003.[12] European Expression organized a conference about the Convention and the future of Europe on 13 May 2002. Moreover, European Expression, through the campaign by the Brussels-based Permanent Forum of Civil Society, introduced in Greece in spring 2003 the idea of abandoning the IGC as the main area for institutional reform and constitution-drafting in favour of the Convention itself; it also introduced the proposal to adopt – through a pan-European referendum – a constitutional treaty binding only those member states that voted for it.

Finally, the Archbishop of Athens, Christodoulos, met President Giscard d'Estaing on 20 February 2003 and submitted a written proposal to include in the constitution a reference to the Christian heritage of Europe, with an emphasis on the Christian intellectual and cultural tradition ('Christodoulos: Reference on Christianity in the Constitutional Treaty', *Eleftheros Typos*, 21 February 2003). At the beginning of the Convention, the Orthodox Church of Greece stated that the EU also had responsibility for the issues of bioethics, environment, migration and social justice.

The Mobilization of Youth

Although quality analysis of the available public opinion surveys shows that young Europeans think particularly positively about European integration – either through their active support (38 per cent) or through their optimistic realism (33 per cent),[13] and that Greek young people anticipate a better future through the EU (37 per cent – the third-highest figure for the 15 member states),[14] the participation of young people, at least in an organized way, in the debate on the future of Europe can only be characterized as weak. The National Youth Council suffered a severe crisis in 2002, and party politics is still a drawback for young people's NGO participation. Moreover, the significant delay in modernizing structures, functions and personalities could very well explain the almost complete absence of Greek youth from the Convention meetings. It is rather characteristic that at the Youth Convention held in Brussels on 9–12 July 2002, a pioneering idea that brought youth and civil society closer to the EU, there were only representatives of the political party youth organizations from Greece – who were appointed without any internal selection criteria and communicated the views of their parties instead of specially elaborated views of their own organizations.[15]

The Greek representative to the Youth Convention, D. Maziotis, argued that the EU has the moral and political obligation to safeguard democracy, stability and safety within the wider European area. He supported 'strong EU institutions' in order to reinforce the notion of European citizenship and have a means of approaching civil society. He finally supported the transfer of youth policy to the EU and the increase of youth mobility. Another representative, Maria Kanata, defined as 'EU goals' the preservation of a more competitive European economy, citizen participation in the EU and a more powerful presence for the EU in the world.[16]

On the other hand, only 23 per cent of the young people in Greece believe in a European government, 20 per cent that the EU guarantees peace and only 15.2 per cent that it guarantees the protection of citizen rights.[17]

Coverage in the Media

The Greek Press did not cover the Convention in detail. Browsing the press clippings from February to December 2002, we can see that there are only 178 publications referring immediately to the Convention in all nation-wide newspapers. This coverage can be summarized as follows:

- 112 refer to the Convention in general in news coverage;
- 17 to the possibility of an EU Directorate;
- 11 to the issue of the EU president (more have been appearing within the first months of 2003);
- 9 to Common Foreign and Security Policy (CFSP);
- 8 to social Europe;
- 7 to the views of the political parties;
- 6 to the Convention procedures in reference to particular members of the Convention,
- 5 to the USA;
- 2 to national parliaments; and
- 1 to the issues of public health, the regions, Community budget and religion.

Of all these publications, 11 were Greek translations of signed views and commentaries which first appeared in foreign newspapers; there were no more than 20 critical texts; 21 dealt with the inauguration of the Convention; 21 with Prodi's suggestions concerning federation; 19 with the Giscard d'Estaing constitution draft; and 22 with the Commission proposals in November 2002. There was only one special report, which comprised four interviews. However, a distinguished place was reserved for Giscard, the president of the Convention, who is particularly popular in Greece ever since his positive intervention in the country's accession to the EC during the 1970s. A special place was also reserved for the federal approach and prospects for its success. The two state-owned broadcast channels presented limited coverage of the Convention, mainly in informative programmes with low viewer ratings.

Public Opinion and Society in Greece

Greek public opinion, during the 20 years of Greek EU membership, has fluctuated greatly regarding the acceptance of Europe. In brief, during the first years – namely 1981–85, Greek public opinion was characterized by suspicion, accompanied by the anti-European rhetoric of PASOK's president (A. Papandreou) and its first term in office. During this period, the highest pro-Europe percentage ever attained was 47 per cent of the population. During the second period, 1986–1991, the picture reversed: in spring 1991, due to a mature PASOK second term and K. Mitsotakis's (ND) term of office, pro-Europeanism reaches its highest levels ever, rising to 76 per cent – a percentage which has not yet been surpassed.

During the period 1991–1996, the development of issues of national interest in the Balkans and to the east of Greece – resulting from the great changes in Europe and the world in 1989 – led to a decline in pro-European sentiment in Greece and mutual distrust among Europeans amidst a climate of insecurity. The return of A. Papandreou to office in 1993 and the weak government in the period that followed, as well as the political system crisis of that time, led to a drop in pro-EU sentiment to 51 per cent in spring 1996. However, from 1996 to date, contrary to the rest of Europe, Greek support of the EU has been revived and seems to have become consolidated. This is directly linked to the fact that the modernizer K. Simitis is prime minister, and K. Karamanlis, the president of the opposition, is undertaking a constructive opposition line with a strong pro-European outlook.

Furthermore, in 1997 Greece won the right to stage the 2004 Olympic Games. The escalating process of materializing this project, along with successful inclusion in the EMU, the 3rd Community Support Programme and resulting economic effects of these two factors – in addition to the positive developments in Cyprus's EU membership and Greek-Turkish relations, caused a significant increase in Greek self-confidence. This, in turn, has engendered a more dynamic and optimistic attitude towards the rest of the world, a focal point of which is Europe.

The Eurobarometer survey for the second semester of 2002 (Eurobarometer 58) shows that public opinion supports the CFSP, favours a European constitution, and disagrees with the proposal to have the president of the European Commission appointed by the heads of state and national governments. The survey also shows, though, that the majority remains against the abolition of the veto by virtue of its support for unanimity in the decision-making process. Greece, moreover, is among the top five countries in terms of level of support for the CFSP (the EU average is 73 per cent), 70 per cent of Greeks expect EU institutions to be reshaped (Greece ranks third; the EU average is 52 per cent) and 78 per cent are in favour of a European constitution (Greece ranks second) – ten per cent higher than the last survey in spring 2002 (Eurobarometer 57).[18] In 23 out of the 26 policy areas mentioned in the survey, the Greek public prefers EU to national decision-making, which amounts to the highest percentage in the EU. These trends, however, are not to be isolated from the manifested dissatisfaction of the Greeks with the way domestic democracy functions (politics, public administration, local government) – in fact, quite the contrary. Thus, a statist and protectionist culture still dominant among the Greeks takes the shape of an EU-centred protectionism. As it is more generously said, 'Overall, Greeks have overwhelmingly viewed the EU polity and bureaucracy as a powerful external agent, forcing domestic adjustment towards higher integrity and efficiency of the national state apparatus' (Pagoulatos, 2003: 25).

The direct election of the president of European Commission by all EU citizens obtains the most support from Greek public opinion (40 per cent) and is the fastest growing preference when compared to the alternatives of being appointed by the heads of state and government (14 per cent), or even of being elected by the EP (28 per cent). Public opinion in Greece, France and Belgium leads the direct election choice in terms of its strength. Nevertheless, Greek public opinion has moved in the opposite direction as far as a federalist arrangement is concerned regarding the unanimity vote/right to veto: instead of an EU average of 53 per cent supporting the veto, which represents an increase of three per cent compared to the responses to the same question in the spring 2002 survey, Greeks are ranked first with a percentage of 82 per cent, which represents an increase of 14 per cent compared to the survey of spring 2002. The paradox of being in favour of both federal power arrangements and a common foreign and defence policy at the same time as exhibiting a pro-veto attitude could eventually be explained by the historical top-down process of European unification (a Europe, in other words, built by diplomats).

In terms of the political unification of Europe, 55.6 per cent of Greeks are in support, but 26.5 per cent disagree.[19] The positive percentage is composed of 61.6 per cent of PASOK voters (centre-left), 52.7 per cent of ND (centre right) voters, 56.2 per cent of SYN (left) voters and 32.2 per cent of KKE (communist) voters. The 25.6 per cent disagreeing with political union is composed of 20.5 per cent PASOK voters, 27.2 per cent ND voters, 23.5 per cent SYN voters and 52.4 per cent KKE voters.

As a conclusion to this section, the survey shows that many Greeks believe that EU membership is a good thing and that the country has taken advantage of its membership: 62 per cent (the Greek percentage) is the most positive response of any country surveyed (the EU average is 55 per cent), although this percentage has dropped by two per cent compared to the spring 2002 survey and is eight per cent lower than respective surveys in 1999 and 2000.[20]

CONCLUDING REMARKS

The Politics of Mobilization in Greece

Greece's interest concerning the future of Europe is by now steadily oriented towards an attempt to contribute to all European issues as well as to participate constructively in the ongoing European integration process. It is not now, then, focused on the typically 'Greek' issues. Of course, it is only natural that specific Greek sensitivities emerged in the Convention. Topics such as safeguarding equality of member states in the decision-making process regardless of their size (unanimity rule, EU presidency, etc.), the CFSP, and solidarity between richer and poorer member states did not fade away. There was, though, also mobilization around new, 'European' issues.

Greece holds strong views on the need for the EU to acquire a federalist structure – starting with the Community system, although the reluctance to abandon unanimity, which is particularly strong among the people, constitutes a departure from federalist beliefs. Greece believes in a common foreign policy as well as in a common defence policy (79 per cent of the population in both cases). An even greater proportion of Greeks – 82 per cent – wants the right to veto to be preserved. This means that Greeks wish for decision-taking on important issues to be transferred to the EU but at the same time they wish to ensure that the EU will not be able to surpass what they want or what they consider to be in the national interest! On the other hand, it is rather interesting that the voters of the conservative ND, the party that prides itself on being the European party that will lead the country into the arms of Europe, are not convinced of the necessity of a political union of Europe, at least not as much as voters of the centre-left parties. In order to interpret this paradox, one should take into account that ND was in office for only three of the 22 years that has elapsed since Greece became a member state of the European Economic Community, and during all these years the PASOK governments were responsible for the Community distribution of resources to Greece, ND being in the opposition.

In terms of the attribution of a legally binding character to the Charter of Fundamental Rights, Greece is in total acceptance, as it is also with the need for a European constitution. Similarly, although a reinforcement to the role of the national parliaments is sought after, the establishment of new institutions in the EU is not favoured (for example, congress). Moreover, Greece does not seem to oppose variable forms of integration, and accepts the importance of an attitude of flexibility – which is based on a non-self-evident precondition that it will be included in a swiftly-moving core group.

In spring 2003, Greece openly declared that it favoured the election of the president of the European Commission by the EP as well as the reinforcement of the Commission. Initially, it was thought that appointing the president of the European Council might lead to conflict with the president of the Commission. However, it is not a question of good relations between the presidencies of the Council, the European

Council and the Commission; it is rather a question of setting the presidency of the European Council competencies. If these competencies are clearly set, Greece is willing to move closer to the hard core of Europe, moving away from the small- and medium-size countries even if this means moving slightly away from the United States. Premier Simitis seems now to believe that Europe risks acquiring a vague attitude and lesser importance compared to the United States because of the rotating Presidency system (P. Troupiotis, 'Τώρα αρχίζουν τα δύσκολα...της Προεδρίας' [Now the Tough Times Begin... for the Presidency], *Isotimia*, 25 April 2003, p.14.). Europe, lacking an institution that will give it a single and cohesive political expression, is called upon to answer whether it is a superpower and has not realized it (Ioakeimidis 2003). 'Joining the EU is not like going into a supermarket where everyone is free to purchase whatever one wishes for' (P. Ioakeimidis, 'Φοβούνται οι ΗΠΑ την Ευρώπη' ['Is the USA Afraid of Europe?' *Ta Nea*, 21 February 2003, p.6).

Within this context, the Greek government[21] as well as the opposition[22] supported the initiative taken by four countries in April 2003 for a special collaboration of certain member states in formulating a common foreign and defence policy even if, in the end, such a project is materialized outside the Community. According to Simitis, European defence can be developed along Schengen lines. The public seemed to realize for the first time the need for a common foreign policy and defence policy after the American attack on Iraq, and demonstrated its strong support for it – seemingly willing to depart from the traditional face of national sovereignty. However, the need to preserve a balance between the European and the Atlantic aspect in Greek foreign policy, stemming from traditional cooperation with the United States, the country's geographical location in the south-eastern Mediterranean, the Balkans in particular, and the problems with Turkey softens the competition between relations with Europe and America; in this way, Greek politics adheres to supporting a relationship based on equality.

Greece did not participate in the initiative taken by seven small states (later to become 16) insisting, among other demands, on keeping the six-month rotation of the presidency as, at the time that this initiative saw the light of publicity, Greece had already undertaken the EU presidency.

Finally, the principle of participatory democracy set out in Article 34 of the Preliminary Draft Constitutional Treaty has been welcomed in principle by civil society in Greece as a good starting point for the recognition of civil dialogue in Europe. However, Women's NGOs in Greece are deeply concerned that the draft does not include a single reference to the equality of women and men in Europe (the inclusion of which would have avoided the treaty appearing to be designed for men only), a treaty with a clear economic and technocratic orientation.

Moreover, a large part of the academic community, in accordance with national ideology, is rather cautious or perplexed in the face of the process of producing a European constitution, let alone a federal one, leaning on national sovereignty and the traditional teachings of constitutional law. In the words of a leading professor of constitutional law:

> [w]hy should it be, in the name of a vast civil society in Europe and a nebulous Charter of Fundamental Rights, or even in the name of an inexistent people of Europe, that we have to sacrifice and eliminate the unity and subjectivity of the Greek people and other peoples in Europe … The European Constitution should incorporate and not abolish national Constitutions, should respect the constitutional autonomy of every state … The federal organizational model of a European polity does not correspond to the historical, institutional and political features of the European integration and does not serve the demands of a European state that aspires to be a meta-state … European sovereignty belongs to European peoples, is exercised by their representatives and the representatives of their governments as provided for in the constitutional treaties. (A. Manitakis (2003): 'Οι αντινομίες και τα λογικά αδιέξοδα της κατασκευής ενός Συντάγματος για την Ευρώπη' ['Antinomies and dead ends in Constitution-Building in Europe'], *Avgi*, 3 March 2003.)

Weak Mobilization of Citizen and Society: A Failure of the Convention and the EU as Political System, or a Problem of State–Society Relations in Greece?

The aim of this essay was to present and analyze the participation of Greek actors, state and non-state, in the Convention for the future of Europe.

For a number of reasons, most of which have been presented here, Greece's membership in the EU is evaluated as a particularly significant *acquis*. In this light, the Convention is seen with a positive eye, although the work and the Convention itself are not particularly known to the greatest part of the population. This does not mean a rejection of Europe. In fact, the situation is quite the contrary. The efforts put into the dissemination of information and debate-generation by the MFA, the parliament and the EU itself (European Commission and EP) produced only limited results; the media coverage has been poor and other issues, some related to Europe (the euro, Cyprus accession), overshadowed the Convention.

Civil society, still weak in Greece, registered its formal participation in the debate without any claims for a dynamic intervention contrary to the anti-globalization movement organized by the 'Social Forum', the trade unions and KKE of Greece or the anti-war movement with its dynamic demonstrations during the Greek presidency in the first half of 2003 – movements focused on European policy and the war against Iraq respectively. Nonetheless, within the small community of experts and those engaged to a certain degree with the Convention, there has been an exhaustive discussion.

The weak participation of citizens in the debate on the future of Europe and the constitution can be attributed to the unsuccessful communication campaign by governments, both national and European,[23] and to the Greek 'consensus' that discouraged public debate as it lacks conflicting positions. However, it can also be attributed to 1) the technical and thus not particularly attractive nature of European institutional issues, and 2) the general lack of legitimization of all European decisions as 'the central institutional framework of the EU retains linkages to governments and citizens which lack legitimization and make it incomplete. Much remains to be done' (Burgess, 2001: 250). The low level of democratic legitimization and the distance between citizens and decision-making has been one of the major issues in theoretical investigations and in political praxis, especially in 2001 when the debate on the future of Europe was carried out (Marhold 2002).

Due to historical, political and economic reasons, the Greek state adopted a centralized structure and a centralistic ideology, which for long has been reinforcing national consolidation while hindering modernization. Greece had never been a federalist state or a democratic one fully respecting civil and human rights at least until 1974. It has only recently started to build a free market economy and to strengthen civil society. Although federalism has not been the preferred option for its domestic political organization, Greece strongly supports a federalist future for Europe, as the debate about the Convention shows. The question concerning how viable it will be to maintain an almost centralized national structure within a European federation in the name of the federalist principle of preserving national identity remains to be answered in the years to come by all member states. In case federalism is taken to mean preserving cultures and identities along with political structures and statist political cultures, problems will arise regarding participation in Europe. The situation will be further aggravated if the EU evolves into a superstate based to a large extent on the French constitutional and political tradition rather than the German federalist model. This development is of great significance for Greece and, indeed, all other European states, regardless of their size.

In other words, the case of European unification can be considered as a test of whether a federation should not only be a democracy of democracies but also, and equally importantly, a federation of federations. The discussion carried out in Greece during 2002–03 in view of the adoption of a European constitution, as well as the public debate during the same year about national issues of high public visibility, shows that the course Greece takes towards a more strengthened political union of Europe will continue to be a major challenge in terms of further modernization and a possible response for unresolved structural problems such as agricultural subsidies, Greek–Turkish relations and the Cyprus issue, the fragile economic stabilization and immigration.

As far as the country's European role is concerned, Greece was in the presidency seat when the initial results of the Convention were presented. In light of this:

> Several European affairs experts said that Greece is not really in a position to be bold in that document. But they said that the European impression of Greece's performance as president could have an impact on efforts, reflected in the convention's work, to adjust the balance between the larger members and its smaller ones, like Greece, which has a population of about 11 million – less than one-seventh that of Germany' (F. Bruni, 'Greece Enters Europe's Spotlight Under Skeptical Eyes', *New York Times*, 11 January 2003).

Furthermore, as former president Delors put it:'It is with confidence and hope that I see the Presidency passing to the country which invented democracy, and which has in recent times seen public support for membership of the EU at record levels and the highest of all fifteen member states' (Pagoulatos 2002). Indeed Greeks are the most impatient Europeans, displaying one of the highest degrees of agreement that the speed of Europe towards political union should be accelerated (Eurobarometer No.56). It should be noted at this point that Greece approached the Convention with increased self-confidence. This is due to the experience of having the EU presidency, the country's membership in the Eurozone and the stabilization role played by Greece in south-eastern Europe.

Certainly, the influence of Greece over the future of Europe cannot be equated with the influence of Europe over the future of Greece. Nevertheless, it becomes a major challenge for both the member states and the EU to each preserve its own significance in a way that guarantees autonomy and participation on the one hand, and democratic accountability and efficiency for all levels of government on the other.

NOTES

1. EKEM was founded in 1988 as an independent research centre, under the institutional supervision of the MFA – to which it is directly linked. Its main objective is the study and research of issues concerning European unification and the European area in general, issues related to the participation of Greece in the European Union as well as general issues that affect Greek foreign policy.
2. From its first appearance in April 2002 to April 2003 there have been 14 issues (approximately one per month). This newsletter is available at www.ekem.gr. In 2002, the website averaged 500 visits per month, 60 per cent of which were from Greece and 40 per cent from other countries.
3. Kostas Simitis, speech delivered in Bruges on 4 February 2002, EKEM.
4. Kostas Simitis, speech delivered in Athens on 13 July 2001 and 1 August 2001, Agence Europe 'It is almost certain that present-day policy reality, even though some institutional solutions were given at Nice, will further strengthen centrifugal forces in a Union of 27 or more Member States ... We must move forward. This is the only option', stated Premier Simitis, noting that at Nice 'we did not speak about how to respond to the need for a new political driving force, a new locomotive, which, in tomorrow's enlarged Union, will be needed more than ever'.
5. EKEM, Newsletter No1, April 2002, on the European Convention and the Future of Europe.
6. The Committee was established in 1990 and today it comprises 31 members, among whom 12 are Greek MEPs – headed by a vice-president of the EP. In this committee, MEPs have the same voting rights as their national counterparts.
7. EKEM, Newsletter No.5, July 2002, on the European Convention and the Future of Europe.
8. The event was organized by the 'Institute for Democracy K Karamanlis', a think tank directly linked to the party. Another meeting was organized on 19 February 2003 by ND in order to discuss the future of Europe.
9. EKEM, Newsletter No.5, July 2002, on the European Convention and the Future of Europe.
10. On 22 April 2002 EKEM organized a conference entitled 'European Constitution: Role, Significance, Content' at Zapion Megaron (the proceedings have been published).
11. 'European Convention', a round table organized by the Greek Centre of European Studies and Research (EKEME) within the framework of the conference 'The 4th Greek Presidency in the EU: The Building of a New Europe: Strong foundations – new concepts', 14.–15 November 2002.
12. The speakers were Th Pangalos, former minister of foreign affairs, P.Avgerinos, member of the Convention, and the MEPs M. Papayanakis and R. Kratsas.
13. 'Quelle est l'image des Européens pour eux mêmes, Regarder le miroir par les recherches de l'opinion publique' [What do Europeans Think of Themselves Looking at the Mirror of Public Opinion Research], European Texts, European Communities, 2001.
14. Eurostat survey, published on March 2003, as quoted in Greek daily newspapers on 27 March 2003.
15. It should also be noted that they did not communicate any of the views of the Greek NGOs regarding the Convention.
16. EKEM, Newsletter No.5, July 2002, on the European Convention and the future of Europe.

17. Eurostat survey, published on March 2003, as quoted in Greek daily newspapers on 27 March 2003.
18. Survey undertaken between 29 March and 28 April 2002 in a sample of 1,002 interviewees (statistical error margin: ± three per cent).
19. A Metron Analysis Survey published in daily newspaper *Kathimerini*, 9 April 2003.
20. 'What do Europeans Think of Themselves Looking at the Mirror of Public Opinion Research', European Commission, Luxembourg 2001. Beyond this survey and the Eurobarometers, there have either been no other public opinion surveys about Greece on the Convention and the European Constitution or they have not been publicized.
21. Prime Minister Simitis, speech delivered at the Greek Parliament, 27 March 2003.
22. Statements of K. Karamanlis following his meeting with J. Chirac, French president, on 28 March 2003.
23. It was only on 2 October 2002 that the EU adopted the 'Communication from the Commission to the Council, the European Parliament, the Economic and Social Committee and the Committee of the Regions on an information and Communication Strategy for the European Union/*COM/2002/0350 final/2 */'.

REFERENCES

Bird, R., B. Dafflon, C. Jeanrenaud, G. Kirchgassner and others (2002): 'Assignment of Responsibilities and Fiscal Federalism', *Federalism in a Changing World – Learning from Each Other*, British Council, Druck: Drucckerei Herzog AG, Langendorf, Herausgeber, pp.407–575.

Burgess, M. (2001): *Federalism and European Union: The Building of Europe, 1950–2000*, London and New York: Routledge.

Chopin, Th. (2003): *La République Unie et Indivisible – Les fondements de la Fédération Américaine, Fondation Robert Schuman*, Plon: Collection Commentaire, www.robertschuman.org.

Ioakeimidis, P. (2003): 'Είναι η Ευρώπη υπερδύναμη' [Is Europe a Superpower?], *Oikonomikos Tachydromos* 10/13 March, pp.26–7.

Marhold, H. (ed.) (2002): '*Le nouveau débat sur l' Europe* [The New Debate on Europe], *H.Marhold*', Presse c'Europe, Nice, Cife.

McGarry, J. (2002): 'Federal Political Systems and the Accommodation of National Minorities', *Handbook of Federal Countries 2002*', Forum of Federations, : McGill-Queen's University Press, pp.416–48.

Pagoulatos, G. (2002): 'Greece, the European Union and the 2003 Presidency', *Notre Europe – Groupement d'Etudes et de Recherche* [Our Europe – Study and Research Group] (President: Jacques Delors), Research and European Issues No.21

Sutter, J. (2002): 'Sovereignty, Self-Government and Global Government', *The Federalist* 44/1, pp.45–53.

The Debate on the Future of Europe in Malta: Moving to Centre Stage

PETER G. XUEREB

INTRODUCTION

It was a cause for some concern in Malta that by December of 2002 the debate on the future of Europe had occupied only a peripheral or subliminal place in public discourse. Indeed, the debating space in Malta was almost entirely taken over by the politically charged issue of Maltese membership of the European Union (EU), and this more in terms of whether Malta should join the European Economic Community (EEC)[1] on the basis of economic considerations ('Debating Europe: What Debate?' *The Sunday Times*, 15 December 2002). In other words, political debate in the run-up to the referendum vote on 8 March 2003 was almost entirely about economic gains and benefits (or the opposite), with some notable exceptions – such as the issue of Malta's neutrality and whether membership of the future EU would be compatible with such neutral status. The Common Foreign and Security Policy (CFSP)/neutrality issue was raised by the 'No to Membership' camp, led by the Labour Party, which argued that the Union of the future would likely be a military alliance requiring member states' participation in military actions under the evolving defence and security policy of the Union and that membership went counter, for that reason, to the neutrality clause in the Maltese constitution.

This prolonged 'peripherality' of the debate on the future of Europe may not be surprising, given that the issue of whether Malta should take up membership at all was hotly debated even after the referendum, which resulted in the casting of 53.6 per cent of all valid votes in favour of membership. We immediately saw the Labour Party, having called on its supporters to do one of three things at the referendum (that is, to vote 'No', to abstain or to spoil their vote), claiming victory for their 'partnership option' on the grounds that a majority of the registered voters had not voted in favour of membership. In light of this, the prime minister immediately called a general election for 12 April 2003 in order to dispel the uncertainty in the country and hoping, on being returned to government, to proceed to the signing of the Accession Treaty in Athens on 16 April. The general election did indeed see the return to government of the Nationalist Party – effectively an endorsement by the Maltese electorate of membership of the EU. Malta was therefore a signatory of the Accession Treaty in Athens on 16 April. At the time of writing (June 2003), the debate in the Maltese parliament on the ratification bill has just been concluded, with the opposition voting 'No' but, in essence, only symbolically, out of an apparent sense of obligation to act loyally to those who had supported it in its pre-election stance. It has been said in the media, then, that the whole of Malta is looking forward to joining the Union on 1 May 2004 and, together, making the most of EU membership (*The Times*, 26 June 2003).

The focus of all political debate up to March 2003 tended to be on the 'membership package' negotiated by the Maltese government, and principally the economic and financial impact of membership and the 'loss', or otherwise, of 'sovereignty'. Nevertheless, the Labour Party made much of Commission president Prodi's speech in December, where he made mention of the concept of a 'ring of friends' and of the reference in the draft constitutional treaty to 'partnership' with proximate non-members, in order to proclaim that their preferred alternative to membership, which they styled as 'partnership', was indeed 'possible' (in the sense of feasible) as well as desirable. Other news items that featured in Maltese political discourse were the Franco-German stance on Iraq and the rather denigratory French comments elicited by certain of their future partners' stances on the crisis.

The relative voting 'strength' in the Council and the European Parliament (EP), as allotted to Malta at Nice, was another point that the Labour Party sought to exploit against the background of proposals to further extend the use of qualified majority voting (QMV) in the next treaty revision. Consequently, much of the media time and space right up to the referendum was taken up with the (mainly economic) merits (or otherwise) of the 'package' negotiated with the EU by the Maltese government, plus some select Convention issues. Attempts to broaden the political debate, including attempts by the government in parliament, were largely unsuccessful. Thus, when the time came for parliament to debate a motion on EU membership and on the question to be posed via the projected referendum, the focus was again on the negotiated package. Only peripherally, once more, did the future shape of the EU enter into the debate.

It may also in part be that this emphasis on the *status quo* was due to the general understanding that should the domestic hurdles of referendum and election go the government's way, then Malta, together with the current members and the other new members, would be playing a full part in revising the treaties and shaping the EU of tomorrow in the intergovernmental conference (IGC) convened in Rome in October 2003. In other words, the understanding was that change to the EU going beyond the Nice Treaty would be for all 25 member states (if things went according to plan) to agree. At that point, the future of the EU would cease to be academic.

Arguably, before the election of April 2003 one could guess that with the Nationalist Party having been returned to power, with a mandate to take Malta into the EU, and the Labour Party playing its oppositional role, the future of Europe debate would erupt onto the political scene and become – by the time of the presentation of the draft constitutional treaty – the subject of political debate like nowhere else in the Union. As it transpired, the Nationalist Party was returned to power, and the Labour Party, after a short period of reflection and restructuring, declared that it will now operate in this new reality. A large degree of convergence is now reported as having emerged between the two parties on the main issues raised by the draft Constitution from a Maltese perspective ('Nationalists and Labour Converge on European Constitution', *The Malta Independent on Sunday*, 15 June 2003, cover story; 'EU debate sees accent on unity from both sides', *The Times*, 26 June 2003, cover story).

THE DEBATE ON THE FUTURE OF EUROPE IN MALTA PRIOR TO APRIL 2003

Although the debate did not erupt onto the political scene, this is not to say that a number of public events had not been organized by the time of the referendum to heighten awareness of the Convention in progress. Nor is it the case that the country's one university, the University of Malta, had not sought to raise awareness of the issues involved.[2] Furthermore, the European Commission delegation supported a number of initiatives, by, for example, supplying speakers on the matter. However, the public debate was never wide-ranging and the future of Europe debate was overshadowed by the immediate issues as defined and described above. The government relied very heavily, as far as the dissemination of information on EU affairs in general and specifically on Malta's membership of the EU was concerned, on the Malta–EU Information Centre (MIC), set up by government with the brief of giving objective information to the public. This applies also to the debate on the future of Europe.

The MIC had indeed organized a few public sessions, and had notably produced a booklet entitled *The Future of Europe: The Debate in Malta* in 2002. This booklet, however, is to some degree in the bipolar tradition of debate. Many of the authors of the essays published therein are protagonists in the pro- or anti-membership debate, hence their contributions tend to take a slant on this score in the sense that they are more or less written in this context. Having said that, also included were essays on the future of the EU by Pierre Muscovici, Nicole Fontaine and Herve Bribosia, and generally attempts were made to give a Europe-wide picture of the future of Europe debate. It also has to be said that the Labour Party had accused the MIC of partiality (in favour of Malta's membership, as opposed to the 'partnership' option preferred by the Labour Party), at least in terms of an alleged lack of coverage regarding the Labour Party's option. The MIC replied to this accusation by stating that the 'partnership' option was not within its brief, as well as that in any case this 'option' remained hypothetical and unclear. Before the general election, the Labour Party had declared that, should it be returned to power, it would negotiate a 'partnership agreement' and then hold a referendum that posed the question: 'Partnership or Membership?'

At the University, besides the conference organized by the EDRC – which was attended by over 250 participants, a programme of seminars also covered aspects of the debate.[3] However, the wider general public requires other information besides the rather academic and technical essays so produced. Furthermore, neither do student-organized events tend to reach the general public. Nevertheless, the student body is sizeable, with some 7,000 students at the University. The Student Representative Council and other student bodies have been active in organizing events on the future of Europe, and some of these have been very well attended.[4] Even so, there is no denying that the student body tended in the first quarter of 2003, like everyone else, to focus on the points raised in the referendum debate by the political parties (highlighted above), rather than carry out a broad, pro-active debate on the range of issues to do with the agenda of the Convention. The apparent reason for this, as always, was that Malta's membership, which the student body supported, was far from a foregone conclusion.

It is clear that the party political agenda and associated arguments tended to dominate and dictate much of the academic and general public debate, as well as the level of the debate. The government did make reasonably frequent (in the circumstances) reference to the future of Europe and the benefits of enlargement as well as the virtues and values of the Union in an era of globalization, but more rarely to the Convention's agenda as such. For their part, the Nationalist parliamentary representative, Dr. Michael Frendo, and the government nominee, Professor Serracino-Inglott, made several interventions in the Convention and sought to contribute actively to the debate – their speeches being reported in the Maltese press. Dr. Frendo published the texts of his interventions in a book entitled *The Future is Europe* shortly before the March 2003 referendum and attempted therein to locate the 'membership debate' in the context of the future of Europe debate. The leader of the opposition party, Dr. Alfred Sant, also attended the Convention, but took the position that as the Labour Party opposed Malta's membership of the EU he felt it would be out of place to participate actively in proposals for EU reform. This bipolar stance, with an 'abstentionist' approach adopted by one of the two main political figures to the future of Europe debate in its primary forum, the Convention, was hardly conducive to creating a thoroughgoing or non-partisan debate about the future of Europe in Malta.

Other bodies, such as the trade unions, tended in their public pronouncements to follow the same contoured lines of debate as set by the political parties, meaning that they would press home the points being made by one side or the other according to the views of their constituencies and thereby made very little attempt to contribute any new angle or dimension such as might relate to the future shape of the Union. The same in general applies to industrial and commercial associations such as the Chamber of Commerce and the Federation of Industry. The Catholic Church, to which most Maltese would turn for moral guidance, welcomed what it saw as important arrangements struck with the EU side in the negotiations (such as relates to a protocol on abortion). It was, though reticent to voice support – in line with papal pronouncements and those of the bishops of some other candidate countries – for the process of European integration and, more specifically, for enlargement, let alone specifically for the country's membership of the Union (such as the Church did in the Czech Republic, Poland and Lithuania). Taking care not to take a position in the membership debate, the bishops exhorted all Maltese to preserve the values which are dear to them, and to inform themselves fully about the issues related to membership and (less clearly) about the Convention debates in order that responsible choices be made when it came to the exercise of one's vote in the 'membership' referendum.

The above is not to say, then, that there had not been – by the time of the referendum or subsequent general election – any debate at all about the future of Europe along the lines of discussion taking place in the Convention. Rather, it is to say that such debate was peripheral, almost accidental, selective, linked to and overshadowed by the more immediate (as perceived) issue of deciding on membership (or otherwise), with the election date as the relevant point of decision and current membership terms, largely, as the focus. Pragmatic politics was in full swing throughout the first quarter of 2003, with most politicians apparently seeing the EU 'post-2004' as something too remote, fuzzy and hypothetical to contemplate (or at least certainly too hypothetical to make prognostications about), even if positions had begun to emerge at the Convention on a number of issues that could be, and should have been, relevant in a membership debate. It is probably fair to say that, apart from the prime minister himself – who might be said for pragmatic as well as visionary reasons to have had cause to emphasize the idealistic and visionary aspects of the enlarged Union, the *Alternattiva Demokratika* Party, the third – but relatively minor – political grouping, was somewhat more visibly prepared to highlight the possible positive impact of the Convention and to discuss it directly. This particular party, however, has no seats in parliament. Thus, a full focus on the range of issues, such as the possible permutations in the Union's institutional structure, was still lacking up until shortly before the time of writing.

Some issues, such as the involvement of the national parliaments in decision-making at European level, were sporadically referred to in the press, especially as reports of Convention working group conclusions came through, but were for the most part quickly submerged again in the wake of the 'bread and butter' issues of membership: net beneficiary status, agricultural support, job competition, removal of levies, and so on. 'Economism', in the sense used by Siedentop (2000), seemed pre-eminent, as in most (if not all) candidate countries, while issues of citizenship and democracy and the place of the EU and European values in the world were in general given a 'Maltese' or Malta-centric twist. On this latter point, the government side claimed that the EU is a bulwark of democracy and a model of solidarity among equal member states in order to counter Labour claims that Malta would have no 'voice', that it would have to apply in all their rigour all the rules of the Union (whose rules were designed for large states and not small ones such as Malta is) and that majority voting would mean that little or no attention would be paid to Maltese interests or needs. On this basis, the Labour Party claimed that 'partnership' (meaning an agreement with the EU tailored to suit Malta's own particular characteristics and needs) would be a better option.

Therefore, politicization and polarization within an inward-looking and short-term perspective were key in the first quarter of 2003, and were manifested in a willingness to engage fully only with the *status quo*. One measure of this is, as I think it is fair to say, that even the Maltese branch of the European Movement had its agenda hijacked to a significant degree by the contours of the membership debate as narrowly drawn by the party political debate. Calls by academics, and some others, for the focus to shift outwards and to the medium- long-term future had not by the time of the referendum on 8 March 2003 had any dramatic impact on the vast majority of politicians, many of whom looked to the future selectively – at least in public. Thus, 'short-termism' might be the best phrase to describe the approach of the first quarter. It has since (that is, after the election) become evident that within the political parties much debate was going on. It surely was also the case that future-gazing was occurring within government circles. However, as far as the general public could see, all resources (or most of them) were at the time of the referendum and in the lead-up to the general election taken up with a 'short-term' debate, conducted most often in *status quo* (that is, predominantly 'the EU as is') terms. This debate possessed an added twist in that the Labour Party sought, but not always successfully, to entirely shift the focus during its general election campaign to so-called 'domestic issues'. Labour, then, downplayed the 'EU issue', which they sought to present as a separate 'foreign policy issue', and sought to relegate the latter to the hypothetical future in the context of a promised future (second) referendum – if, that is, they were returned to government.

Even so, as indicated above, not all key issues in the future of Europe debate were ignored, even in this climate. For example, assurances – as given to Ireland – that neutrality can be maintained even after 2004 featured in the referendum debate. The Maltese government secured, in the membership negotiations, the inclusion in the Accession Treaty of a declaration to similar effect; several of such issues remain salient. Neutrality featured as a key issue in the post-Thessaloniki parliamentary debate on the Accession Treaty ratification bill. The emphasis made in the Convention on the principle of subsidiarity and on the value of solidarity, as underlying the future (as the present) Union, was also the foundation of key arguments made by the government – whose campaigns were spearheaded by Prime Minister Fenech Adami himself in the referendum and general election campaigns.

In the same context one could also mention respect for national identity, values and culture, which emerges as a fundamental Union principle to be preserved into the future. Such 'positive messages' emanating from the Convention were not lost on the government, which pressed them in the referendum debate. However, we have seen that the Labour Party's election campaign strategy was to downplay the 'EU membership issue' and focus on attacking the government's record on the environment, education, inward investment, infrastructure and other so-called 'domestic' issues. The Nationalist Party, on the other hand, focused on reminding the people that their 'yes to membership' vote in the referendum would come to naught if they did not re-elect a Nationalist government and on pointing out the benefits already visible from the raft of laws and measures already adopted in the pre-accession phase as a direct result of the preparation for membership.

Since the election, which returned a Nationalist government, and the signing of the Accession Treaty, the Labour Party has gone through a period of reflection. This period saw something of a redrawing of the party hierarchy. Dr. Alfred Sant remains leader, but the two deputy leaders have been replaced, and one of the politicians who had been tipped as a possible new leader is now opposition spokesman on the EU. The debate which took place at the end of June 2003 on the Accession Treaty ratification bill – the law that is necessary to give effect to the Accession Treaty (and therefore the *acquis*) in Malta – was interesting as the Labour members of parliament felt unable to vote in favour of it. The final speeches from the Labour benches underscored the line that the EU membership question is now settled, and that the Maltese should not expend any further energy on issues of the past but work together to face the challenges of membership with success.

In the course of that debate, with much reference to certain perennial constitutional questions such as neutrality, the focus can be said to have been 'actualized': at last, the politicians can debate the impact of membership in the context of the constitutional treaty, which was presented to the Thessaloniki summit just a few days before the parliamentary debate on the Accession Treaty ratification bill began. Consensus has arguably emerged in the course of the debate on some salient issues: the determination to safeguard Malta's neutrality, to exercise the fullest national parliamentary scrutiny of proposed EU legislation, to seek the greatest representation and voice in the institutions – and, in particular, in the EP, and to fully involve the whole of civil society in policy-making – with all that this entails in the membership context.

CONCLUSION

In the light of the above discussions, one could conclude by contemplating that there is only so much with which a nation cast in the role of an electorate can be asked to cope at any particular moment in time. From that perspective one might say that the timing of the Convention was rather unfortunate! Visitors to Malta have always been impressed by the vigour of political debate and public participation in it, and by the volume and range of information and media coverage on the EU, although it often takes discernment and pinches of salt for the formation of a rounded opinion.

Objective, unbiased and researched material is not as readily available in a country with one University as in a country with many more. One result of this is that very important analyses and studies kept filtering through until the very last moment before the referendum vote. The level of journalism is high but not as high as it might be, with journalists ready to report but rarely ready or able to probe effectively, and there are few independent newspapers. Much unmitigated drivel, produced by individuals with a dubious grasp of the issues and little or no qualification or experience, is published by otherwise reputable newspapers for fear of accusations of bias. Even worse, as the editor of one of the daily newspapers, *The Malta Independent*, recently remarked, the Maltese media had made themselves conspicuous by their absence from the Convention (he was one of the few to have attended at all). This must explain a great deal.

Yet, the political climate in Malta has changed since the election. EU membership is by all accounts accepted by all as a new fact of life. Still, given our tradition of two-party partisan politics, it is inevitable (as well as desirable) that the future of Europe and the EU in the round – and therefore the constitutional treaty and all its implications, including whether or not a referendum on it should be held – will be vigorously debated in Malta. What is historically and sadly true, is that the future of the EU did sometimes feature in the membership debate in the run-up to the April general election with a view not to achieving national consensus on the preferred nature of the future EU (both in the abstract and the Maltese perspective) nor with the all-important aim and effect of contributing 'as a nation' to that debate, but rather as ammunition in the pro- or anti-membership debate. While EU membership itself remained the central election issue for the Nationalist Party, it was declared a non-issue by the Labour Party, which argued that the election was 'about' the government's track record in addressing 'real' issues such as the public deficit and the cost of living. This general strategy/approach on the part of the Labour Party, treating membership of the EU – and therefore the EU itself – as though it simply was not on any 'domestic' agenda, may have been a pity (to use an understatement uncommon to the Maltese) in itself, for candidate country status did give Malta a place at the Convention. Moreover, whether Malta decided to join the EU or not, it had (as it has and always will have) a great stake in the 'shape' of the Union. Even so, no great harm appears to have been done as a result.

That, as they say, is now history. The Maltese (led by the politicians on all sides) appear set to turn now to the present and very different reality as Malta is now set to join the Union at the next enlargement in May 2004. In this respect, the membership issue is being treated as settled, and the consensus is that the best must be made of membership. There has been no suggestion, in the course of the post-Thessaloniki debate on the Accession Treaty ratification bill in the Maltese parliament, of anything other than a determination to make membership work in the long term. Political and public debate in Malta in the context of the IGC and beyond is set to be at least as vigorous as elsewhere in Europe. This will be to the benefit of Malta, the EU and the Mediterranean region.

NOTES

1. The reference to the EEC is deliberate.
2. For example, the annual European Documentation and Research Centre (EDRC) Conference organized in conjunction with the Jean Monnet Chair and the Malta European Studies Association in April 2002 on the theme 'The Future of the European Union: Unity in Diversity', proceedings published under that title (Xuereb, 2002)
3. Further information is available at the EDRC website: www home.um.edu.mt/edrc.
4. Notably, the UNIDEBATE organized by AEGEE VALLETTA on the theme 'Where are the Borders of Europe?' held on 16 November 2002. Also, a series of debates in the series 'Generation Europe: Debating Europe's Future Together', organized by the Student Representative Council.

REFERENCES

Frendo, M. (2003): *The Future is Europe*, (published by the author).
Malta–EU Information Centre (MIC; www.mic.org.mt) (2002): *The Future of Europe: The Debate in Malta*, available from euinfo.mic@magnet.mt
Siedentop, L. (2000): *Democracy in Europe*, London: Allen Lane: The Penguin Press.
Xuereb, P.G. (ed.) (2002): '*The Future of the European Union: Unity in Diversity*', Malta: Publishers Enterprises Group.

English-language electronic newspapers

The Times of Malta/The Sunday Times; www.timesofmalta.com
The Malta Independent/The Independent on Sunday; www.independent.com.mt
The Malta Business Weekly; www.maltabusinessweekly.com
Maltatoday; www.maltatoday.com.mt
The Malta Financial and Business Times; www.businesstimes.com.mt
Maltastar; www.maltastar.com

Old and New Patterns of Domestic Politics in the European Perspective: The Debate in the Republic of Cyprus

KALLIOPE AGAPIOU-JOSEPHIDES

INTRODUCTION

The ongoing debate on the future of Europe with respect to constitution-building and the process of treaty reform in the European Union (EU) has attracted significant international attention and sparked substantial research among EU specialists, mainly in the context of the Nice and post-Nice agenda (Piris 2000; Weiler 2000; Schmitter 2001; Hoffman 2002; Philippart 2002; Reh and Wessels 2002; Smith 2002; Shaw 2003). Nevertheless, the implications of the Convention on the future of Europe for 'domestic politics' have not attracted similar scholarly interest.

European integration is a complex phenomenon and indeed a unique experience in human history for several reasons: the number of countries and peoples involved,[1] the scope and breadth of cooperation considered, and the methods used and visions shared. Research into the future of European integration, either from a theoretical or empirical perspective, has its own merits, which stem both from methodological concerns and the determination of this social and political experiment's defining properties. The aim of this essay is to provide a clear and enhanced understanding of those key socio-political features that characterize the symbiotic relationship between the European polity and the polity of an accession country – the Republic of Cyprus. Debates taking place within domestic institutions regarding the future of European integration constitute an interesting and as yet unexplored unit of analysis for understanding the missing links between European citizens and European institutions.

According to a survey conducted immediately after the Thessaloniki European Council in June 2003 and focused on the results

The author is grateful to Danae Agathocleous (MA, College of Europe) for her research assistance and to Christopher L. Griffin (graduate student at Brasenose College, Oxford) for his assistance in matters of language and style.

of the Convention, people's awareness of the latter remains very hazy: 45 per cent of people in the enlarged EU have at least heard of the Convention, 55 per cent said they had never heard of the Convention, and 52 per cent were unaware of what kind of text the Convention had come up with. Among genders, we can note that far more men than women have heard of the Convention on the future of Europe, both in the EU member states (men 52 per cent; women 38 per cent) and, to a lesser extent, in the adherent countries (men 47 per cent; women 40 per cent). Among the adherent countries, Cyprus has the highest rate of respondents having heard of the Convention (54 per cent).[2] The case of Cyprus underscores the fact that, until now, no European debate with such a broad agenda has been given so much attention at the national level nor involved as many national stakeholders and grass-roots organizations.

The Convention, as a method and as a means of bolstering the legitimacy of the European political system, is unprecedented in the history of European integration (Deloche-Gaudez 2001; Hoffman 2002; and Shaw 2003). More specifically, it facilitates progress in three crucial areas: citizens' involvement, clear interpretation of the EU's founding documents and the relevance of their provisions. With regard to enlargement, one of the main breakthroughs of the Convention method is the participation of accession candidate countries on a nearly equal basis with current EU member states. The Laeken Declaration on the Future of the European Union states that: 'The accession candidate countries will be fully involved in the Convention's [sic] proceedings. They will be represented in the same way as the current member states (one government representative and two national parliament members) and will be able to take part in the proceedings without, however, being able to prevent any consensus which may emerge among the Member States'. This particular feature of the Convention has increased significantly the legitimacy of the whole process, both among the Cypriot members of the Convention and public opinion in Cyprus.

Although the Convention is only the second established by the EU, it is the first to deal directly with constitutional issues and the first to call for a large-scale public debate in all participating countries. In that same spirit of local involvement, on 28 February 2002 (the same day of the Convention's inaugural session) the House of Representatives of the Republic of Cyprus celebrated its launch by convening an official meeting at a plenary session, which was attended by a diverse set of representatives from governmental and non-governmental organizations (NGOs). As a result, the Cypriot parliament successfully introduced an innovative, interactive feature into its consultations on key European issues and, more importantly, into its rapport with civil society. The event was well covered by the mass media,

154 MOBILIZING POLITICS AND SOCIETY?

thereby facilitating a swift, direct flow of information to the general public. To be sure, Cyprus has participated in this debate with particular interest due to its search for a new constitutional framework following United Nations' (UN) efforts to resolve 'the Cyprus problem'.[3]

An empirical analysis of the ways in which South European countries are participating in the EU Convention on the future of Europe will hopefully shed more detailed light on the interaction between domestic politics and international institutions. Within that analytical framework, this essay examines the case of Cyprus and attempts to highlight the gradual yet profound developments in constitutional discourse in southern Europe. It is no easy task for a small accession country with limited human resources to follow complex negotiations on the EU constitution-building process. Will the Convention method, through its open and transparent work, pave the way for a new, legitimized constitutional process for the enlarged EU of 25 member states? How can a small accession country, like Cyprus, make a significant contribution to these complex processes?

CONCEPTUAL AND ANALYTICAL FRAMEWORK

Deliberations at previous intergovernmental conferences (IGCs) have been interpreted primarily from two theoretical perspectives: the rational choice-based *liberal intergovernmentalism* and the more idealistic *neo-functionalism*. In his work on EU treaty reform, Smith (2002) outlines a third approach, that of *incrementalism*, which is characterized by the following four elements: ambiguity among member governments regarding their negotiating objectives, a period of indirection in the negotiation process, unintended outcomes and a propensity to postpone discussion of sensitive issues until a future constitutional IGC or post-negotiation period.

Although the IGC model has proved to be a remarkably successful method for deepening the integration process, it seems to have been less effective in tackling the current wave of intricate constitutional and institutional issues facing an enlarged EU. It has been unable to ensure that debate and negotiations over these issues is both transparent and fully participatory. Cyprus favours the Convention method and a more federal governance structure in the enlarged EU.

The decision to organize the Convention on the future of Europe, which sets the stage for the IGC 2004, implicitly reflects the inadequacy of IGCs as vehicles for treaty reform – mainly on the grounds of efficiency and legitimacy. They have been criticized as ill-suited to the conduct of negotiations over constitutional texts. In terms of efficiency, subtle political compromises reached overnight are quite difficult to translate into the legal language of treaties. As a result, legal and political clarity are sacrificed. Recent major shifts in international relations and the currently high degree of integration are further evidence of the incompatibility of IGCs with the needs of individual actors. The legitimacy of the process has also been challenged on a number of grounds, the most prominent of which is the paradoxical establishment of a *sui generis* organization on a purely conventional basis. Evidently, then, the EU is much more than a conventional international organization. The European Court of Justice (ECJ) has explicitly recognized constitutional value in the EU treaties primarily because their scope extends beyond those of conventional international treaties and contains important constitutional elements.[4] Since the EU is mainly a collective management system of separate, national sovereignties, it is obvious that a solution to the legitimacy question will not be an easy one – neither for member states nor for accession countries.

The composition of the Convention is in many respects radical and innovative. It includes representatives of heads of state or national governments, members of national parliaments (MPs), Members of the European Parliament (MEPs) and a limited number of European Commission representatives. This new format, although modelled on the previous one (which produced the Charter of Fundamental Rights of the European Union), does exhibit some notably different features.

First, its composition is significantly more political (though less so in the case of Cyprus): both the representative of the head of state and his or her alternate are high-ranking diplomats. The Convention, moreover, represents one of the first instances in which the enlarged EU will attempt to achieve consensus in such a heterogeneous setting. For applicant countries, this represents their first and most challenging collective exercise. The potential benefits of 'learning-by-doing' for government officials, civil servants, business and trade union representatives, and ordinary citizens participating in the process should not be underestimated. Hence, their *political socialization* within the EU system is a fundamental first step towards full participation.

According to Crum (2002), the success of the Convention depends on its ability both to produce innovative proposals that resolve the current deadlock on EU reform and to attract broad public support for the Convention's final document, as well as obtain political legitimacy for the project in order to prevent the IGC from ignoring the conclusions or recommendations proposed by the Convention.

Second, the scope of the new Convention is not limited to a single topic (fundamental rights in the previous version) but instead covers a wide array of constitutional issues. Thus, the involvement of citizens from all participating countries becomes a more crucial factor, elevates the importance of the dialectical relationship between European and national citizenship and points to ways in which the EU polity can overcome the dual challenge of promoting unity and diversity. As Nick Bernard notes, 'Union citizenship must be not just accepting of, but rooted in the diversity of the EU polity and there should not be distinct, hermetically sealed, spheres for the expression of national and Union citizenship but a more symbiotic relationship between the two' (Bernard 2002: 207).

Creating 'an ever closer union' among European peoples within an intergovernmental structure and building a *sui generis* institution on the foundations of international treaties is indeed an unprecedented phenomenon. Moreover, it is evident that the relatively short history of community-building in Europe has been highly idiosyncratic. After more than fifty years of successful integration and in the absence of major external threats, citizens' demands for greater transparency in democratic processes have risen to the forefront. The Single European Act and the three IGCs (held in Maastricht, Amsterdam and Nice), coupled with plans for enlargement and concomitant increases in diversity and heterogeneity, have revealed the true extent of the EU's democratic deficit.

The Convention framework analysed in this section reflects a decidedly new perspective in European politics: it is shifting the locus of debate not entirely away from the IGC method, but certainly towards a more constitutional path. As stated above, the most compelling evidence of this is the nearly balanced participation of member states and candidate countries. As a result, the governments of 28 countries are now involved in the dialogue and attempting to elicit the support and participation of ordinary citizens. Having explored the conceptual framework surrounding the Convention, we now turn to a case study of Cyprus's involvement in that process and its implications for domestic politics.

DOMESTIC POLITICS: OLD AND NEW PATTERNS

The EU: A Driving Force for Domestic Change

There is common agreement that European integration has called into question many features associated with traditional politics in member states. Europeanization is an incremental process reorienting the direction and the shape of politics to the degree that EU political and economic dynamics become part of the organizational logic of national politics and policy-making (Ladrech 1994), although there is a growing literature on the impact (or non-impact) of 'Europeanization' upon domestic political management in EU member states (see Pagoulatos 2002).

The large-scale *adaptation pressure* on domestic polity and politics allows for distinction among three levels of influence (low, moderate and high), according to the area and intensity of the EU *acquis* in question (Knill 2001: 41). In short, the domestic ramifications of European politics and policies depend upon the institutional compatibility of European policy requirements and relevant national cultures.

Over the last ten years, the EU has undoubtedly proved to be the single most important driving force for Cyprus's socio-political, economic and institutional modernization: hundreds of new laws were adopted, numerous new institutions were set-up and a great number of structures in the public and private field were adapted to the country's accession perspective.

There is strong support among Cypriot policy elites and the public for the view that the EU has served, not only as a catalyst for change and modernization, but also as a motivating and unifying force towards a more peaceful coexistence among the different communities inhabiting the island, alongside the UN secretary general's efforts to devise a solution to the Cyprus question between 1999 and early 2003. The fact that Cyprus's accession has been massively supported both by Greek-Cypriots and Turkish-Cypriots has also opened new perspectives for peace in the country, which has been divided since 1974. In a Eurobarometer survey in 2003, 72 per cent of people in Cyprus indicated that they think membership in the EU is 'a good thing' and 84 per cent would vote in favour of the country's accession to the EU, if a referendum were to be held (Eurobarometer 2003.2 'Public Opinion in Candidate Countries': 69–72). According to a 2002 Eurobarometer ('First Results – Northern Cyprus'), 88 per cent of adults and teenagers think that membership would be 'a good thing' and 88 per cent of the voting-age population would definitely vote for EU membership.

The influence of European norms in the country can also be identified in the easing of restrictions against movement across the Greek–Turkish dividing line in April 2003 – just one week after the Accession Treaty was signed. As Günter Verheugen, the European commissioner for enlargement, stated, this experience has clearly disproved the myth that the two ethnic communities 'can't live peacefully together' and reminded the observers of the fact that 'the solution to the Cyprus problem is *not* a zero sum game'.[5]

As a matter of fact, all political parties in the Republic of Cyprus are in favour of the country's accession to the EU. In such a context where people unanimously agree on the European perspective of their country, it is not surprising that the debate on the future of Europe is less controversial than any other in the national arena. Such cooperation is also sustained by three additional factors. First, public opinion has been swayed by the favourable stance towards European integration adopted by Cypriot intellectuals. Second, the business community, which from the outset embraced a clear, proactive position towards Cyprus's accession bid, and the trade unions, at a later stage, have been extremely instrumental. Finally, and perhaps most importantly, the fact that so many citizens are aware of the country's accession perspective and eager to participate in the debate on the future of Europe has been integral in maintaining cooperation throughout the process.

The Innovative Initiatives of the Cypriot House of Representatives: a Pluralistic and Gender-balanced Approach

As mandated by the Laeken Declaration, four members of the Cypriot parliament were selected as delegates (two full and two deputies) to the European Convention. Parliament sought to achieve the widest possible political representation and nominated the two full members from the two largest political parties (*Anorthotiko Komma Ergazomenou Laou* (AKEL; Progressive Party of the Working People) and *Dimocratikos Synagermos* (DISY; Democratic Rally)) and the two deputy members from two smaller political parties (*Dimokratiko Komma* (DIKO; Democratic Party) and *Enomenoi Dimokrates* (EDI; United Democrats)). This model reflects fully the interests of both the government and the opposition and, more surprisingly in Cypriot politics, is equally representative in terms of gender. At the macro level, the gender dimension seems to have been neglected by the majority of governments and parliaments sending delegates: only 17 out of 105 Convention members were women. In the Cypriot case, the outcome with respect to gender is neither a coincidence nor a direct effect of the Laeken Declaration. It is best understood within the wider context of domestic changes as a result of what can be called 'Europeanization' (Ladrech 1994; Featherstone and Kazamias 2001) in the sense of large-scale adaptation pressure: the percentage of women in politics and decision making positions in Cyprus, which is less than 10%, is much lower than the EU average.

Cyprus's pioneering Convention launch: Participating governments were urged by the Laeken Declaration and the Convention itself to organize a series of events and inaugurate national debates on the future of Europe. In response, the Cypriot House of Representatives invited an assortment of organizations, associations and unions to attend the launching ceremony and various conferences. This explicit attempt to involve grass-roots institutions signals an innovative if not radical shift in the political culture of Cyprus, once again inspired by the prospect of imminent EU accession.

Parliament celebrated the launch of the Convention on the future of Europe by calling an official meeting at its plenary session on 28 February 2002. The president, Mr Dimitris Christofias, addressed MPs and the general audience, officially inaugurating the public dialogue. In attendance were representatives of governmental and NGOs, mass media, foreign embassies, and other important bodies. This was the first time that so many social strata were represented at a parliamentary plenary session devoted exclusively to Europe. All the MP delegates and deputy delegates, Eleni Mavrou (AKEL), Panayiotis Demetriou (DISY), Marios Matsakis (DIKO) and Androulla Vassiliou (EDI), as well as the government's Michael Attalides, participated in several radio and TV programmes focusing on the debate on the future of Europe.

A successful opening to civil society: In order to focus the country's outreach efforts regarding the debate on Europe's future, the Cypriot parliament made a conscious decision to stimulate public debate on the future of Europe by encouraging grass-roots organizations to participate. The Parliamentary Committee on European Affairs developed an impressive and original set of activities. The committee organized its communication with citizens both through conventional methods and more innovative campaigns such as extensive website links to relevant EU internet pages, a special forum to promote public dialogue and a regular newsletter. The various workshops and conferences organized by parliament also extended beyond the usual format; certainly, they achieved the loftier goal of connecting the parliament directly to civil society.

On 5 April 2002, the parliament organized a special conference on the future of Europe. During that session, three workshops were sponsored, each with a unique focus: the cultural aspects of European integration, the role of national parliaments and European institutions. It is worth emphasizing that this conference attracted a large number of participants from a wide range of social organizations: representatives of the Chamber of Commerce and technical guilds; local authorities; trade unions; higher education institutions and university students' organizations; organizations representing the interests of women, consumers, agriculture, human rights advocates and scientists; and the mass media.

The relatively high participation of women and youth signifies how groundbreaking the conference was, as it opened up new patterns of interaction between the parliament and civil society. Indeed, by examining the dialogue stimulated in those workshops, one easily understands the general sentiments and initial reactions of the Cypriot people. In the workshop on cultural aspects, the views expressed underscored the common values and principles of European citizens: democracy, political stability, legitimacy, human rights, the protection of minorities and tolerance. The contribution of European citizenship to the development of a communal ethos and European identity was also emphasized. Participants stressed the fact that the European programmes promote European civilization through inter-cultural learning and contribute to the cultivation of an appreciation of other societies. They also proposed further ideas for educational and cultural programmes and inter-cultural communication. Participants in the session on national parliaments stressed the vital role of those bodies as points of liaison between European institutions and domestic populations with the potential to reduce the perceived democratic deficit. The third workshop, on the role of European institutions, gathered individuals who concurred that European institutions should follow transparent procedures in daily business that can be easily comprehended by the general public.

The second conference, which took place on 24 April 2002, was entitled 'The Future of Europe and Youth: Expectations and Concerns', and its participants were representatives from the youth organizations of Cyprus. The young people who attended the conference stressed the fundamental importance of the 'White Paper on Youth' and its role in addressing such pervasive problems as youth unemployment, xenophobia and lack of equal opportunities. The participants also accentuated the fact that keeping the country's youth informed about European issues on a consistent basis is a prerequisite for ensuring its active participation in European affairs.

The third conference took place on 15 May 2002 and investigated 'Local Administration and Subsidiarity'. The parliament, recognizing the essential role of local democracy, invited representatives from local authorities to discuss the issue of subsidiarity.

The fourth conference, held on 25 June 2002, examined fundamental rights and assembled representatives of numerous organizations interested in the protection of human rights. Its participants favoured the incorporation of the Charter of Fundamental Rights into the Constitutional Treaty. They acknowledged, however, that the European Convention on Human Rights possesses a wider scope for implementation and is more progressive than the Charter of Fundamental Rights, mainly because of its legally binding status. They also agreed that the EU should – given its imminent plans for enlargement – enhance the Charter of Fundamental Rights with specific implementation mechanisms and incorporate the rights of minorities. The government of Cyprus favours the incorporation of the Charter of Fundamental Rights in EU treaties so that its citizens have a clearer idea of their rights and obligations.

The Cypriot members of the Convention invested significant political capital in order to fulfil its stated objectives. They shared the codified conclusions reached at all conferences with local organizations in Cyprus and their colleagues in the Convention. Public participation in the conferences organized by the parliament was remarkably high and unique for Cypriot domestic politics. The activities sponsored by the parliament contributed greatly by introducing efficient mechanisms for exchanging information, opinions and experiences. One should note, however, that apart from the conferences organized, the proposal for a permanent information disseminating mechanism, which was embraced politically, has not yet been implemented due to a lack of financial resources. The Committee nevertheless reiterated its intention to continue promoting such successful activities and eventually secure the necessary financial resources, either through the executive or directly from the EU.

The Initiative of the Ministry of Foreign Affairs

As early as June 2001, the minister of foreign affairs, Ioannis Kasoulides, took the lead in announcing the start of public discourse on the future of Europe, stressing the potential benefits from contributing to the debate.[6] Under the tutelage of his successor, Georges Iacovou, Cyprus's position regarding fundamental Convention issues has not changed significantly. The uncontroversial nature of the debate on the future of Europe has been confirmed by the fact that the government's representative at the Convention has not been replaced nor has its position changed in the wake of presidential elections in February 2003 and the subsequent change in government.

A weak support mechanism: In order to provide assistance to the government team that was to represent Cyprus at the Convention, the Ministry of Foreign Affairs (MFA) established a special secretariat aimed at providing administrative assistance to the government representative. Whereas many other countries appointed a team consisting of high-ranking civil servants, diplomats and intellectuals in order to provide the members of the Convention with substantial support, Cyprus offered its delegates mainly the services of the secretariat. The government's delegates, therefore, had to rely in large part upon their own skill, resources and creativity.

In terms of a communication strategy, the MFA created a special page on its website dedicated to the debate on the future of Europe (www.mfa.gov.cy/debate) with the aim of informing and involving civil society in the discussion. Citizens can browse its content to access contributions of the government's representative to the Convention as well as the government's own position on various issues. In the context of supporting open dialogue, the MFA made this technology available to allow the public to submit their opinions, observations and comments regarding the European Convention.

An integrationist approach: The Government of Cyprus has advocated the 'Community method' in its stance towards the Convention, most notably by defending the preservation of supranational institutions. Indeed, it envisages a strong, democratic and prosperous Union capable of assuming leadership roles in the international arena and maintaining peace, security, sustainable development and respect for human rights.[7] Cyprus also appears to support the development of a common European identity and the concept of a larger European family while simultaneously preserving Europe's underlying diversity of cultures, identities and ethnicities. The country also believes that the EU must possess a developed and coordinated defence and security policy and speak with a clearer, more unified voice in world affairs. Along these lines, Cyprus affirms that the Europe of the twenty-first century must be intelligible to national populations and responsive to their needs and expectations; democratic legitimacy and transparency in decision-making processes must be guaranteed. In the government's opinion, this can be achieved via the principles of subsidiarity, solidarity and proportionality.

In terms of competences, the Cypriot government favours neither the creation of a *kompetenzkatalogue* (catalogue of competences) nor the strict demarcation of competences between member states and the EU because they potentially deprive the EU of necessary flexibility in the face of shifting needs and future challenges. Moreover, it would be nearly impossible to draft lists of issues that fall within the exclusive competence of either the member states or the Union. The introduction of rigid delineations would inevitably and unnecessarily constrain the development of EU policy. Nevertheless, those issues which are supranational and impact the entire Union, such as international terrorism, defence, cross-border crime, global financial crime, global humanitarian crises, money laundering, drug trafficking, migration and asylum, seem to fall under the jurisdiction of the Union rather than individual member states.

The concept of 'institutional balance' within the Union should be upheld as well. The role of the European Parliament should be reinforced just as the involvement of national parliaments in European affairs is strengthened. The European Council should continue directing the Union's political agenda, establishing priorities and setting new courses for action. Increased access to the legislative work of the Council of Ministers would be instrumental in eliminating the now pervasive opinion that the EU operates behind closed doors and that Brussels is overly bureaucratic. The right of every country to appoint a commissioner upholds the principle of equality among member states and fosters an atmosphere of mutual trust. Finally, the Commission should not be subject to the vicissitudes of party politics.

Cyprus favours the enhanced participation of national parliaments in European affairs as a means of bolstering the democratic legitimacy of the European legislative process. Domestic legislatures should exert stronger control over EU affairs within their borders, especially when the Council of Ministers wields legislative authority. Furthermore, they should scrutinize the executive in order to ensure democratic control in each member state. The Commission should be required to distribute information directly to member state governments. Also, it is worth exploring opportunities for increased intra-Union exchange through the Conference of the Community and European Affairs Committees of the EU (COSAC). The creation of a superfluous second chamber could lead to greater delays, reduce efficiency, introduce unnecessary complications and perhaps signal a move towards re-nationalization.

The MFA emphasized that the future of Europe should cease to be perceived to be driven by elitist interests. Rather, it should take into account the real preferences, doubts and anxieties of Europe's citizens. As mentioned above, the debate on the future of Europe explicitly seeks to embrace the general public in a closer, more symbiotic relationship with the Union and its institutions. Individuals must be directly and personally involved in the dialogue if it and any decisions taken at the European level are to be considered legitimate. Moreover, such participation would increase the probability of widespread approval of the European experiment and infuse the EU with a social and human face. The Cypriot minister of foreign affairs has called upon civil society, grass-roots organizations, political parties, universities, think tanks, and research centres to contribute actively to the debate.[8] Specific examples include cooperation with the House of Representatives, the Jean Monnet chair of the University of Cyprus, the European Institute of Cyprus (www.eic.ac.cy) and other stakeholders in order to organize public lectures, discussions and conferences on the issues taken up by the European Convention. Radio and television stations have broadcast several forums on the Convention and the Cypriot position. Although these initiatives to widen participation are still in their infancy, the debate has reached local and regional audiences.

GRASS-ROOTS INVOLVEMENT OR ELITIST DOMINATION?

The importance of involving local and regional actors such as unions, NGOs, business leaders and academia was highlighted in the Laeken Declaration and acknowledged in the European Commission's White Paper on Governance. The intended outcome was to make a sincere attempt at widening participation within member states and candidate countries. To be sure, this is not an easy task due to the difficulties of organizing representative democracy on a transnational basis. Systems of interweaving alliances and cross-cutting interests are developing gradually and could eventually strengthen the democratic character of the EU. Yet, just how easy is it to stimulate public interest in issues facing an enlarged Europe? To what extent was it possible to generate such attention to relatively unfamiliar issues?

In Cyprus, various stakeholders, mainly at the national level, have assumed primary responsibility for answering these questions. This suggests a landmark turning point in the sense that the parameters of the debate have shifted from bilateralism – that is, between Cyprus and the EU – to multilateralism. Cypriots are therefore better equipped to understand and participate in general European affairs, particularly when it comes to relations with citizens of other EU member states. Furthermore, these initiatives have helped, at least in theory, bridge the gap between the masses and the European institutions shaping their lives. Nevertheless, the topics discussed in the Convention have, in practice, been relegated to secondary public importance and are at risk of being completely overshadowed by the prospect of a comprehensive settlement. Thus, despite the existence of growing general interest, it is not surprising that in 2002–03 the 'Cyprus problem' has been dominant among issues of social consequence.

However, the Jean Monnet Chair in European Political Integration at the University of Cyprus has organized several seminars on the future of Europe. The very first public debate on the subject was co-organized on 3 April 2002 by the chair in conjunction with the parliament, the MFA and the students' association. The president of the parliament and the permanent secretary of the MFA addressed the colloquium, and three Cypriot members of the Convention shared their experiences. The second forum was organized after the Copenhagen European Council in December 2002 and was devoted to the collective futures of Cyprus and the EU. The third seminar was exclusively devoted to youth and the future of Europe and was held in May 2003.

As a measure of grass-roots involvement in the debate on the future of Europe, we have chosen to examine the involvement of youth, political parties and local authorities with the aim of isolating the most important factors that influence awareness and involvement. We have selected Cypriot youth culture because of its already growing presence in European affairs. The methods employed by political parties to draw ordinary citizens into the debate are of central concern because of their role in mediating between the public and political power. Finally, local authorities are in close contact with the political base, thereby providing a third source of useful empirical evidence.

The Role of the Youth Board of Cyprus in the Debate on the Future of Europe

The Youth Board of Cyprus has an important role to play in the debate on the future of Europe because of its key position in mediating between youth and the European polity. The Youth Board designated two representatives of the government of Cyprus to the Youth Convention on the Future of Europe on the basis of a formal application procedure. The four national MPs participating in the larger Convention selected the other four participants, one from each youth political organization (Progressive Party of the Working People, Democratic Rally, Democratic Party and United Democrats).

The Youth Convention was held in Brussels in early July 2002. Participants had the opportunity to discuss topics including missions and visions, democracy and participation in the EU, and Europe in a globalized world. The three workshops organized yielded a number of innovative ideas and proposals. Although the Youth Convention involved the region's young citizens at the European level, it has not achieved much success in continuing and strengthening their negotiations at the national and local levels. As a matter of fact, the event received scant media attention in Cyprus. It is worth underlining the fact that the reportage on youth and the Convention, although produced in time, was only presented on the occasion of the end of the Convention proceedings.

The Youth Board of Cyprus also selected one individual to participate in the Youth 2002 Conference in July of that year, which gathered 1,000 young Europeans from 33 countries. Attendees stayed at 13 Danish Folk

High Schools and were charged with answering the opening question: 'If a European Constitution comes into being, what then, would we want it to contain?' The delegates formulated their own document – the final version of which was a combination of proposals from the groups at the 13 high schools.

Furthermore, the Youth Board also elected six young Cypriots to attend the 'Youropa – The Future of Europe' conference in December 2002 in Copenhagen (www.youropa.dk/conference). Three participants were chosen through the political parties. Two of them were officials working for the Youth Board, and the third was selected on the basis of previous participation in the Youth Convention. The spirit of the Laeken Declaration served as the thematic backdrop to the conference – the objective of which was the encouragement of more active youth participation in the debate on the future of Europe. The in-depth discussions at the conference covered, among others, the following topics: EU enlargement, the EU and globalization, democracy and European civil society, a charter on fundamental rights, xenophobia and discrimination at the European level, youth organizations and integration, European culture and identity, the role of youth organizations in decision-making processes, and formal and informal education. The conclusions reached at these and other workshops were submitted to the Danish minister of European affairs.

The European Youth Programme seeks to bring young people in Europe closer together by facilitating their full integration into social networks. It encourages ingenuity, knowledge and aptitude, fosters youth solidarity in the face of racism and xenophobia, promotes appreciation for common European culture, heritage and principles, and promotes equality and informal education. The Youth Programme also encourages the participation of underprivileged youth from different cultural, geographical and socio-economic backgrounds as well as people with disabilities. Five hundred Cypriots between the ages of 15 and 25 have participated in this programme and enjoyed the opportunity to exchange opinions on the future of Europe.

Therefore, the Youth Board of Cyprus has played a vital role in promoting dialogue on the future of Europe through the nomination of delegates to various European conferences. Those participants developed high expectations for the public debate within Cyprus and observed that much more can be done to reach non-familiar youth audiences. To that end, the Youth Board of Cyprus planned several conferences in 2003 and, as part of its communication strategy, plans to inform youth organizations about the White Paper on Youth and stimulate public debate on the future of Europe.

Political Parties: The Predominance of Domestic Politics

The Commission White Paper on Governance recognizes the potential benefit of political parties when attempting to bridge the gap between European institutions and member state populations. All the political parties of Cyprus[9] are in favour of Cyprus' accession to the EU, and thus no political party is anti-European or Euro-sceptic.

The process of Europeanization has presented a number of challenges to political parties and affected them in both subtle and explicit ways. Five areas of party activity have been influenced: policy and programmatic content, organizational structures, patterns of inter-party competition, party–government relations and relations beyond the national party system (Ladrech 2001).

In terms of the course of Cypriot accession and in recognition of the need for rapid harmonization, all parties reached a significant level of consensus. As a result, out of the 620 bills concerning harmonization, 614 passed unanimously.[10] This atypical behaviour on the part of political parties could be attributed to what Kreppel calls a 'sign of institutional maturity' as evidenced by their respect for compromise in the name of the greater good (Kreppel 1999). Moreover, collective fear of anti-European accusations served as an implicit constraint against excessive ideological tension during parliamentary discussions.

Another interesting aspect of the transformation of Cypriot political parties through the European integration process has been the educational role they perform. Increased awareness of European issues and the training of partisan political elites as they confront more complicated problems in the European political system, are two significant features of this role. All political parties are performing this role, with varying degrees of intensity and success.

Cypriot political parties have viewed European integration not only as a means of pursuing their own self-interested goals, but also as a potentially positive factor in the quest for internal reunification of the island. This belief has had far-reaching consequences for their overall assessment of EU integration as well as cross-community (Greek–Turkish) and cross-party cooperation.

However, debate on the future of Europe stimulated by Cyprus's political parties has been rather subdued because they have directed their attention and efforts more towards the accession negotiations and adoption of the *acquis communautaire*. In addition, the Annan Plan for a comprehensive settlement to the Cyprus question and external pressures to agree upon a resolution before the Copenhagen European Council in December 2002 have contributed to this prioritization. Political parties in Cyprus created links on their websites to the homepage of the EU but have not done so in order to devote electronic resources to the debate on the future of Europe, nor have they posted the contributions of MPs to the negotiations.

The Limited Role of Local Authorities and Municipalities

So far, local authorities in Cyprus have still not organized any activities nor adopted any communication strategy regarding the debate on the future of Europe. The survey conducted for this essay to measure the involvement of local authorities demonstrated that the discussion did not even reach local elites. At the end of January 2003, only a few of the 33 municipalities planned to host a series of seminars on issues concerning European citizens during the first half of 2003. Large municipalities have arranged special lectures on the EU within existing public events. Only as the Convention was concluding its work and as the Accession Treaty was signed, did several municipalities (including some small and rural ones) organize public lectures and cultural events focusing on Europe and Cyprus's European perspective. This was indeed a noteworthy step forward in the effort to raise public awareness, and local authorities discovered creative ways of achieving that goal. Using limited financial resources made available by the government of the Republic of Cyprus, they organized these events with the close cooperation of grass-roots NGOs.

It is abundantly clear that municipalities lacked the informational networks necessary for full involvement in the debate on the future of Europe. The presence of local authorities, therefore, has been restricted to the attendance of some officials at lectures on local administration and Cyprus's EU accession organized by the Union of Cyprus Municipalities. Others have taken part in seminars organized by the Cyprus Academy of Public Administration and training seminars on European affairs in Brussels. A few municipalities have discussed local administration and subsidiarity in events organized by the Committee of the Regions and the Council of Europe, and many more are members of the Eurocities network – which collaborates with local and regional authorities to advance the role of micro-level administration in EU governance and enhance its presence in the draft European Constitution.

As Michalis Attalides, the government's delegate to the Convention on the future of Europe stressed, public interest in the details of Convention business is negligible outside the House of Representatives, the MFA, the European Institute of Cyprus and the University of Cyprus.[11] As previously noted, the attention of politicians and citizens has been focused on the accession negotiations and adoption of the *acquis communautaire*. The relative intensity of and excitement surrounding the accession process had a major impact on the public response. If the *status quo* is to change at all – that is, if there is to be a genuine shift from an elite-driven to a grass-roots-oriented public debate on the future of Europe – the full participation of the country's economic, social and political organizations must be secured. The real challenge is how to identify incentives and disincentives of civic participation in the context of domestic 'gatekeeper system' (Tofarides 2003) in order to move beyond 'elitist citizenship' (Magnette 2001).

CONCLUSION

Widespread civic participation in political dialogue is naturally limited, even in the strongest of democracies, due to the sheer numbers involved and the complexity of the modern political landscape. Individuals have many competing interests and concerns, and politics – being only one – may not represent the most important of them. Hence, it should not come as a surprise that the general public's contributions to the debate on the future of Europe in accession candidate countries have been neither extensive nor substantial. Rather, active participation has been predominantly restricted to political elites and organized nationally.

It would be naive to expect that the EU Convention on the future of Europe could generate extensive and rapid changes in patterns of domestic politics. Due to its dynamic nature, EU adaptation pressure – whether low, moderate or high – may eventually produce far-reaching changes in domestic politics but at a gradual pace. In the case of the Republic of Cyprus, a number of innovative features has been introduced into its political culture: new relationships between parliament and society, more transparent and participatory political processes, a more visible role for women and youth, and, perhaps most importantly, an environment conducive to future peace and cooperation among Greek-Cypriots and Turkish-Cypriots.

The involvement of local authorities, NGOs and other social groups is still very limited, but the process of enhancing their roles has been initiated. Escalating public awareness is following a dynamic process that is aimed at reaching non-familiar audiences. The Youth Convention, though, has attracted scant media attention in Cyprus and EU member states, despite its innovativeness. Nevertheless, what remains important in the long term is this vibrant progression, this clearly expressed determination to involve citizens from a wide range of social strata in the debate on the future of Europe.

One of the less apparent but truly far-reaching benefits of the Convention exercise has been its contribution to the legitimacy of European integration through the promotion of general agreement and understanding of the basic principles according to which European citizens wish the EU to operate and evolve in member states and applicant countries. Citizens of both sets of countries embarked on a common journey from an equal standing. It has provided a framework for creative and consensual approaches to future integration endeavours. Even if a significant gap exists between the results of the Convention and the positions of member states at the start of IGC 2004, this first constitutional experiment of the European *demos* with the participation of all national governments will be long remembered. Given this symbiotic relationship between the European core and its constituent members, there is scope for additional research into the importance of domestic politics for the future of European integration – for 'the way to Ithaca' is probably equally important as 'Ithaca' itself:

> When setting out upon your way to Ithaca,
> Wish always that your journey be long,
> Full of adventure, full of lore.
> For Ithaca has given you the marvellous journey.
> Without her you would not have set your course.
> There is no more that she can give.
> And if you find her poor, Ithaca will not have deceived you.
> Wise as you will have become, so full of experience,
> you will have understood by then what these Ithacas mean.[12]

The journey towards an 'ever closer union' of European nations will, without a doubt, be a long and arduous one. Yet, along the way it will be paved with experiences of great political and historical importance regardless of whether Ithaca turns out to be poor or fails to meet expectations. Indeed, the most significant challenges for participating countries like Cyprus and its citizens are still to come.

NOTES

1. It involves (at the time of writing) 15 member states, ten accession countries (by May 2004), three candidate countries and a large worldwide network of nations engaged in close cooperation.
2. Survey conducted for the European Commission by Taylor Nelson Sofres/EOS Gallup. It covered the period 23 to 29 June 2003 and encompassed 25,000 people from all the countries in the enlarged EU. Further information can be found at: www.europa.eu.int/comm/public_opinion/index.htm.

3. See 'Basis for a Comprehensive settlement of the Cyprus Problem' (Annan Plan), which includes a constitution for Cyprus, 26 February 2003, www.pio.gov.cy, and Report of the Secretary-General to the Security Council of the United Nations on his mission of good offices in Cyprus, S/2003/398, 1 April 2003, www.un.org.
4. Judgement of 23 April 1986 in the Case 294/83, Les Verts.
5. Günter Verheugen, 'Bringing People Together', speech delivered at the Cyprus Chamber of Commerce and Industry in Nicosia, 17 June 2003.
6. 'Federalizing Europe-Federations within the EU and the Path of Cyprus', Nicosia, June 2001.
7. Views expressed by the minister of foreign affairs of Cyprus, Ioannis Kasoulides, European Policy Centre, Brussels, 4 June 2002.
8. Conference on 'Federalizing Europe – Federations within the EU and the Path of Cyprus', Nicosia, 29 June 2001.
9. Parliamentary election 2001: AKEL 34.71 per cent, DISY 34 per cent, DHKO 14.84 per cent, KISOS (EDEK) 6.51 per cent, NEO 3 per cent, EDI 2.59 per cent, ADIK 2.16 per cent, Environmentalists 1.98 per cent, Others 0.21 per cent.
10. Proceedings from the parliamentary discussions regarding the state's budgets (8–10 Jan. 2003).
11. Comments made at the 'Copenhagen European Council: Public Debate on the Future of Europe and on the Future of Cyprus', Jean Monnet Chair, University of Cyprus, Nicosia, 16 December 2002.
12. The poem 'Ithaca' was written in 1911 by Konstantinos P. Kavafis, a highly distinguished Greek poet. Ithaca is a Greek island in the Ionian Sea and the birthplace of the hero Ulysses (Odysseus in Greek). His ten-year adventure home after the Trojan War has been recounted in Homer's epic poem *The Odyssey*. See www2.thphy.uni-duesseldorf.de/ ~ likos/ithaca.shtml for an English version.

REFERENCES

Bernard, N. (2002): *Multilevel Governance in the European Union*, The Hague: Kluwer.
Crum, B. (2002): 'Laying Building Blocks or just Window-Dressing? – The First Half Year of the Convention on the Future of the EU' Centre for European Policy Studies, Brussels, www.ceps.be/Commentary/Jul02/crum.php.
Deloche-Gaudez, Fl. (2001): *La Convention pour l'elaboration de la Chartre des droits fondamentaux: une methode d'avenir?*, Paris: Groupement d'Etudes et des Recherches Notre Europe.
Featherstone, K. and G. Kazamias (eds.) (2001): *Europeanization and the Southern Periphery*, London: Frank Cass.
Hoffman, L. (2002): *The Convention on the Future of Europe: Thoughts on the Convention Model*, Jean Monnet Working Paper, Nov.
Hoskyns, C. (2003): *Gender Equality and the Convention*, Federal Trust for Education and Research.
Knill, C. (2001): *The Europeanization of National Administrations. Patterns of Institutional Change and Persistence*, Cambridge: Cambridge University Press.
Kreppel, A. (1999): 'Rules, Ideology and Coalition Formation in the European Parliament: Past, Present and Future', EPRG Working Paper, No.4, APSA Annual Meeting, Atlanta, Georgia, September 2–5.
Ladrech, R. (1994): 'Europeanization of Domestic Politics and Institutions: The Case of France', *Journal of Common Market Studies* 32/1, pp.69–88.
Ladrech, R. (2001): *Europeanization and Political Parties: Towards a Framework of Analysis*, Queens Papers on Europeanization, Feb.
Magnette, P. (2001): 'European Governance and Civic Participation: Can the European Union be politicised?' NYU/Jean Monnet Working Paper, June.

Pagoulatos, G. (2003): *Greece, the European Union and the 2003 Presidency*, Paris: Groupement d'Etudes et de Recherches Notre Europe.

Philippart, E. (2002): *The Convention on the Future of the EU*, CEPS Policy Brief_No.11.

Piris, J.-C. (2000): *Does the European Union Have a Constitution? Does It Need One?* NYU/Jean Monnet Working Papers, May.

Reh, Ch. and W.Wessels (2002): 'Towards an Innovative Mode of Treaty Reform? Three Sets of Expectations for the Convention', *Collegium* 24, pp.17–42.

Schmitter, C.P. (2001): 'What Is There to Legitimize in the European Union … and How Might This Be Accomplished? NYU/ Jean Monnet Working Papers, June.

Shaw, J. (2003): *What's in a Convention? Process and Substance in the Project of European Constitution-Building*, Vienna: Institute for Advanced Studies (IHS), Political Science, 89.

Smith, B. (2002): *Constitution Building in the European Union*, The Hague: Kluwer Law International.

Tofarides, M. (2003): *Urban Policy in the European Union. A Multi-Level Gatekeeper System*, Aldershot: Ashgate.

Weiler, J.H.H. (2000): *Federalism and Constitutionalism: Europe's Sonderweg*, NYU/ Jean Monnet Working Papers, Oct.

Turkey on the Edges of the Convention on the 'Future of Europe'

KEMAL KİRİŞCİ and ZEYNEP GÜLŞAH ÇAPAN

INTRODUCTION

Turkey was the sole candidate country at the 'Convention on the Future of Europe' that had not yet started its accession negotiations for membership to the European Union (EU). Turkey's efforts to gain admittance to the Convention were an uphill battle that met considerable resistance from a number of EU governments. Government and civil society participation (compared to the other countries surveyed in this issue) was, on balance, more limited and subdued. Moreover, public interest in the Convention was limited to a very small number of elite-led non-governmental organizations (NGOs) and a very restricted part of the media. In the media, the debate generally focused on the place of Turkey in Europe and Turkey's membership prospects. There was hardly any debate concerning institutional reform in the EU and the future of the EU itself, and discussion of the content of the draft constitution released by the Praesidium of the Convention in October 2002 was entirely lacking.

Nevertheless, the remarks in November 2002 of the president of the Convention, Valery Giscard d'Estaing, that on cultural grounds there was no place for Turkey in the EU did precipitate interest and debate.[1] Surprisingly, the efforts of the Pope in July 2002 and November 2002, as well as in February 2003 to include a reference to the Christian roots of Europe in the draft constitution did not receive much attention.[2] Initially, Turkey's official participation at the Convention was led by the centre-right *Anavatan Partisi* (ANAP; Motherland Party), the junior partner in a governmental coalition that included *Demokratik Sol Partisi* (DSP; Democratic Left Party) and the right-wing *Milliyetçi Hareket*

The authors would like to express their thanks to representatives of NGOs who have shared their experiences about the Convention with us. They would also like to extend special thanks to the current Turkish representatives of the Convention and those officials associated with Convention activities who have shared their experiences with the authors.

Partisi (MHP; Nationalist Action Party). This coalition government experienced frequent internal disagreements over relations with the EU.[3] The absence of public interest and awareness about issues debated at the Convention coupled with a divided government that lacked a strong supportive will on EU-related issues led to a weak and subdued governmental participation at the Convention. The political parties represented in the governmental coalition were swept out of office at the November 2002 elections. Their members of parliament (MPs) failed to gain any seat in the new parliament. The new parliament is composed of the conservative *Adalet ve Kalkınma Partisi* (AKP; Justice and Development Party) and the social democrat *Cumhuriyet Halk Partisi* (CHP; Republican People's Party), as the sole opposition party.[4]

Both of these parties are committed to Turkey's EU membership, and the formation of the new government coincided with a revived and lively debate on Turkish–EU relations in the media during the weeks preceding the European Council summit in Copenhagen in December 2002. Both the government and civil society became engaged in an energetic effort, during the run up to the summit, to lobby for a date for accession negotiations to start. The failure to get a clear date for accession talks was received as a great disappointment by the public. This was accompanied by a debate in the media that the EU was biased against Turkey on cultural and religious grounds. Civil society groups that had been very active during the run up to the summit subsequently became subdued. Furthermore, early in 2003, the government's and the public's attention was dominated first by the crisis and then by the war on Iraq. In any event, the public continued to remain aloof to the developments at the Convention after the formation of the new government. Yet, the new representatives of Turkey to the Convention were on balance more active participants in the debate surrounding the future of the EU than their predecessors. They were engaged in articulating views and seeking to gain support for various amendments to the draft constitution. Participation at the Convention provided an opportunity to develop contacts and to participate in the activities of European Parliament (EP) political party groupings operating there.

Turkey has long been on the edges of the EU, both in geographical and political terms. Yet, it has also long aspired to become a member of the Union and over the last three years has embarked on a series of political reforms in an effort to meet the Copenhagen Criteria for accession negotiations to begin.[5] Participation at the Convention has been seen by both the government and interested civil society groups as one aspect of Turkey's uphill battle to gain recognition and support for its membership aspirations. This essay argues that, regardless of these aspirations,

Turkey's participation at the Convention was relatively muted. In spite of the high level of public support for membership, public interest in the work of the Convention was almost non-existent. This is not surprising considering that Turkey's prospective membership date is put at around 2011–12.[6] This clearly weakens immediate interest in substantive public debate about the EU itself. Active attention was limited to a group of very specialized NGOs and youth groups. Even then, only a very few of the participants representing these groups possessed substantive knowledge about the issues at the Convention, let alone the debates surrounding these issues. In order to understand how Turkey approached the Convention, it is useful to provide some background information on its relationship with the EU – which comprises the first section proper of this contribution.

HISTORICAL BACKGROUND

Turkey's relationship with Europe and her quest to become part of Europe and later the EU has been a long one. A westernization and modernization process started as early as the late eighteenth century in the Ottoman Empire. However, it was with the establishment of the Turkish republic in 1923 and with Mustafa Kemal Atatürk's reforms that Turkey embarked upon a systematic and profound modernization process. Atatürk defined his efforts to achieve a modern, secular and western society as a process of catching up with contemporary civilization. This process was itself manifested in the form of an aspiration to become part of Europe (Lewis 2002; Ahmad 1993). For Atatürk and his supporters, the primary aim – right from the early days of the foundation of the Turkish republic – was to see the country recognized as a respected European power (Hale 2000: 57).

In 1949 Turkey became a founding member of the Council of Europe and joined the North Atlantic Treaty Organization (NATO) in 1952. Turkey's relationship with Europe gained an impetus when her relationship with the European Economic Community (EEC) started in 1959 as the government applied for associate membership (Karluk 1996; Eralp 1997; Balkır and Williams 1993; Tekeli and İlkin 1993, 2000). This application resulted in the signing of the Ankara Association Agreement on 12 September 1963. The provisions of this agreement envisaged a gradual process of economic integration between Turkey and the EEC. Article 28 also raised the prospect of eventual Turkish membership of the EEC. In 1970 the Additional Protocol was signed. The Protocol envisaged a 22-year transitional period that would end with the establishment of a customs union. Yet, Turkey's relationship with the European Community (EC) started to experience problems from the mid 1970s onwards because of economic problems and political instability in Turkey. The military coup of 1980 worsened relations between Turkey and the EC. Moreover, in the early 1980s Greece became a member of the EC and then proceeded to raise regular objections to any improvement in EC–Turkish relations because of Greek–Turkish bilateral problems and Cyprus. Nevertheless, transition to democracy and economic liberalization led Turkey in 1987 to apply for membership. The Commission in its opinion on the Turkish application in 18 December 1989 concluded that Turkey was not ready to be a member of the EU for economic, political and social reasons (Arat and Baykal: 326; Hale 2000: 174–9, 233–45).

After the end of the cold war, most of the 1990s were a very difficult period for Turkey as violence in the south-east of the country increased and the Kurdish problem together with widespread human rights violations led to a marked deterioration in EU–Turkish relations (Kirişci and Winrow 1997; Kirişci 2004). Nevertheless, in spite of the considerable resistance from human rights circles and the EP, Turkey and the EU succeeded in signing the Customs Union Agreement that came into force in January 1996 (Klauss 2000). In Turkey this new treaty was perceived as a vital step towards eventual full membership (Arat and Baykal 2001: 341). Therefore, when Turkey was not included among the list of candidate countries for the next round of enlargement at the Luxembourg summit of the European Council in December 1997, there was considerable governmental and public disillusionment as well as anger. In protest, the Turkish government went as far as breaking off political dialogue with the EU and refusing to attend any of the meetings it was invited to. As a result of Turkey's exclusion from the list, the Turkish government feared that the EU wanted to develop a 'special' relationship with Turkey falling short of membership (Buzan and Diez 1999; Müftüler-Bac 1998).

However, the major breakthrough for Turkey came at the December 1999 EU Helsinki summit when it was granted candidate status. There were many factors that played a role in this dramatic turn around of the EU's position (Rumford 2000). The arrival of the social democrat government of Gerhard Schröder in Germany in 1999, replacing Helmut Kohl's Christian Democrat-dominated government, had a major impact on the Helsinki decision. Christian Democrats have traditionally been much less sympathetic to Turkish membership to the EU. The end of the violence surrounding the Kurdish problem in Turkey and early governmental steps towards improving democracy as well as a growing *rapprochement* in Greek–Turkish relations also played a role. Most importantly, the conclusions of the Helsinki summit foresaw the preparation of an accession partnership document that outlined the economic and political reforms that had to be adopted by Turkey in order for it to meet the Copenhagen Criteria. In return, Turkey prepared her national programme, outlining the reforms she would make in the short and long term.

In the summer of 2001 the Turkish parliament finally went into action and adopted a series of critical amendments to the Turkish constitutions as a means of facilitating political reforms in order to meet the Copenhagen Criteria (Oder 2002). These reforms were welcomed by the progress report published by the European Commission in 2001, even if the report also noted that there was still a lot of ground to cover before the Copenhagen Criteria would be met (Commission of the European Communities 2001). These developments also coincided with continued improvement in Greek-Turkish relations as well as a major breakthrough on Cyprus – Turkish Cypriot and Greek Cypriot leaders, Rauf Denktaş and Glafcos Klerides, meeting in December 2001 with the intention of restarting negotiations for the settlement of the Cypriot problem. The compromise agreement reached between Turkey, the United Kingdom and the United States in respect to the use of NATO facilities for operations in the context of the European Security and Defence Policy (ESDP) added to the positive climate for EU–Turkish relations (Udum 2002). This climate played a critical role in resolving the objections among some members of the EU in the Council of Ministers to Turkey's participation in the 'Convention on the Future of Europe' (Avcı 2002: 101). This was reflected in the decision of the Laeken European Council summit in December 2001, which confirmed that Turkey had finally gained access to the Convention. This was, in Turkey, received as a very positive development, considering that the country had been completely left out from the new institutional arrangements to accommodate the new wave of enlargement introduced by the Nice Treaty of 2000.

TURKISH PARTICIPATION IN THE CONVENTION

As Lucarelli and Radaelli explain in their introduction to this issue, the Convention had tasks relating to both process and outcome. We will consider the latter. The Convention was asked to address a number of questions and prepare a draft proposal for the intergovernmental conference (IGC) which opened in Rome on 4 October 2003. Turkish participation mostly focused on debates concerning articles of the draft constitution that address issues such as the actual future legal shape of the EU, the place of religion among the values that would represent the Union, the borders of Europe, the question of the powers of the institutions of the EU and the role of national parliaments in EU decision-making. Turkish participation at the Convention was led by government representatives and Turkish members of the parliament, together with the occasional appearance of activists from NGOs. The larger public and the media were generally on the sidelines. Rarely, moreover, did interest in the Convention go beyond very occasional news reports, with hardly any public debate emerging on the broader issues addressed at the Convention. Public and media involvement was obviously higher in issues directly pertaining to EU–Turkish relations.

Governmental Participation

The main governmental players were the Ministry of Foreign Affairs (MFA) and the Secretariat General for European Union Affairs (*Avrupa Birliği Genel Sekreterliği* – ABGS). ABGS is the main agency responsible for coordinating EU–Turkish relations among Turkish ministries and government agencies; this included coordinating Turkish participation at the Convention. The ABGS is the most specialized agency in terms of the Convention, and has a section focusing solely on the work of the Convention. It was established in 2000 with the responsibility for drafting Turkey's National Programme for the Adoption of the Acquis as well as coordination of the harmonization projects across different government agencies and the parliament. The General Secretary of the agency was Ambassador Volkan Vural; in late December 2002 he was replaced by Ambassador Murat Sungar.[7]

For a governmental agency, the ABGS has been exceptionally open to cooperation and interaction with representatives of Turkish civil society interested in the Convention. In the early days of the Convention, the agency organized a number of public meetings to discuss and debate what Turkey's official position on Convention related issues should be. Besides government representatives, academics, journalists and civil society representatives were also invited to these meetings. These meetings, by traditional Turkish standards, were unprecedented in their transparency and openness to civil society participation. The agency also established a portal where views and comments about the Convention can be openly exchanged.[8] However, participation in this debate was limited.

Until the elections of November 2002, Turkey's official representatives at the Convention were the then deputy prime minister and ANAP leader Mesut Yılmaz, the *Doğru Yol Partisi* (DYP; True Path Party) MP Ayfer Yılmaz and DSP MP Ali Tekin. Subsequent to the formation of the new government, Abdullah Gül, the minister of foreign affairs, accompanied by the AKP MP Zekeriya Akçam (his alternate is İbrahim Özal) and CHP MP Kemal Derviş (his alternate Necdet Budak) became Turkish representatives.

Most importantly, the previous governmental participation was led by the leader of the political party that had the smallest number of seats in the parliament and hence the least political weight. In that coalition government it was Mesut Yılmaz who was politically most supportive of Turkish membership of the EU and keenest to support political reforms to meet the Copenhagen Criteria. Furthermore, the issue of reforms had become a major source of tension within the governmental coalition. The MHP resisted the adoption of some of the more sensitive reforms such as the lifting of the death penalty and the introduction of legislation to allow broadcasting and education in Kurdish. In August 2002, though, the parliament did succeed in adopting a reform package that included these issues too. This precipitated a crisis within the coalition government that culminated in a decision to call an early election in November. Hence, for Yılmaz, the Convention also became a forum to promote his own political agenda and raise his profile as an advocate of EU membership in the hope of attracting votes for his party.

The form of participation in the Convention was also determined by the fact that during the previous government's participation, the draft constitution had not yet been released. Hence, participation for the Turkish representatives was, by and large, limited to making general declarations and speeches. In terms of substance, the common denominator to these declarations and speeches was the preference for the continuation of the *status quo*, or incremental change at most, as far as the institutional structure of the EU was concerned. Particular emphasis was put on the preference to see the future of the EU in terms of the continued centrality of member states rather than an increase in supranationalism. In respect to addressing the problem of democratic legitimacy in the EU, an enhancement of the role of national parliaments was advocated. There was a reluctance to see the EP being granted the right to initiate legislation even if an expansion of the issue areas to which the 'co-decision' procedures could apply were entertained. Actually, the scene for such a conservative approach on substantive issues was set by the then minister of foreign affairs, İsmail Cem, when, at the very onset of the Convention in June 2002, remarked that 'we should not lose sight of the fact that the existing institutions, structures and working methods of the Union are the by-product of more than four decades of common experiences. On that basis, care should be taken not to take high risks for the sake of change' (Cem 2002).

In general terms, the position of the new government in terms of substance has not been too dissimilar from the preceding one. Nevertheless, in terms of the form of participation as well as the content there are some differences of nuance and emphasis. Most importantly, the new government has had the benefit of commanding a large majority in the parliament. This has also been accompanied by a clear will to support Turkish accession to the EU. The representative of the political party in power, Zekeriya Akçam, and his alternate, Ibrahim Özal, were quite active in associating themselves with various efforts to bring amendments to the draft constitution. Interestingly, in terms of the politics surrounding the Convention, they found themselves cooperating closely with members of the European Liberal, Democrat and Reform Party (ELDR). Their concern was particularly directed towards enhancing the role of national parliaments as well as ensuring that the final version of the draft constitution would not have references to Christianity. They were keen to make sure that the Constitution retained its secular characteristics. Furthermore, they were also very much against the introduction and acceptance of any amendments that could throw Turkey's membership into doubt, hence objected to any *a priori* definition of the borders of Europe.

The representative of the opposition party, Kemal Derviş, and his alternate, Necdet Budak, generally shared similar views with the exception of the issue of the role of national parliaments. Derviş, though, consciously refrained from supporting an ELDR amendment aimed at enhancing the role of national parliaments on the grounds that his party wished to see a stronger EP with greater powers. Instead, he cooperated very closely with his social democrat counterparts in the Party of European Socialists (PES). This is surprising because his party, CHP, has a long tradition of being strongly associated with national sovereignty. In many ways, though, this may well be a sign of the degree of independence and leeway that the party leadership has allowed its representatives to enjoy; it may also be a sign of the little importance or salience attributed to the Convention itself by the party.

Lastly, no Turkish representative took the initiative to prepare an amendment to the draft constitution. One representative explained this as a product of an absence of expertise in the area of constitutional law and lack of experience in parliamentary politics and networking at the European level.[9] Most interestingly, representatives of AKP and CHP pointed out that in spite of a limited Turkish participation at the Convention their presence helped them to develop contacts with party groupings from the EP.

Political Parties

The programmes of political parties in the previous as well as current parliament do not state any specific position on the issues that are being discussed at the Convention. Neither do they, with the exception of ANAP, provide any forum for discussing the issues. In contrast, most political parties (one way or the other) express support for membership of the EU.

However, a party that stands out from the others is MHP. This party is known for its nationalist views and the importance it attributes to national sovereignty. It considers many aspects of European integration and the Copenhagen Criteria as a threat to national independence. It has long objected to a relationship with the EU where Turkey is compelled to make one-sided compromises (Nationalist Action Party 2002; Avcı 2003). Furthermore, its preference is more in support of a relationship that would be based on intergovernmental cooperation rather than a relationship that invokes supranationalism. The party energetically resisted some of the critical reforms, including the abolition of the death penalty and the provision of broadcasting and education rights in minority languages. Nevertheless, this uncompromising and nationalist stand towards reforms and the EU in general did not prevent the party from losing the national elections in November 2002.

The AKP and CHP programmes also did not say much about the Convention. This is very surprising, considering that both parties have been keen to continue with political reforms to meet the Copenhagen Criteria and attribute great importance to Turkish membership of the EU. Furthermore, even though the leader of the governing AKP party, Recep Tayyip Erdoğan, and the then prime minister, Abdullah Gül, mounted energetic campaigns in Europe during the run-up to the Copenhagen summit in order to mobilize support for a date to start accession negotiations, they did not express any opinion concerning issues discussed at the Convention. Subsequently, as minister of foreign affairs, Gül participated in the sessions of the Convention (The European Convention 2003).

In spite of the regular participation of both AKP and CHP representatives at the proceedings of the Convention, the Convention itself and the issues which it addressed – including the matter of the draft constitution – have not been that high up the agenda of both parties and their leadership. Instead, both parties, during the first half of 2003, were absorbed in the politics of the preparation of another round of EU-related political and economic reforms. Furthermore, the political parties, particularly AKP – the party in government, were deeply engaged during the first three months of 2003 in the politics surrounding the Iraqi war. The governing party also had the added challenge of having to manage the aftermath of parliament's decision early in March not to allow US troops to use Turkish territory in their war against Saddam Hussein. Moreover, Turkish politicians and members of parliament are not particularly well versed in the intricacies of the politics of the EU, let alone the Convention.[10] They do not have close contacts with European politicians or members of the EP.

Against this background, it is not surprising that participation at the Convention was left by AKP to two young members of the parliament with a good command of a foreign language and considerable familiarity with the EU, if not the Convention. CHP, on the other hand, preferred Kemal Derviş, a relatively well-known figure in Europe from the previous government, and his alternate Necdet Budak, a former trade unionist to represent them at the Convention. Interestingly, both political parties encouraged their representatives to develop closer contacts with their European counterparts and participate in political party group activities at the Convention. CHP instructed Damla Gürel, one of the few female members of the Turkish parliament, to develop relations with PES and informally participate at the Convention.

NGOs and Civil Society

It is only over the last decade or so that civil society has started to flourish in Turkey. (Norton 1995, 1996; Toprak 1996). The EU has had a direct, contributing influence in this development by providing funds for NGOs and indirectly by encouraging greater democratization in Turkey (Yerasimos 2001; Rumford 2001; Tarih Vakfı 2001). However, it would be wrong to assume that civil society enjoys the kind of presence and influence that is generally associated with civil society in EU member states. Turkish civil society suffers from various weaknesses, ranging from being mostly elite-driven to structural difficulties such as diminishing – yet still prevalent – state control and supervision of NGOs (Kalaycıoğlu 2001, 2002a, b).

There are several NGOs and civil society groups that have mobilized their attention and members on EU issues, such as the European Movement 2002.[11] In 2002, it rallied support for the adoption of political reforms and Turkey's accession into the EU. The Movement was most known for its publicity campaign in support of political reforms in the country based on the slogan '*Başka Yarın Yok*' [There is no other tomorrow]. The Movement consists of several working groups, which have produced a common text supporting Turkey's accession into the EU. This text was published and opened to signature by the public in order to rally support for Turkey's accession. It is difficult to gauge its influence. Nevertheless, Emre Kocaoğlu, a former member of the Turkish parliament, did cite the Movement during a conference organized by civil society groups on Turkish and EU relations as an important source of pressure on members of the previous parliament. He argued that the Movement's activities and efforts did have some role in the adoption of the reform package of August 2002.[12]

Türkiye Ekonomik ve Sosyal Etüdler Vakfı (TESEV; The Turkish Economic and Social Studies Foundation) was established in 1961 as a non-profit organization and became a foundation in 1994. TESEV (www.tesev.org.tr) carries out research in policy areas concerning Turkey and has expanded its scope by having a special focus on Turkey–EU relations. The results of a public opinion survey on Turkish preferences and attitudes towards the EU and the Copenhagen Criteria run by TESEV was presented at a conference that brought together leading members of the parliament, academics, NGOs and the media. The results of the research precipitated a wide debate in the media about Turkey's membership of the EU and are widely believed to have contributed to the political debate that helped the adoption of the reform package of August 2002 (TESEV 2003).

Another important NGO is *İktisadi Kalkınma Vakfı* (İKV; Economic Development Foundation; www.ikv.org.tr). It worked like an umbrella organization for leading discussions centring on the initial stages of the Convention. The İKV was established in 1965 on the initiative of the Istanbul Chamber of Commerce and Istanbul Chamber of Industry to help the Turkish private sector with regard to the EU and improve Turkish–EU relations. On EU affairs, ABGS, the government and the Convention have closely consulted the İKV. Another very important and politically influential NGO is *Türk Sanayiciler ve İş Adamları Derneği* [TUSİAD; Turkish Industrialists' and Businessmen's Association]. TUSİAD has been a forceful advocate of EU membership. It has been actively involved in mobilizing support for membership at both the governmental as well as civil society level in Turkey. It is also a member of the Union of Industrial and Employers' Confederation in Europe. TUSİAD has actively used this membership to lobby support for Turkish membership within the EU. However, unlike İKV, it did not participate actively in Convention-related events.

Youth organizations were active both on wider European issues and the Convention. Here, it suffices to mention the Istanbul branch of AEGEE and Youth Association for Habitat. AEGEE (*Association des Etats Generaux des Etudiants de l'Europe*) is the European Students' General Forum (see www.aegee.org; the Istanbul branch website is www.aegee-istanbul.org). It is an international youth organization that was established in April 1985 in Paris by a group of students. Today, it has organizational branches in 271 cities in Europe and more than 17,000 members. The branch in Istanbul was established in 1992 and is one of the most active student NGOs on Turkish campuses. Members of both organizations participated at student and youth activities in Europe addressing Convention topics.

NGOs have generally been very supportive of Turkish membership of the EU, although few of them have developed extensive knowledge on issues concerning the European Constitution. In December 2002 during the run-up to the Copenhagen European Council summit, 175 NGOs came together to adopt a declaration called '*Türkiye'nin yeri Avrupa Birliği'dir, kaybedecek zaman yoktur*' [Turkey's place is in the EU, there is no time to waste].[13] Another conspicuous civil society engagement in EU issues occurred on 27 November 2002. On that occasion, in an effort to mobilize support for Turkey's position at the upcoming Copenhagen summit, representatives of more than 200 Turkish NGOs travelled to meet with 187 EU NGOs (İktisadi Kalkınma Vakfı 2002a, d). Yet, among these Turkish NGOs there were actually very few who had engaged themselves in Convention-related issues.

Among Turkish civil society, there are also NGOs that have expressed strongly sceptical views about the EU. A group of these NGOs formed a platform in response to the pro-EU stance and issued a declaration, which was published in various dailies. The most striking of them has been *Türk İşçi Sendikaları Konfederasyonu* (TÜRKİS; Confederation of Labour Unions of Turkey; see www.turkis.org.tr). In a report published by TÜRKİS in December 2001 (TÜRKİS 2001), it went as far as to claim that the EU intended to usurp Turkish national independence and that the EU's ultimate aim was to territorially dismember Turkey. Euro-sceptics consisting of NGOs such as DİSK (*Türkiye Devrimci İşçi Sendikaları Konfederasyonu* – Confederation of Progressive Labour Unions of Turkey), KESK (*Kamu Emekçileri Sendikaları Konfederasyonu* – Confederation of Public Service Employees' Union), TMMOB (*Türk Mühendis ve Mimar Odaları Birliği* – Union of Chambers of Turkish Engineers and Architects), İHD (*İnsan Hakları Derneği* – Human Rights Association of Turkey) and TÜMTİS (*Türkiye Motorlu Taşıt İşçileri Sendikası* – Turkish Road Transport Workers' Trade Union) prepared a declaration stating that unconditional support will make Turkey dependent on the EU.[14] However, no representatives from these NGOs really followed the Convention. In this respect, then, the Convention did not mobilize any particular anti-EU sentiment.

One concrete example of civil society and government interaction in the context of the Convention occurred early in 2002. Two public meetings were organized by the government, bringing together different civil society groups. The meeting chaired by the minister of foreign affairs, İsmail Cem, on 11 January 2002 was organized by the Foreign Ministry. The meeting chaired by the deputy prime minister Mesut Yılmaz on 19 February 2002 was held by the ABGS. The aim of these meetings was to bring together NGOs, academics, and representatives of the media and interest groups in order to discuss the issues to be raised in the Convention (The European Convention 2002b). These meetings launched a mobilization campaign, which sought to attract more public attention and participation. The İKV took on the role of an umbrella organization coordinating the activities of several working groups that were discussing the issues on the agenda of the European Convention and presented a report summarizing the conclusions that were reached during the working group meetings (İktisadi Kalkınma Vakfı 2002).

The report is the only one of its kind which provides a fairly developed opinion about a possible constitutional agreement for the EU. It supports the merging of the constituting agreements of the Union into a constitutional agreement rather than the development of a separate draft constitution (İktisadi Kalkınma Vakfı 2002b, c). It is noteworthy here that the position of the report with respect to institutional reform did not demonstrate a great divergence from the conservative, *status quo*-oriented governmental position. Not surprisingly, the report also argues for an enhanced role for national parliaments. Many themes in the report were subsequently taken up by the Turkish government as well as parliamentary representatives at the Convention.

Overall, the number of NGOs interested in the work of the Convention was limited, so one should look for quality – rather than quantity – of societal mobilization. Seventeen NGOs attended the initial meeting organized by ABGS and contributed to the efforts of İKV to develop a common approach to the Convention (The European Convention 2002). One great difficulty was that few NGO members were knowledgeable about the Convention to any significant degree. Hence, the views adopted on these issues were restricted to generalities and often to ideas borrowed from opinions expressed by others at the Convention. NGOs, moreover, remained ambivalent on issues of federalism and supranationalism. However, this ambivalence was more often than not the product of the absence of a thorough understanding of the issues involved rather than any ideological preference. Furthermore, in general, it has also been difficult to identify an original civil society stance on the Convention. Indeed, on many issues, the views and opinions of most of the NGOs were quite similar to those held by the government and the parliamentary representatives.

Public Debate and Public Opinion

In contrast to the low interest in the European Convention, there is a lively debate in Turkey on EU–Turkish relations and Turkey's prospects of membership. However, even then this topic has not yet produced robust mobilization. There have been times when the public has been energetically engaged in a discussion of EU related issues – followed, however, by periods of lack of attention. High interest coincided with periods preceding governmental and parliamentary activity to adopt reforms in support of the Copenhagen Criteria or critical EU meetings dealing with issues pertaining to Turkish accession. It would not be an exaggeration to say that the only time the Convention received extensive attention in the eyes of the public was when Valery Giscard d'Estaing made his remarks about Turkey's cultural incompatibility with Europe and the need to keep Turkey out of the EU. Otherwise, the Convention has only received brief and thin media coverage, mostly to report Turkish parliamentary and governmental participation. Surprisingly, even the repeated efforts of the Pope to include references to Christianity in the Constitution went almost unreported and were hardly debated.[15]

There have been several opinion polls conducted on Turkish citizens about the EU. Although none of these surveys dealt with the Convention, they can nevertheless give an idea about Turkish public opinion in respect to some of the critical issues debated – and especially on Turkish membership. According to the results of a survey conducted by TESEV on 3,060 respondents across Turkey during late May and early June 2002, the Turkish public is very supportive of membership and primarily sees integration with Europe as a process that will improve Turkish democracy and economic prosperity. Yet, the survey also demonstrates that Turks have little detailed knowledge about the EU. Furthermore, they also feel that the EU is biased against Turkey and doubt that it would ever accept Turkey for membership even if it were to meet all the necessary criteria. This doubt was also accompanied by 49 per cent of respondents who thought that the EU was an exclusively Christian Club with no room for a Muslim Turkey (TESEV 2002).

CONCLUSION

Since Turkey received candidate status for EU membership, interest in European integration and the EU has been increasing. Furthermore, the public at large and many sections of Turkish civil society have expressed extensive support for membership of the EU, as well as for domestic political reforms needed to meet the Copenhagen Criteria. In the run up to the Copenhagen summit of December 2002, there was a concerted effort both by the government and civil society groups to mobilize support among member countries for a date for accession talks to start. However, this intense activity and enthusiasm has not spilled over to the constitutional debate on Europe. Political mobilization on the Convention was limited to a number of MPs and representatives of government agencies. With the exception of the deputy prime minister, before the November 2002 elections political party leaders did not pay attention to the Convention. The contributions of Turkish official representatives to the debate surrounding the main issues addressed by the Convention were conservative and *status quo*-oriented. The few inputs provided into the future of Europe debate did not reveal much enthusiasm for supranationalism and the deepening of integration. Turning to state–society relations, we are able to conclude that the Convention was instrumental in raising domestic standards of transparency and consultation.

Civil society interest was limited, with some exceptions. As we argued above, mobilization was scarce in terms of quantity. What about quality, then? Frankly, the impact of Turkish social mobilization on the discussions and deliberations taking place within the Convention (see, for example, Piana, this issue) were negligible. Furthermore, there were no distinct contributions to the debate on institutional reform, the future of the EU and the draft EU constitution that would set civil society opinion apart from those advocated by the official representatives. General public interest, on the other hand, was close to zero. There was very little media coverage, and no debate around the central issues being addressed at the Convention.

One theme raised by Lucarelli and Radaelli in their introduction to this issue is whether poor mobilization is the result of poor state–society relations or the consequence of an elitist Union. We would like to stress the latter point in this conclusion. The elitist nature of the work of the Convention was quite succinctly put by the *Economist* when it suggested that the Constitution of the EU should start with the 'WE THE elites …' rather than 'We the people …' (*Economist*, 2 March 2002). This elitist nature of the exercise clearly also accounts for an important aspect of the lack of interest – an interest that would require quite a sophisticated understanding of what is after all a very complex project. This is the kind of understanding that is only beginning to develop in Turkey. For now, the Turkish government, civil society and the public at large will see the Convention solely through the perspective of how the debates and decisions of the Convention relates to Turkey's place in Europe and its prospects of eventual EU membership. Under these circumstances, Turkey was more at the margin of the Convention rather than at the centre of the debates and decision-making processes.

However, participation in the Convention proceedings gave Turkish MPs, political parties and some NGOs an opportunity to develop links with their European counterparts and start to become, even if in an extremely modest way, part of the politics of European integration. As for the general public's interest in EU affairs, it will undoubtedly increase in 2005 if Turkey starts its accession negotiations at that time.

NOTES

1. *'Pour ou contre l'adhesion de la Turquie a l'Union europeenne'* [For or against the accession of Turkey into the European Union], *Le Monde*, 8 November 2002, online edition, www.lemonde.fr/article/0,5987,3210-297386-,00.html; 'Turkey is not a European country, says Giscard', *EUObserver*, 8 November 2002, online edition, www.euobserver.com/index.phtml?aid = 8315.
2. 'Pope urges Europe to remember religious heritage', *EUObserver*, 15 November 2002, online edition, www.euobserver.com/index.phtml?aid = 8378; 'Pope: Christian roots in future EU constitution', *EUObserver*, 17 February 2003, online edition, www.euobserver.com/index.phtml?aid = 9404.
3. A further analysis of the problems experienced within the coalition with respect to the EU is provided by Avcı (2003).
4. AKP was formed by politicians who had previously been associated with two political parties – *Refah* (Welfare) and *Saadet* (Prosperity) – that had Islamist political leanings. However, during the election campaign and since they have been in power, the leadership has been trying to distance itself from this Islamist past. The party is supportive of further democratization in Turkey and the adoption of the remaining reforms to meet the Copenhagen Criteria of the EU. The party is also publicly committed to EU membership and is energetically engaged in efforts to achieve this end. See Çarkoğlu (2002).
5. For a recent evaluation of EU–Turkish relations, see Çarkoğlu and Rubin (eds.) (2003).
6. On 14 April 2003 Gunter Verheugen, the commissioner responsible for EU enlargement, noted that if Turkey completes its reforms and gets its accession negotiations started in 2005 then membership should occur around 2011 or 2012.
7. *'Vural gitti Sungar Geldi'* [Vural is gone. Sunar came], *Radikal*, 28 December 2002, online edition, www.radikal.com.tr/veriler/2002/12/28/haber_61025.php.
8. The website of the agency is www.euturkey.org.tr, which has a special page on the Convention.
9. Based on interviews with parliamentary representatives. A similar observation was also made by Zeynep Göğüş (*'Konvansiyon'daanayasahukukçusudaolmalıydı'* [There should have been a Constitutional Lawyer in the Convention], *Hürriyet*, 21 Jan. 2003, online edition; www.hurriyetim.com.tr/arsivim/1,p ~ 1,00.asp).
10. For an analysis of the views of Turkish parliamentarians about the EU, see McLaren and Müftüler-Baç (2003).
11. See www.avrupahareketi2002.org.tr.
12. *'Avrupa Birliği Üyeliği Sürecinde Siyasi Kriterler: Sivil Perspektif'* [The Political Criteria on the Accession Process to the European Union: A Civil Perspective], 2–3 May 2003, The Marmara, Istanbul. The conference was organized by the Turkish branch of the Helsinki Citizens Assembly and the Turkish branch office of the Heinrich Böll

Foundation. It was attended by almost one hundred representatives of NGOs, prominent members of the media and academics.

13. *Radikal*, 6 December 2002, online edition, www.radikal.com.tr/veriler/2002/12/06/sayfa_4.php.

14. '*Bu da AB karşıtı* cepheden bildiri' [This is the declaration from the Euro-sceptic front], *Radikal*, 4 July 2002, online edition, www.radikal.com.tr/veriler/2002/07/04/haber_42318.php.

15. The only references that we could find in a large number of Turkish newspapers surveyed was: '*Avrupa Hıristiyan mı?*' [Is Europe Christian?], *Abhaber*, 2003, available at www.abhaber.com/nilgun/nilgun_yorum4.htm; '*TanrıAB'ye köstek oluyor*' [God is obstructing the EU], *Radikal*, 01 March 2003, available at www.radikal.com.tr/veriler/2003/03/01/haber_67619.php; and '*Papa : AB AnayasasıHıristiyanlığı esas almalı*' [Pope: The EU Constitution should be based on Christianity], *Zaman*, 8 July 2002, available at www.zaman.com.tr/2002/07/08/dis/h1.htm.

REFERENCES

Ahmad, F. (1993): *The Making of Modern Turkey*, London and New York: Routledge.

Arat, T. and S. Baykal (2001): '*AB'yle İlişkiler* [Relations with the EU]', in B. Oran (ed.), *Türk dış politikası: Kurtuluş Savaşından bugüne olgular, belgeler, yorumlar* [Turkish Foreign Policy: phenomenon, documents and interpretations since the Independence War], İstanbul: İletişim, pp.326–65.

Avcı, G. (2002): 'Putting the Turkish EU Candidacy into Context', *European Foreign Affairs Review* 7/1, pp.91–140.

Avcı, G. (2003): 'Turkey's Slow EU Candidacy: Insurmountable Hurdles to Membership or Simple Euro-scepticism?', *Turkish Studies* 4/1, pp.149–70.

Balkır, C. and M.A. Williams (eds.) (1993): *Turkey and Europe*, London: Pinter Publishers Ltd.

Buzan, B. and T. Diez (1999): 'The European Union and Turkey', *Survival* 41/1, pp.41–57.

Cem, I. (2002): 'Turkish Reflections on the Future of the European Union', available at www.europa.eu.int/futurum/documents/contrib/conturkey_en.htm.

Commission of the European Communities (2001): 'Regular Report on Turkey's Progress Towards Accession', available at www.europa.eu.int/comm/enlargement/report2001/tu_en.pdf.

Çarkoğlu, A. (2002): 'Turkey's November 2002 Elections: A New Beginning', *Middle East Review of International Relations* 6/4, pp.30–41.

Çarkoğlu, A. and B. Rubin (eds.) (2003): *Turkey and The European Union*, London: Frank Cass.

Dunér, B. and E.Deverell (2001): 'Country Cousin: Turkey, the European Union and Human Rights', *Turkish Studies* 2/1, pp.1–24.

Eralp, A. (1997): '*Soğuk Savaş'tan Günümüze Türkiye – Avrupa Birliği İlişkileri*' [Turkey – EU Relations since the Cold War], in A. Eralp (ed.), *Türkiye ve Avrupa* [Turkey and Europe], İstanbul: İmge Yayınları.

The European Convention (2002): 'Report on National Debate on the future of Europe: Turkey', 28 June, available at: www.register.consilium.eu.int/pdf/en/02/cv00/00166en2.pdf.

The European Convention (2003): 'Address by Mr. Abdullah Gül, Minister of Foreign Affairs of the Republic of Turkey at the Plenary Session of the Convention', 15–16 May, available at www.european-convention.eu.int/docs/speeches/9091.pdf.

Hale, W. (2000): *Turkish Foreign Policy, 1774–2000*, London: Frank Cass.

İktisadi Kalkınma Vakfı, (2002a): '*16–30 Nov. 2002 IKV Bülteni*' [İKV Bulletin], available at www.ikv.org.tr.

190   MOBILIZING POLITICS AND SOCIETY?

İktisadi Kalkınma Vakfı (2002b): 'Türk Sivil İnsiyatifi Perspektifinden AB'nin Yeniden Yapılanmasına Katkılar] [The contributions to the restructuring of the EU from the perspective of the Turkish Civil initiative], available at www.ikv.org.tr/turkiye-ab/guncel/turkce-konvansiyon.htm.

İktisadi Kalkınma Vakfı (2002c): 'Speech of Meral Gezgin Eriş, European Convention Civil Society Session, Development Group, 24-25 June 2002', available at www.ikv.org.tr/faaliyetler/temsil-faaliyetleri/temsil.html.

İktisadi Kalkınma Vakfı (2002d): 'Türkiye Platformu Brüksel Toplantısı açıklaması' [The Brussels declaration of the Turkish Platform], 27 November 2002, available at www.ikv.org.tr/faaliyetler/toplantilar/toplantilar.html.

Kalaycıoğlu, E. (2001): 'Turkish Democracy: Patronage versus Governance', Turkish Studies 2/1, pp.54-70.

Kalaycıoğlu, E. (2002a): 'State and Civil Society in Turkey: Democracy, Development and Protest', in A.B. Sajoo (ed.), Civil Society in the Muslim World, London: I.B Tauris Publishers.

Kalaycıoğlu, E. (2002b): 'Civil Society in Turkey Continuity or Change?', in B. Beeley (ed.), Turkish Transformation: New Century – New Challenges. The Eothen Press.

Karluk, R. (1996): Avrupa Birliği ve Türkiye [The European Union and Turkey], İstanbul: İstanbul Menkul Kıymetler Borsası.

Kirişci, K. (2004): 'The Kurdish Question and Turkish Foreign Policy', in L. Martin (ed.), The Future of Turkish Foreign Policy, Cambridge, MA: MIT press, pp.277-314.

Kirişci, K. and G. Winrow (1997): The Kurdish Question and Turkey, London: Frank Cass.

Klauss, S. (2000): 'European Parliament in the EU External Relations: The Customs Union with Turkey', European Foreign Affairs Review 5/2, pp.215-37.

Lewis, B. (2002): The Emergence of Modern Turkey, 3rd edn, New York: Oxford University Press.

McLaren, M.L. and M. Müftüler-Baç (2003): 'Turkish Parliamentarians' Perspectives on Turkey's Relations with the European Union', Turkish Studies 4/1, pp.195-218.

Müftüler-Bac, M. (1998): 'The Never Ending Story: Turkey and the European Union', Middle Eastern Studies 34/4, pp.240-58.

Nationalist Action Party (2002): Parti Programı [Party programme], available at www.mhp.org.tr/Tanitim/Prg&Tzk/Program.htm#_Toc511564256.

Norton, R.A. (ed.) (1995): Civil Society in the Middle East, Vol.1, Leiden: Brill.

Norton, R.A. (ed.) (1996): Civil Society in the Middle East, Vol.2, Leiden: Brill.

Oder, B.E. (2002): 'Enhancing the Human Face of Constitutional Reality in Turkey through Accession Partnership with the EU', in B. Dunér (ed.), Turkey: The Road Ahead?, Stockholm: The Swedish Institute of International Affairs.

Rumford, C. (2000): 'From Luxembourg to Helsinki: Turkey, the Politics of EU Enlargement and Prospects for Accession', Contemporary Politics 6/4, pp.331-43.

Rumford, C. (2001): 'Human Rights and Democratization in Turkey in the Context of EU Candidature', Journal of European Area Studies 9/1, pp.93-105.

Tarih Vakfı (2001): 'VIII. STK Sempozyumu 'Türkiye-AB Bütünleşmesinde STK'ların Rolü" [The Eighth Civil Society Symposium 'The Role of Civil Society Organizations in the Integration of EU-Turkey'), May, Istanbul.

Tekeli, İ and S. İlkin (1993): Türkiye ve Avrupa Topluluğu [Turkey and the European Community], Vols 1-2, Ankara: Ümit.

Tekeli, İ and S. İlkin (2000): Avrupa Birliği ve Türkiye [European Union and Turkey], Vol.3.

TESEV (2002): 'Türk Halkının Avrupa Üyeliğine Bakışı' [The Perspectives of the Turkish Public on Membership to the European Union], available at www.tesev.org.tr/temmuz2002/t1.html.

TESEV (2003): 'Türk Halkının Avrupa Birliğine Bakışı – Haziran 2002' [The Perspectives of the Turkish Public on membership to the European Union – June 2002], available at www.tesev.org.tr/basin/ab2002.php.

Toprak, B. (1996): 'Civil Society in Turkey', in A. Norton (ed.), Civil Society in the Middle East, Vol.2, Leiden: Brill.

TÜRKİS (2001): 'AB Türkiye'den Ne İstiyor?' [What does the European Union want from Turkey?], December 2001, available at: www.turkis.org.tr/AB%20RAPORU.doc.
Udum, Ş (2002): 'Turkey and the Emerging European Security Framework', *Turkish Studies* 3/2, pp.69–103.
Yerasimos, S. (2001): '*Sivil Toplum, Avrupa ve Türkiye* [Civil Society, Europe and Turkey]', *Türkiye'de Sivil Toplum ve Milliyetçilik* [Nationalism and Civil Society in Turkey], İstanbul: Fransız Anadolu Araştırmaları Enstitüsü.

Regions and the Convention on the Future of Europe

MICHAEL KEATING

INTRODUCTION: EUROPE AND THE REGIONS

The theme of a Europe of the Regions is a recurrent one (Keating and Hooghe 2001; Bullman 1994; Jeffery 1997). It first emerged in the 1970s, with concerns, particularly on the part of the German Länder, that the concentration of powers in the Council of Ministers would allow their domestic government – by going through Europe – to encroach on matters of Land competence (Gerstenlauer 1985). It reappeared from the mid 1980s, with the advance of the European Community (EC) into new functional areas as a result of the Single European Act; the fear in peripheral regions that the single market could marginalize them at the expense of wealthy and more developed regions; and the bargaining over the reformed Structural Funds. This phase persisted until the Treaty of European Union, which perhaps represented the high tide of regional mobilization. In the reforms of 1988 and 1993 the size of the Structural Funds was increased and the Commission sought to transform them into an instrument of genuine Community policy, rather than an intergovern-mental transfer mechanism, and partnership arrangements were put in place to allow regions to engage in a dialogue with Europe. This certainly contributed to regional mobilization and introduced Europe as a central theme in debates on regionalism within member states (Hooghe 1996). The Treaty on European Union established the Committee of the Regions (CoR), and met a long-standing demand of the Länder by permitting a regional minister to represent a state in the Council of Ministers where matters of regional competence were at stake (Jeffery 2000). Since this phase, there has perhaps been a certain renationalization of regional policies and representation. CoR, while becoming an established part of the European Union (EU) architecture, has not satisfied the more ardent regionalists and suffers from a division between regional and municipal representatives (Christiansen 1996). Member states have reasserted their role in the design and implementation of Structural Funds measures, although the policy has by no means been completely renationalized.

The debate has now been reopened, largely as a result of three factors: the new debate on a European constitution and the challenge of democratizing the EU; the Commission's need to reduce its administrative overload while improving efficiency; and the rise of strong regions within several member states. Further impetus is given by the pressures of enlargement and changing thinking about regional development and policies.

The big questions at stake here, as in the debate over Europe more generally, are those of efficiency, democracy and solidarity. More specifically, debate has focused on the political and constitutional role of the regions, and on the future of regional policy. It is these issues that this contribution addresses.

THE RISE OF REGIONS IN EUROPE

In the last 20 years European space, dominated for so long by nation states and their boundaries, has been transformed by the twin processes of supranational integration and the rise of regions as new spaces within states – and, in many cases, across the old state borders. Regions have emerged in several distinct but related ways (Le Galès and Lequesne 1997). The first relates to functional change, notably in economic development and change, which is increasingly recognized as a territorial process in which the distinct characteristics of regions and localities are a vital element in adaptation. Regions are now presented as production systems located not just within national economic space but also within the European and global marketplace, where they compete with other regions for investment, markets and technology. The traditional model of regional policy in which regions were seen as complementary within national economies has largely given way to one in which regions compete within European and global markets, undermining the integrative capacity of the state.

Regions have also emerged as political spaces, especially where there is a strong culture or sense of identity – as in the historic or stateless nations. Europe has had an effect here too. In some cases it has transformed demands for autonomy or self-determination by providing a new political and discursive space in which they might be articulated. Ideas of shared and limited sovereignty, at the heart of the European debate, have struck a chord in stateless nations and regions which cannot or do not wish to aspire to full independence; they also chime well with historic traditions of mixed and limited sovereignty in many of these places. So, both in the Europe of the 15 and in the accession countries, minorities and regions have invested a lot in the idea of a new Europe of multiple levels.

Regions, moreover, have developed as distinct civil societies, with a decentralization of interest articulation, while social movements have often been attracted to the local and regional level as one that is less dominated by existing political elites, hence is potentially penetrable. At the same time, European issues are increasingly appreciated and judged within a regional or local – rather than a purely national – framework. In some cases, therefore, the region is becoming a significant level for interest intermediation and social compromise.

Finally, regions have been institutionalized in all the large member states and to some degree in the smaller ones as well (Loughlin 2001). There is a wide range of types of regional government across the EU. In Northern Europe, the larger states have established general-purpose regional governments. Germany, Belgium and Austria are federal states, although their form of federalism varies considerably. Belgium has devolved power both to regions and to language communities, which largely correspond in Flanders but not on the French side. In Southern Europe, regions have served in part as a way of reforming Napoleonic state structures, with their strong central-municipal linkages. Spain and the United Kingdom are multinational states with a devolving of power to the nations and regions. In Spain, there is universal devolution, albeit with some differences among the autonomous communities. Notably, the Basque Country and Navarre have a large measure of fiscal autonomy. In the United Kingdom, Scotland has a Parliament with legislative and administrative powers over all matters not reserved by the centre; Northern Ireland has an Assembly with a similar but not identical pattern of competences; and Wales has a National Assembly with administrative powers only. In the regions of England there are indirectly elected advisory assemblies, but pressure is being applied to convert these into elected governments. France and Italy are regionalized unitary states, although there are movements of change here. In France, proposals for a special status for Corsica were advanced by the Jospin government. While these did not survive the change of government in 2002, the new prime minister, Raffarin, has come up with a new set of proposals which would constitutionalize regions and allow them more autonomy, including some ability to modify national norms. In Italy, the direct election of regional presidents has raised the political profile of regions and they are in the process of gaining more powers under a process initiated by the centre-left government but radically reoriented by the centre-right after 2001. The remaining states are unitary, but in the Nordic countries there is a strong role for municipal government.

The powers and responsibilities of regional governments also vary greatly. Some have primary legislative powers while others have only administrative competences. All have a growing role in economic development and planning while some have more extensive social, environmental and regulatory responsibilities. In some regions, there are distinct and well-articulated civil societies, with a range of territorial interest groups and a sense of common identity among the population and economic and social actors. Some are well organized around a development project, drawing in actors from public and private sectors, while others are have shown a lesser capacity for collective action in the face of competitive pressures. Within some states, the main focus of territorial identity and collective action is the city or city region; in others, the state itself remains the overwhelmingly most important point of reference. This all makes it very difficult to provide for a single or uniform treatment of regional or local government across the EU. Complicating matters still further is the fact that government itself is changing as part of the transformation of the nation state.

THE TRANSFORMATION OF GOVERNMENT

European integration and regional/local decentralization are now recognized as two aspects of the same process. This is the transformation of the old model of the nation state into a complex, multilevel polity. National economies are both internationalizing and regionalizing. New economic regions are emerging across national boundaries. Spatial planning and infrastructure provision must take account both of emerging regional economic spaces and of the wider European picture. Environmental problems are transnational in scope but local in their impact. Social cohesion is potentially undermined by economic globalization and European integration as regions and localities compete for investment, with the risk of 'social dumping'. On the other hand, regions and localities may represent new spaces of social solidarity and cohesion.

The EU is emerging as a powerful level of government in its own right, while government is being decentralized – with the establishment of an intermediate or regional tier and the strengthening of local levels. Civil society is also being reconstituted at multiple levels. It is increasingly autonomous from the state and an important site for citizen expression and collective action. A new system of governing is emerging, which is not organized hierarchically like the old state with a clear division of competences among levels. Rather, tasks are shared among all levels (European, state, regional and local) and between the state and civil society.

This gives us a new model of government, which is difficult to fit into the conventional categories – whether of federal or unitary states. Attempts to theorize the new dispensation with ideas like 'governance' or 'multilevel governance' have not provided us with a new paradigm to replace the old one. The changes to the political order do, however, raise five key issues. 1) There is the 'democratic deficit', as policy-making becomes more complex and escapes the limits of national political institutions and citizens find it harder to participate. 2) There is a problem of efficiency, as policy making and implementation becomes more complex and spans several levels. Old frameworks and levels for policy-making no longer correspond with the requirements of changing social and economic systems. The EU, in particular, faces questions about the efficiency of its administration and the efficacy of its policies. 3) Despite the trend of decentralization in individual states, centralization may increase as there is a tendency to respond to transnational integration by taking more powers and competences to the European level. 4) Social solidarity may be threatened as regions compete for investment and the nation state loses its redistributive capacity. 5) Finally, European integration and the single market may threaten cultural diversity and pluralism.

Various responses to these problems have been suggested. One is a renationalization of functions and a reinforcement of the intergovernmental method of policy-making. This, though, is to ignore the shift of basic functions from the state level to Europe and to the regions and localities. Member state governments are not capable of reflecting the diversity of Europe, nor of delivering policies geared to the needs of localities. Another repeated suggestion is a list of competences at several levels so as to constitute a new federal polity with clear lines of authority and accountability. German Länder have often been keen on this model. Yet, it ignores the changes in the way government operates in the modern world. Traditional divisions of competences are no longer relevant and needs are constantly changing. Any list of competences would have to be framed in rather general terms, and would have to recognize the role of local and regional governments as well as member states. A third approach recognizes the complexity of European policy-making and the need for cooperation and deliberation at all levels. Rather than trying to limit the intrusion of Europe into the regions, it seeks to increase the role of the regions and localities in Europe across the range of matters that have a regional and local impact. There needs to be a partnership across levels and spheres of action in order to seek the best solutions to problems and to encourage innovation and the diffusion of best practice. It is in this third approach, which characterizes the Community method, that regions and local governments have most to contribute, since they have long had to work in much the same way. This is also an approach that comes more instinctively to Southern European countries, used as they are to working in systems of centralized government in which there are complex patterns of influence, including territorial influence, and no clear division of powers.

DEBATING THE CONVENTION

Despite its relevance to the broader challenges facing regions, the Convention on the future of Europe has not featured prominently in political debate in most European regions, nor been the subject of much media attention. Such media attention that the Convention has received has often been misleading, perhaps due to a lack of understanding of the way it works – for instance, on the role of working groups or the search for consensus. This, it should be said, is equally true at member state level. Nonetheless, a number of regions established forums and working groups on the Convention. These were often opened to civil society, as in the Basque and Catalan Conventions on Europe and the Forum on the Convention in Tuscany. In some cases, academics played a prominent role in producing proposals. Academics were active in the Catalan Convention, and the Flemish government's proposals were produced by a working party with a strong academic presence. Political parties were also active to varying degrees. State-level political parties gave relatively little attention to the regional dimension of the Convention. Regionalist and sub-state nationalist parties, mostly represented in the European Free Alliance, were more concerned, but often tended to confine themselves to generalities rather than coming up with specific proposals.

The impact of regional debates was reduced by the fact that many of them were launched in the second half of 2002, simultaneously with the Convention and too late to influence its early debates. For example, reports from the Catalan and the Basque conventions appeared in the early part of 2003, along with the debate on the draft treaty – rather late to introduce new ideas (see León, Mateo Diaz and Meseguer, this issue). The Basque report itself was caught up in the polarized politics of the region and was voted down in the parliament by an unholy alliance of unionists and extreme nationalists. Not all of the regional debates, though, focus on the role of regions in the decision-making process of the EU. In Tuscany, for example, the emphasis was on citizenship and rights across the board.

Furthermore, debates at the regional level were not generally linked well to debates at the member state level, which tended to focus on the link between the EU and the member states. In some states, domestic matters have dominated discussion of regional issues, crowding out the European dimension. Italy has had a vigorous debate over current constitutional reforms, pitting the centre-right government against the centre-left opposition, but the European Convention has rarely been mentioned in this debate. Spain has been preocuppied by the Basque conflict, but this is presented at the state level as a purely Spanish question – although the Basques have sought to Europeanize it. In the United Kingdom the devolution reforms of 1999 were explicitly designed to include a European dimension, and there has been a debate on how well Scotland is represented in Europe, particularly on agriculture and fisheries matters – but this was not channeled into the Convention. The British parties in Scotland rely on keeping good relations with London, while the Scottish National Party sees the answer as independence in Europe rather than a stronger regional role in a multilevel system. Belgium is an exception, since the structure of national politics makes it impossible to ignore the regional question. There has been some linkage in Germany, although Länder are divided between more Europhile and Euro-sceptic attitudes. More often, however, there has been a vague tendency to invoke Europe in order to justify positions in domestic politics, or to call for a radical reordering of the European order as a means of escaping the state straitjacket, without offering a detailed consideration of exactly what the Convention could and could not offer.

Clearly, the Convention was of greater importance to those regions that cannot easily access Europe through their national political systems. In Germany, Austria and Belgium, the main focus continued to be the national level and a concern to retain their present status, with the right to participate up to the Council of Ministers. Southern European countries, without this channel of access, tended to stress the need for new opportunities in the proposed constitution. In the smaller countries without a regional level, debate was focused on the local and municipal level. This is notably true in the Nordic countries, where there has been an emphasis on citizenship issues.

In contrast to the poor linkage of regional debates into national debates, there has been a substantial pan-European debate linking regions and localities and generating some new ideas. There is CoR, with its various subcommittees, and a series of bilateral and multilateral contacts. These include meetings among regional parliaments and their European committees. Inter-regional associations have been active in the debate, notably the Council of European Municipalities and Regions (CEMR), a federation of national associations, the Assembly of European Regions (AER), the Conference of Peripheral Maritime Regions (CPRM) and Eurocities. In addition, there is the more loosely organized conference of Regions with Legislative Powers (RegLeg) and the consortium of Constitutional Regions.

CoR was not given the right to nominate members to the Convention, but did have six observers. In practice, like the observers from candidate countries, these had full speaking rights and, as no votes were taken, this amounted to much the same as membership. Policy was made by the plenary meetings of CoR, through its Commission on Constitutional Affairs, and by meetings of the delegation itself. The fundamental cleavage between legislative regions and the rest made consensus difficult to attain and diminished the impact of CoR, but there was a continuing debate and the delegation was able to table a series of amendments to the draft constitution.

The European Parliament (EP) has traditionally been rather friendly to regional interests, as both were trying to secure a position against the intergovernmental logic of the Council and the weight of the Commission. More recently, they have turned not precisely into rivals, but into the focus for distinct visions of Europe. Ambitions to turn CoR into a second chamber, which would clearly undermine the EP, have largely disappeared, but there is still suspicion of regions among some parliamentarians. The Parliament's main contribution to the regional dimension of the Convention was the 2003 Napolitano Report, which contained some of the regions' demands about subsidiarity and access to the Court for CoR (see below), but caused wide offence by its generally suspicious tone. Perhaps excessively influenced by Italian experience, Napolitano wrote that regional lobbying 'can hardly be interpreted as a sign of solidarity towards other regions', and claimed that the regions with the strongest demands for autonomy were the richest, implying some rather base and selfish motives. Napolitano also suggested that fuller involvement of regions might overburden and complicate the decision-making process (Napolitano 2002). After discussion with CoR, these conclusions were modified, but the Parliament has not in general been a strong supporter of regional interests.

THE REGIONAL AGENDA

In the lead-up to the Maastricht Treaty of European Union, there was an important regional input, and three key concessions were gained: CoR; the right of regions to participate in the Council of Ministers according to national regulations; and the acceptance of subsidiarity, albeit in a rather vague form open to different intepretation by member state governments. This time around, there was less consensus on the demands, and a greater variation in approaches and strategies. This reflects the wide variation in the status and role of sub-member state governments and the different goals and strategies of regional and local actors.

Within plurinational states like the United Kingdom, Spain or Belgium, there are many people who see Europe as a means of accommodating the nationalites question in a new, asymmetrical and open order. They point to the diffusion and sharing of sovereignty as an essential element of the EU and look to a 'third way' between historic demands for independence on the one hand, and decentralization within the state on the other. The emphasis here is on a new model of the state and Europe, beyond the usual nation state, federalist, or intergovernmental formulas. This underlay the strategy of the Catalan Convention, the Flemish proposals and recent proposals from the Basque Country. It is also widely favoured within the parties of the European Free Alliance. The United Kingdom, which already has a highly asymmetrical constitution, is perhaps moving in this direction, although the fact that the same political party currently dominates at all levels has reduced the scope for differentiation and variety. The Basque government ties this new model into the search for peace and stability by calling for a European capacity for intervention in nationality conflicts. Such a Europe would be asymmetrical and highly differentiated by culture, constitutional status and divisions of powers. Most members of the Convention, including those from regions without a strong cultural identity or national aspiration, found this argument unacceptable.

Others, like many of the German Länder, look to a federal Europe organized on similar lines to Germany, with two linked layers of government or, in federal states, three. In Italy, on the other hand, there has been a rather confused debate about federalism, which most politicians support rhetorically but which they interpret very differently. For many on the centre-left, it seems to mean no more than administrative decentralization, while on the centre-right there is a barely concealed division between the former separatists and old-fashioned centralists. In France, while there has been a recent initiative for regional decentralization, the word 'federalism' is still largely taboo.

A third position is found among municipal governments, which put less emphasis on constitutional issues and more on the key role of localities in service delivery and implementation of national and European regulations. They also emphasize the role of municipalities as democratic spaces and expressions of citizenship and participation.

Besides these diverging ideas, there is also division over the future of Europe itself. Some regions, including some German Länder, have become a little Euro-sceptic and emphasize the dangers of Europe extending its competences at their expense. They have sought to limit the competences of the EU, demanding a strict and exclusive division among the three levels and a retrenchment of EU powers. The Resolution of the Presidents of Parliaments of the German Federal States, 3–4 June 2002, is a powerful expression of this attitude. Other regions have emphasized the need for greater participation within European institutions. They accept that exclusive divisions of competence are not possible in modern systems of government and that flexibility is needed to cope with new demands. The important point is that regions should be part of the emerging system of complex and multilevel policy-making. One might sum up the difference in saying that some regions want to get Europe out of the region, while others want to get the region into Europe.

A persistent division has occurred between the Regions with Legislative Powers (RegLeg) and the other regional and municipal governments. The RegLeg group include regions in Germany, Belgium, Austria, Italy and the United Kingdom. Their argument is that they have direct responsibility for the transmission of directives and implemention of a wide range of EU policies, putting them in some respects in the same category as member states. Much the same distinction is made by the Constitutional Regions (a group founded by Bavaria, Catalonia, North Rhine-Westphalia, Salzburg, Scotland, Flanders and Wallonia), who have argued for specific recognition in a European constitution. This would include rights of consultation, involvement in the legislative process, access to the Court of Justice and protection for subsidiarity. Parliaments of legislative and constitutional regions have also argued for recognition in a number of ways, including membership of the Conference of Community and European Affairs Committees (COSAC) and links with the EP. They also demanded equivalent rights for those that might be conceded to member state parliaments in the constitution, including participation in any second chamber or subsidiarity mechanism.

Other regions and municipalities object to any idea that the RegLeg should have special status. It is also objected that it is impossible to distinguish between legislative and non-legislative regions since the significance of legislation in modern government has changed so much and that regions with strong administrative powers may have as much real discretion as those with weak legislative powers. Further complications arise in the case of the National Assembly for Wales, which has only powers of secondary legislation, although this arguably puts it in the same category as Italian regions – which can only legislate within the limits of national law. Both are different from the Scottish parliament, which can repeal or amend any state law not lying within specified reserved powers. Nordic municipalities have been particularly resistant to the idea of regions with legislative powers – pointing out their extensive administrative responsibilities. RegLeg regions in turn note that they have municipal government, too, but that this is a different matter; indeed, in the German Länder and in Scotland the structure of municipal government itself is under the control of the Länder and the Scottish parliament. The categories of Regions with Legislative Powers and Constitutional Regions do not, it should be emphasized, correspond with that of stateless nations, but there is a strong link between the two as both have been arguing for a form of asymmetry, and in the case of Scotland or Catalonia, for example, the two criteria do come together and reinforce each other.

ISSUES IN THE CONVENTION

While there is, as noted above, a certain emerging Euro-scepticism among some regions, the majority feeling is that regionalists and Europhiles remain allies in the building of a new complex system of representation and government. Regions, with the exception of some of the German Länder, have continued to favour the Community method and supra-nationalism, but have emphasized that this must be within a decentralized and pluralistic Europe. Specifically, they have been concerned with six types of issue in which they can demonstrate a common interest.

Recognition

There has been a persistent effort to insert the regions and localities into the architecture of the new Europe. This runs against a general assumption that the Convention was about clarifying the division of responsibility between the EU and the member states, but it is a precondition both for the recognition of diversity and for more concrete proposals on individual items. Early drafts of the treaty, including Giscard d'Estaing's skeleton and the first drafts of the articles, made no mention of regions and localities, provoking a series of amendments that aimed system-atically to insert regions and localities alongside member states. Clauses on diversity and pluralism also attracted amendments, expanding these to include regional and local diversity. Many regions and CoR itself suggested a reference to the Council of Europe's Charter on Local and Regional Self-Government.

There was also considerable debate around terminology. Regions tried to avoid suggestions that the Union should be a Europe of the states – or nation states, preferring instead formulations such as 'peoples of Europe'. The use of the term 'nation' to apply only to states attracted particular criticism from the European Free Alliance, representing the stateless nations and minorities. The Catalan Convention demanded recognition for stateless nations as well as for Regions with Legislative Powers. For itself, CoR, demanded recognition as an 'institution', although this is of more symbolic than practical importance.

Consultation

Regions and localities have consistently complained about having to implement policies over which they have not been consulted and which can involve considerable cost. They have encountered some opposition here on the grounds that consultation is expensive and time-consuming and creates complexity. The response has been that consultation can improve the quality of policies, help them take into account diversity of conditions, enhance efficiency and secure better implementation. There can also be a democratic benefit. The impact of European policies is often felt by citizens in a local and regional context, and consultation in advance can improve the transparency of decision-making. Regions and localities are also important democratic spaces, providing the opportunity for citizens and stakeholders to make an input into policy.

The main vehicle for consultation is CoR, and it and other regional delegates therefore pressed for more advance consultation, including on draft legislation, and on extending the right of consultation into new fields. They also demanded that a failure to consult CoR on time and in full should result in the suspension of the action by the responsible institution pending transmission of CoR opinion.

Regions and CoR also asked for policies to be costed for their impact on regions and localities. In some versions, there was a demand that the EU provide financial resources for costs imposed by regulations, a measure obviously derived from some national practices. Since the EU does not have substantial free resources, however, this was unrealistic and was changed to a demand that the cost of regulations should at least be recognized and measured.

Subsidiarity

Subsidiarity has appeared repeatedly in the debate over the role of regions in the EU, despite the tendency of states to see it as referring only to them. Hitherto, it has remained more of a political than legal principle, although it did feature in the treaties. In the Convention there was a broad consensus on giving it legal force through a right to go to the Court of Justice when a government or parliament feels that an EU act has violated subsidiarity. Regions have demanded that, in addition to national parliaments, they should have the right to initiate such proceedings, but there is some disagreement as to how this would work. The RegLeg regions saw the issue as particularly relevant to themselves, given the danger of EU infringement of their legislative prerogatives, and demanded the same right for themselves. Other regions and municipalities saw this as another example of the RegLeg regions seeking special status, and insisted that the right be reserved to CoR, with an understanding within the Committee that it would take up cases passed on by legislative regions if asked. This proposal was included in the draft constitution, where its application is confined to CoR.

Decision-Making

European laws and directives often impinge on matters of regional competence, and this will continue no matter how competences are defined in a new treaty. Partnership among all levels will therefore continue to be the normal decision-making method. This applies particularly to regions with legislative powers, which often have the primary responsibility for applying directives and translating them into law. In practice, participation in decision-making is usually via member states, and it is there that regions need to exert pressure. There was no need for the Convention to introduce a clause allowing regional participation in the Council of Ministers, since this already exists, but at the discretion of member states. The Catalan Convention demanded that this should become the norm for regions with legislative powers, but there was no chance of the Convention trying to impose this on member states. The Spanish government regards participation by the Basques, in particular, in the Council as an impossibility. There was also a demand for early consultation on legislation, as opposed merely to policy proposals, and for a right of CoR to propose amendments. More ambitious still was a demand for participation by CoR in the legislative conciliation procedure where regional matters are at stake.

Implementation

It is often regional and local authorities who have the task of implementing EU policies over a range of matters. Yet, in the interests of simplicity, verification and control, the EU has tended to charge member states with responsibility for implementing policies and being accountable for any failure. Regions, on the other hand, have argued that efficiency, transparency and accountability can be enhanced by recognizing their role in this, and giving them greater freedom in interpreting directives, designing the appropriate instruments, and integrating them with their own policies and programmes. Member states have argued in favour of the greater use of framework laws, now recognized as a category in the proposed constitution. Regions, especially the RegLeg, have urged that similar latitude be given to them in interpretation and implementation. This is easy to concede as a general principle, as long as it is accompanied by statements about the constitutional requirements proper to each state, but in practice there are two problems: member states continue to be responsible for non-implementation and it is they who must answer to the Court of Justice; and the EU has also been unwilling to recognize intra-state as opposed to inter-state diversity in the application of laws and regulations. Yet, the different conditions that might justify different application may be as much between regions as between states, and the primary legislative responsibility might be at the regional and not the state level.

A more elaborate proposal has been pressed by French Member of European Parliament (MEP) Alain Lamassoure and already featured in the Commission's White Paper on Governance. This is that regions could be invited to become partners of the Union, with more room for manoeuvre in the implementation of programmes. From the White Paper this was taken forward in the form of tripartite contracts among the Commission, the member state and the region, which are being pioneered in environmental policy. Lamassoure, as a member of the Convention, continued to press the idea, but it did not have a prominent place in the debate. Some regions, moreover, have expressed the fear that tripartite contracts are a way for the member states to get into fields that are properly shared by the EU and the regions.

Radical Options

Most radical of all are proposals that will enable regions to use Europe to escape from the state altogether. For a long time, the Basque government has demanded 'direct' participation in the EU without specifying what this could mean; it might be anything from recognition as a member state to using the provision for regional participation in the Council of Ministers. In 2002, the Basque president unveiled a more detailed plan, which would provide for a 'freely associated state' with links both to Spain and to the EU. It is not clear exactly how this would work in practice, but it certainly goes beyond anything the Convention could discuss. Although the Basques say that the proposal is an elaboration on the Lamassoure proposal, it clearly exceeds this form of administrative decentralization. Proposals from the Flemish government and the Catalan Convention, that states be allowed to split their votes in the Council where the regions are participating rather than having to agree a common state position, were also outside the remit of the Convention and did not feature in the debate. More radical still and completely beyond the Convention was the idea of the European Free Alliance of 'internal enlargements' – that stateless nations should be able to accede to the Union by becoming independent.

REGIONS IN THE CONVENTION

The most consistent regional input into the Convention was through CoR, which insisted on its role as the only body speaking for all regional and local governments in Europe. It also insisted on the need to distinguish regional and local governments – as elected bodies – from civil society in general, despite various efforts to place it alongside voluntary groups and social movements. Yet, it remains internally divided, as noted, and there are other bodies and individuals speaking for specific regional and local concerns. The regional question was not high on the agenda from the beginning of the Convention, and an early decision was made not to set up a working group in this area, which would have provided a focus for the debate. There was one plenary session devoted to the regional and local issue, but even this was delayed as the previous session overran and there was an emergency debate on foreign and security policy linked to the crisis over Iraq. The session itself produced a disparate set of interventions rather than a focused debate. For example, representatives from the Åland islands, the Azores and the French overseas territories managed to raise their specific concerns before the broad issue of regions could be broached.

This was never expected to be the constitutional round for the regions, and they made modest progress. The alliance among regions that produced important gains at Maastricht has been partly broken by the strengthened position of some Northern European regions in their own national systems. Southern European regions still lack the possibility of representing the state in the Council of Ministers and so have pressed for a new multilevel Europe. Even within states, regions are divided on their interests and strategies. So in Spain, the Basques have been rather isolated because of domestic political conditions. Italian regions are divided between those controlled by the left and the right. Radical ideas about reconstituting Europe at multiple levels entered the debate only at the level of rhetoric, if at all. Stateless nations have gained no recognition and have been almost unrepresented within the Convention. The demands of the Legislative or Constitutional Regions – which sometimes overlap with stateless nations – for special recognition and a corresponding role in European policy-making, were articulated but not heeded. On the other hand, demands for renationalization and the drawing up of a rigid list of competences to keep Europe out of the regions made little progress either. Instead, CoR pressed a small number of issues, including symbolic recognition, a role in policing subsidiarity and greater consultation for regions in various ways. These modest demands were largely conceded at the Convention and are unlikely to be challenged at the Intergovernmental Conference. CoR may also gain symbolic recognition as an institution, so reinforcing its role as the channel of sub-member state representation. Given the scale of state transformation and the constitutional shifts visible within member states, this will hardly satisfy in the long term, and the issue is bound to come back in future rounds of constitutional reform.

REFERENCES

Bullman, U. (ed.) (1994): *Die Politik der dritten Ebene. Regionen im Prozeß der EG-Integration*, Baden Baden: NOMOS.

Christiansen, T. (1996): 'Second Thoughts on Europe's "Third Level": The European Union's Committee of the Regions', *Publius* 26/1, pp.93–116.

Gerstenlauer, H.-G. (1985): 'German Länder in the European Community', in M. Keating and B. Jones (eds.), *Regions in the European Community*, Oxford: Oxford University Press, pp.191–214.

Hooghe, L. (ed.) (1996): *Cohesion Policy and European Integration*, Oxford: Clarendon.

Jeffery, C. (ed.) (1997): *The Regional Dimension of the European Union: Towards a Third Level in Europe?* London: Frank Cass.

Jeffery, C. (2000): 'Sub-National Mobilization and European Integration', *Journal of Common Market Studies* 38/1, pp.1–24.

Keating, M. and L. Hooghe (2001): 'By-Passing the Nation-State? Regions and the EU Policy Process', in J. Richardson (ed.), *European Union. Power and Policy Making*, 2nd edn, London: Routledge.

Le Galès, P. and C. Lequesne (eds.) (1997): *Les paradoxes des régions en Europe*, Paris: La Découverte, [The Paradoxes of the Regions in Europe].

Loughlin, J. (2001): *Subnational Democracy in the European Union*, Oxford: Oxford University Press.

Napolitano, G. (2002): *Le rôle des pouvoirs régionaux et locaux dans la construction européenne*. PE 313.402.

The Participation and Representation of Women in the Debate on the Future of the European Union

MERCEDES MATEO DIAZ

INTRODUCTION

While the process of the Constitutional Convention in itself may well have represented a wide consultative and participatory exercise aimed at inclusion and dialogue (see Lucarelli and Radaelli, this issue), it is notable that the involvement of women participants was relatively small and low level. This raises the possibility of a democratic deficit in the process of European Union (EU) constitutional reform. Yet, with the questions of parity, quotas and gender mainstreaming high on the political agenda of a number of member states, it is rather surprising that the issue of women's participation (or lack of it) in the reform process was not highlighted more effectively.

This contribution will succinctly discuss some of the principles stated on paper, such as inclusion, participatory democracy and democratic equality, and what seems to appear as a gap in their effective accomplishment – at least by looking at very simple facts such as the composition of the Convention group itself. The discussion then briefly moves onto the arguments and empirical evidence that have been put forward to encourage an institutional sex-balance in other political and decision-making bodies. The contribution ends with a normative positioning on the issue.

STATEMENTS AND PRINCIPLES IN THE DEBATE ON THE FUTURE OF THE EUROPEAN UNION: A GAP BETWEEN THE DECLARATIONS 'ON PAPER' AND AN EFFECTIVE POLITICAL WILL?

The process of the Constitutional Convention was advertised as a widely consultative and participatory exercise aimed at inclusion and dialogue

This contribution has been developed from a seminar held by the Robert Schuman Centre for Advanced Studies at the European University Institute (EUI), Florence, on 19 November 2002, hosted jointly by the Gender Studies Programme and the EUI's Working Group on the Constitutional Convention. This research was supported through a European Community Marie Curie Fellowship. The author is solely responsible for information communicated and the European Commission is not responsible for any views or results expressed.

(see Shaw 2002). It was underpinned by two documents – the Laeken Declaration and the Charter of Fundamental Rights, which acted as building blocks in the dialogic process and which, importantly, address the Union's commitment to gender equality and participatory democracy. The Charter was accorded a special place in the debate on constitutional revision. Within its chapter on 'Equality' it sets out the principle of equality before the law (Article 20), the non-discrimination principle (Article 21), and the principle of equality between men and women (Article 23). Together with the Charter, the EU's Community Framework Strategy on Gender Equality (2001–05) – supposed to be one of the guiding lines of all EU activities, presents democracy as a fundamental value and establishes, as a condition for its full realization, equal participation and representation of women and men.[1]

The Laeken Declaration invokes the democratic challenge facing the EU and the acknowledgement that rethinking the Union is a process which must involve citizens and meet their expectations. Bringing the EU closer to its demos by improving and monitoring its democratic legitimacy and transparency is a theme which runs as a leitmotif through the Declaration and appears to require above all else a simplification of the Treaties. To this end, the preliminary draft of a constitutional treaty drawn up by the Praesidium and presented by its president at the plenary session on 28 October 2002 (CONV 369/02) and the draft Articles 1–16 presented on 6 February 2003 (CONV 528/03) provided a clarification of the constitutional basis of the EU. Furthermore, the draft text of 6 February 2003 already provided space in Article 5 for inclusion of the Charter of Fundamental Rights and, therefore, could be seen to envisage the principle of equality between men and women at the level of a constitutional right. After a significant amount of discussion on how and where it should be included, the Charter has finally been given space within Part II of the last version of the draft treaty, as submitted to the president of the European Council in Rome on 18 July 2003 (CONV 850/03).[2] A reference to the Charter was also added in Part I, Title II on fundamental rights and citizenship of the Union (Article 7-1).

Moreover, in Title VI of the draft of 28 October 2002, which concerned the democratic life of the Union, articles 33 and 34 provided respectively for the principles of democratic equality ('all Union citizens are equal *vis-à-vis* its institutions') and participatory democracy ('the institutions are to ensure a high level of openness, permitting citizens' organizations of all kinds to play a full part in the Union's affairs'). In its last version of 18 July 2003, former articles 33 and 34 have been both maintained and renumbered into articles 44 and 46 respectively. Interestingly enough, an intermediate article 45 was added providing for the principle of representative democracy, which, in its third paragraph, reinforced the former principle of participation ('every citizen shall have the right to participate in the democratic life of the Union').

There is, however, a distinct gap between this rhetoric of gender equality, democracy and participation and the reality of the Convention process. Despite the articulation in textual form of the twin principles of equality and participatory democracy, it is notable that the involvement of women participants in the Convention itself was relatively small and low level (see tables 1 to 3 below). This denotes a democratic deficit in the debate on EU constitutional reform which paradoxically coincides with the increasing visibility on national political agendas of initiatives regarding parity, quotas and gender mainstreaming.[3] These are emerging in recognition of the fact that national assemblies are basically unrepresentative of the major socio-economic components of society, to the point that political representation has been said to have an 'aristocratic character' (Manin 1996), and the composition of parliaments to be biased (Norris and Lovenduski 1995). That this bias is identifiable at the EU level too, despite the spirit and rhetoric of inclusion in the Convention process – and the texts which underpin it and are now being produced by it, is disappointing. Moreover, the gender gap looks decidedly at odds with Council Recommendation 96/694 EC on the balanced participation of women and men in the decision-making process and the Commission Decision of 19 June 2000 which addresses the gender balance of committees and expert groups within the Commission and contains a commitment to achieving a target of 40 per cent of women members.[4]

THE CONVENTION'S SEX-COMPOSITION

The composition of the Convention was constantly changing via new nominations. The Convention group was composed of 15 representatives of the heads of state or government of the member states (one from each member state), 13 representatives of the heads of state or government of the candidate states (one per candidate state), 30 representatives of the national parliaments of the member states (two from each member state), 26 representatives of the national parliaments of the accession countries (two from each candidate state), 16 members of the European Parliament (EP), and finally two representatives of the European Commission.[5] The Convention group members were then functionally distributed around three main bodies: a praesidium, a secretariat and the working groups.

TABLE 1
THE COMPOSITION OF THE CONVENTION BY SEX (FIGURES FOR
21 OCTOBER 2002)

Presidency	President: Mr Valéry Giscard d'Estaing	Vice-Presidents: Mr Giuliano Amato, Mr Jean-Luc Dehaene
	FEMALE MEMBERS	FEMALE ALTERNATES
Representatives of the heads of state or governments of the member states	3/15 20%	3/15 20%
Representatives of the national parliaments	3/30 10%	4/30 13.33%
Representatives of the European Parliament	5/16 31.25%	7/16 43.75%
Representatives of the European Commission	0/2 0%	0/2 0%
Representatives of the governments of the accession candidate countries	3/13 23.08%	1/13 7.69%
Representatives of the national parliaments of the accession candidate countries	3/26 11.54%	9/26 34.62%
Total	17/105 16.19%	24/105 22.85%
Observers	COMPOSITION	PER CENT
Committee of the Regions	2/6	33.3
Economic and Social Committee	1/3	33.3
European Social Partners	0/3	0
European Ombudsman	0/1	0
Total	3/13	23

Source: Own elaboration from primary data.

The figures in Tables 1, 2 and 3 represent the gender balance on 21 October 2002. Another check of the composition was made on 19 February 2003. While the difference is not great with regard to the members themselves, the number of female alternates was reduced notably among the candidate countries and there was also a cut in the number of women observers. The overall number of female members rose by one (up to 18/105, or 17.14 per cent). This change resulted from two women from Latvia being introduced as substitute representatives of the government and the national parliament, and a Turkish male parliamentary representative replacing a previous female nominee.

TABLE 2

THE COMPOSITION OF THE CONVENTION BY COUNTRY AND SEX (FOR THE 15 EU MEMBER STATES)

(FIGURES FOR 21 OCTOBER 2002)

COUNTRIES	Representatives of the heads of state or governments of the member states		Representatives of the national parliaments		Representatives of the European Parliament		TOTAL	
	FEMALE MEMBERS (1)	ALTERNATES (1)	FEMALE MEMBERS (2)	ALTERNATES (2)	FEMALE MEMBERS	ALTERNATES	FEMALE MEMBERS (1+2)	ALTERNATES (1+2)
Belgium	0	0	0	1	1		1/4 25%	1/3 33.3%
Denmark	0	0	0	0	0	2/2	0/4 0%	2/5 40%
Germany	0	0	0	0	1/3	0	1/6 16.6%	0/4 0%
Greece	0	0	1	0			1/3 33.3%	0/3 0%
Spain	1	1	0	0	0	0	1/4 25%	1/4 25%
France	0	0	0	0	0	1/2	0/4 0%	2/5 40%
Ireland	0	0	0	0		0	0/3 0%	0/4 0%
Italy	0	0	0	1	1/2	1	1/5 20%	1/4 25%
Luxembourg	0	0	0	1			0/3 0%	1/3 33.3%
Netherland	0	0	0	0	1		1/4 25%	0/3 0%
Austria	0	0	0	1	0	1/2	0/4 0%	2/5 40%
Portugal	0	0	1	0	0	1/2	1/4 25%	1/5 20%
Finland	1	0	0	1	0	1/2	1/4 25%	2/5 40%
Sweden	1	1	0	0			1/3 33.3%	1/3 33.3%
United Kingdom	0	1	1	0	1/3	0/2	2/6 33.3%	1/2 20%
Total	3/15 20%	3/15 20%	3/30 10%	4/30 13.33%	5/16 31.25%	7/16 43.75%	11/61 18%	14/61 22.95%

Source: Own elaboration from primary data.

TABLE 3
THE COMPOSITION OF THE CONVENTION BY COUNTRY AND SEX (FOR ACCESSION CANDIDATE COUNTRIES)
(FIGURES FOR 21 OCTOBER 2002)

COUNTRIES	Representatives of the governments of the accession candidate countries		Representatives of the national parliaments of the accession candidate countries		TOTAL	
	FEMALE MEMBERS (1)	ALTERNATES (1)	FEMALE MEMBERS (2)	ALTERNATES (2)	FEMALE MEMBERS (1+2)	ALTERNATES (1+2)
Cyprus	0	0	1	1	1/3 33.3%	1/3 33.3%
Malta	0	0	0	1	0/3 0%	1/3 33.3%
Hungary	0	0	0	0	0/3 0%	0/3 0%
Poland	1	0	0	2	1/3 33.3%	2/3 66.6%
Romania	1	0	1	0	1/3 33.3%	0/3 0%
Slovakia	0	0	0	1	1/3 33.3%	1/3 33.3%
Latvia	0	0	0	1	0/3 0%	1/3 33.3%
Estonia	0	0	0	1	0/3 0%	1/3 33.3%
Lithuania	0	0	0	1	0/3 0%	1/3 33.3%
Bulgaria	1	1	0	0	1/3 33.3%	1/3 33.3%
Czech Republic	0	0	0	0	0/3 0%	0/3 0%
Slovenia	0	0	0	1	0/3 0%	1/3 33.3%
Turkey	0	0	1	0	1/3 33.3%	0/3 0%
Total	3/13 23.08%	1/13 7.69%	3/26 11.54%	9/26 34.62%	6/39 15.4%	10/39 25.6%

Source: Own elaboration from primary data.

Among the alternates the number of women was reduced by three overall (down to 21/105, or 20 per cent). This change comprised the loss of a female Swede among the representatives of the heads of state or government and the loss of three female representatives of the national parliaments of the accession states (Latvia, Lithuania and Slovenia) but with the addition of a Czech female representative of the government. Among the observers there was a loss of one woman representing the Committee of the Regions (CoR), reducing the total to 2/13 – or 15.38 per cent. Whereas in February there remained two women in the Praesidium, a final look at the composition made on 14 June 2003 revealed that just one woman remained.

Table 1 reveals the extent of women's under-representation in the Convention. In February 2003 only 18 out of 105 (17.14 per cent) members of the Convention were women. Women comprised 20 per cent (3/15) of the representatives of the heads of state or government of the member states; ten per cent (3/30) of the representatives of the national parliaments; zero per cent (0/2) of the representatives of the European Commission; 30.77 per cent (4/13) of the representatives of the governments of the accession candidate countries; and 11.54 per cent (3/26) of the representatives of the national parliaments of the accession states. The highest percentage of female representatives comes, not surprisingly, from the EP (31.25 per cent, or 5/16), reflecting the relatively high percentage of women Members of the European Parliament (MEPs).[6] Among the observers at the Convention (six from CoR, three each from the Economic and Social Committee and the European Social Partners, together with the European Ombudsman) there were only two women (15.38 per cent). Within the 12-member Praesidium, which directs the agenda of the Convention, there were just two women (16.7 per cent) – and no women among the three-man presidency. Not surprisingly, the absence of women at the top merely perpetuates general employment patterns.

Tables 2 and 3 shed some light on the individual member states and accession countries' choice of male and female representatives. This rather confounds expectations that those countries with relatively good records of female participation in their national assemblies, or at least constitutional commitments to securing this end, should score well in the number of female representatives they sent to the Convention. For example, France, despite its constitutional commitment to gender parity in public office, sent no women as members and just one as an alternate. This, perhaps, is not as astonishing when one considers that France continues to have one of the lowest figures in the EU of female members in the national assembly (only 12.1 per cent). What is more surprising is that a country like Denmark, which has a fairly large representation of women in the national parliament (38 per cent) sent no women as members, and only 2 alternates from the EP. Germany is another example of a member state which, despite a relatively high percentage of women members in the national assembly (32.2 per cent), sent a much lower number of women in percentage terms to the Convention (16.6 per cent). Many other member states mirror this pattern, Sweden, Finland and the Netherlands sent, in proportion, less women to the Convention than they have in their national assemblies (33.3 per cent/45 per cent; 25 per cent/36.5 per cent; and 25 per cent/34 per cent, respectively). On the contrary, five countries do better in terms of female representation at the Convention than at the domestic level, namely: Greece (33.3 per cent/8.7 per cent), the United Kingdom (33.3 per cent/17.9 per cent), Italy (20 per cent/9.8 per cent), Portugal (25 per cent/19.1 per cent), and Belgium (25 per cent/23.3 per cent).

Significantly, moreover, women feature relatively strongly among the representatives of the accession countries. On 19 February 2003 – a few months after the date in Table 3 – Latvia, with two out of three female representatives (66.6 per cent), sent a much higher proportion of women than sits in its national parliament (18 per cent). Bulgaria, Poland, Slovakia, the Czech Republic, Cyprus and Romania all sent one out of three female representatives (33.3 per cent), thus scoring better than at the domestic level (26.2 per cent; 20.2 per cent; 17.3 per cent; 17.0 per cent; 10.7 per cent; and 10.7 per cent respectively). Conversely, Estonia sent no female representatives to the Convention; it has a figure of 17.8 per cent for women in the national parliament. Hungary and Turkey, also with no female representatives at the Convention, simply mirrored their poor rates of female parliamentary participation at the domestic level (9.1 per cent and 3.6 per cent, respectively).

Turning now to the internal organization of the Convention group, it has been mentioned already that there was a Praesidium (with a chairman and two vice-chairmen, plus nine members drawn from the Convention group), a secretariat (composed of the Secretariat, the chairman's private office, and the members of the Secretariat), and the working groups. The 105 members mentioned above were therefore functionally distributed within the different bodies of the Convention. The top of the Praesidium was occupied by three men, whereas among the nine other members (three representatives of governments holding the presidency,[7] two national parliament representatives, two EP representatives, and two Commission representatives) there was, in the last stage of the works (June 2003), only one female representative left (nine per cent of the entire

TABLE 4
THE COMPOSITION OF THE SECRETARIAT BY SEX (FIGURES FOR 14 JUNE 2003)

		Number of Female Members	Total Number of Members	Percentage of Female Members
Secretariat		1	3	33.3
Chairman's private office		1	2	50.0
Members of the Secretariat	Drafters	5	11	45.5
	Consultants	2	2	100.0
	Other members	1	2	50.0
	Total	10	20	50

Source: Own elaboration from primary data.

Praesidium's composition). Quite the opposite, as Table 4 shows, the Secretariat was perfectly balanced.[8]

The above observations are particularly relevant when one considers the tasks each of the bodies was supposed to fulfil within the Convention process. Starting with the Praesidium, its responsibility was that of 'lending impetus to the Convention and providing it with a basis on which to work' and 'preparing draft agendas for plenary sessions, and in overseeing the activities and organization of the Forum'.[9] That is to say, the Praesidium had the fundamental role of agenda-setter, of scrutiny, the capacity of initiative, and that of drafting. Conversely, the Secretariat was mainly supposed to support the Convention and the Praesidium, to provide assistance to all members, to prepare discussion documents, to draft reflection papers, and to draw up syntheses of the debates.[10] The Secretariat was basically responsible for the logistical and practical arrangements. It is interesting to note, then, a perfect correspondence with the traditional distribution of tasks between men and women at work.

Finally, the working groups were embedded in the task of examining and deliberating upon specific matters related with some of the cornerstones of the Convention work. At the end of the process, one could count up to six working groups deliberating on the following matters: subsidiarity, the Charter of Fundamental Rights, the legal personality of the Union, the role of national parliaments, the complementary competences and economic governance. Table 5 shows the composition of the six working groups by sex.

The first pertinent observation is that only one working group (WG), national parliaments WG, had a woman as a chairperson. As a second

TABLE 5
THE COMPOSITION OF THE CONVENTION WORKING GROUPS BY SEX
(FIGURES FOR 14 JUNE 2003)

	Number of female members	Total number of members	Percentage of Female Members
Group I Subsidiarity	2	35	5.7
Group II Charter of Fundamental Rights of the European Union	6	33	18.2
Group III Legal personality	7	30	23.3
Group IV National parliaments*	10	35	28.6
Group V Complementary competences	6	33	18.2
Group VI Economic governance	10	36	27.8
Total	41	202	20.3

Source: Own elaboration from primary data.
Note: *means that the working groups had a female chairperson. Chairpersons have been included within the totals.

observation, there exists a significant heterogeneity in terms of composition among the six groups: whereas the WG on subsidiarity had barely five percent of female representatives, the working WG on national parliaments had reached almost 30 per cent.

One can wonder to what extent this unbalanced composition – and obvious discordance between the way the Convention has been presented as a deliberating process, and the reality of the Convention in which the presence of women has been small and low level – has also been reflected in some of the gender outputs of the Convention.[11] This issue will not be discussed in any depth here, but it is interesting to briefly mention that in the draft version of 27 June 2003, the principle of gender neutrality was not respected throughout the constitutional text. For instance, in its Title IV on the Union's institutions, the role of the Union minister for foreign affairs was described as follows:

1. The European Council, acting by qualified majority, with the agreement of the President of the Commission, shall appoint the Union Minister for Foreign Affairs. *He* shall conduct the Union's common foreign and security policy. The European Council may end his tenure by the same procedure.
2. The Union Minister for Foreign Affairs shall contribute by *his* proposals to the development of the common foreign policy, which *he* shall carry out as mandated by the Council of Ministers. The same shall apply to the common security and defence policy.
3. The Union Minister for Foreign Affairs shall be one of the Vice-Presidents of the Commission. *He* shall be responsible there for

handling external relations and for coordinating other aspects of the Union's external action. In exercising these responsibilities within the Commission, and only for these responsibilities, the Union Minister for Foreign Affairs shall be bound by Commission procedures (Part I, Title IV, Chapter I, Article I-27. See CONV 820/03 25).

No need to stress the particular importance of the description, given that the key players of the Union are here introduced. This considerable mistake has been rectified in the final draft treaty submitted on 18 July 2003.

ON WHAT GROUNDS IS A BALANCE SUITABLE?

Having observed the factual gender imbalance in the Convention, the question as to why this matters and what might be its effects needs to be addressed. While previously more attention has been paid to the utilitarian arguments as reasons for increasing the presence of women in elected and nominated office,[12] I would suggest that greater concentration on rights-based arguments might now be in order. This is because the debate on the future of the EU clearly points towards a more constitutionalized framework for decision-making and, within this context, it is important to stress that women quite simply have a right to participate fully, rather than that they could bring in new issues and decision-making styles. Viewed within the framework of individual civil and political rights, women – like men – are entitled to be politically active and present in national and European decision-making processes in the name of democratic equality and participatory democracy (as per articles 33 and 34 of the draft Constitutional Treaty).

In this regard, it is important to note some of the dangers that may ensue from insisting on a utilitarian justification for more women representatives. One is that the newcomers may themselves be used instrumentally for political ends. This is because it is very likely that the new representatives will temporarily profit from a rise in popularity. Parties and existing institutions will employ them and their popularity to increase their own prestige and use them as a way of increasing legitimacy. We need to be careful, therefore, that gender balance is not used purely for politically strategic aims and that a real commitment to promoting the role of women in public life lies behind the push for increased gender equality. Furthermore, we need to be wary of a backlash against the new representatives if the expected renewal of political culture does not materialize, or does not occur in the ways anticipated or indeed quickly enough. A further reason to insist on the *right* of women to participate rather than pure utility is that to do the latter may reduce the autonomy of the female representatives. If their political legitimacy comes from complying with certain expectations in terms, for example, of the issues on which they campaign or for which they have responsibility, this will severely limit the scope of their political action and would create a strong determination of what being a female representative entails.

Put simply, new actors such as women have a basic right to take part in the political decision-making processes which affect them, and this goes as much for the EU as for domestic politics. The question for the future development of gender relations in the EU is not so much, therefore, one of why more women should be involved in the political process but rather one of how to bring an end to those structural factors which work in contradiction to their effective political involvement. The absence of women's participation in the future development of the EU reveals a clear disparity between principle and practice. If one presents democracy as a fundamental value and establishes, as a condition for its full realization, equal participation and representation of women and men, one also needs to implement the subsequent mechanisms ensuring its full realization. If the pre-defined principles of participation and inclusion fail to materialize, this raises the possibility of a democratic deficit in the political decision-making processes. For the principle of participatory democracy to be meaningful, a change has to be brought about which will generate better female participation.

The evident disparity in the composition of the Convention shows that gender equality cannot be taken for granted. It does not just happen but requires effort and positive measures to bring it about. Without this effort, the process of natural selection takes over, reproducing networks of national elites. It is not simply a case of the constitutionalization of quotas or principle of parity (which, in some member states, such as France, has not been tremendously effective in reducing gender imbalances in public office, especially at the higher levels), but rather a widespread, transparent and hard-hitting gender mainstreaming strategy running through the work of all European institutions in their decision-making and policy-making processes. Ultimately, then, the European Convention did not take gender equality seriously.

NOTES

1. The text reads as follows: 'Democracy is a fundamental value of the European Union, Member States, EEA States and applicant countries It is also a key part of external

development policy in the Union. Its full realization requires the participation of all citizens women and men alike to participate and be represented equally in the economy, in decision-making, and in social, cultural and civil life. The EU has a long-standing commitment to promoting gender equality, enshrined in the Treaty since 1957. The Community legal framework ensures that women and men are equal before the law. The promotion of gender equality is an important element of the European Union's external relations and of its development cooperation policies and, in particular, the promotion and protection of women's rights is an integral part of the EU's human rights policies in third countries. Moreover, equal treatment legislation is a firmly established integral part of the *acquis communautaire* that countries applying for EU membership have to respect.' EU, Community Framework Strategy on Gender Equality (2001–05), www.europa.eu.int/comm/employment_social/equ_opp/strategy_en.html#demo, as of 12 May 2003.

2. This final version draws on the following preceding documents: CONV 820/1/03 REV 1, CONV 847/03 and CONV 848/03.
3. See the individual member state studies in Beveridge, Nott and Stephen (2000).
4. Council Recommendation 96/694/EC of 2 December 1996 on the balanced participation of women and men in the decision-making process, OJ 1996 L 319/11; Commission Decision of 19 June 2000 relating to gender balance within the committees and expert groups established by it, OJ 2000 L 154/34.
5. The website is www.european-convention.eu.int/organisation.asp?lang = EN.
6. Since the European parliamentary elections in June 1999, there have been 194 out of 626 women MEPs – a figure which represents 31 per cent of the total membership. On the capacity of this 'critical mass' to effect change, see Freedman (2002).
7. Spain, Denmark and Greece.
8. See the composition of the Working Groups in CONV 77/1/02 at www.register.consilium.eu.int/pdf/en/02/cv00/00077-r1en2.pdf (as of 7 July 2003).
9. www.european-convention.eu.int/praesidium.asp?lang = EN.
10. www.european-convention.eu.int/secretariat.asp?lang = EN.
11. A more thorough analysis of this issue has been made in, for instance, Leon, Mateo Diaz and Millns (2003).
12. From a utilitarian perspective, there exist positive benefits in more broadly based assemblies, as what results from this diversification of the *res publica* is a greater capacity for change in terms of a renewal of the political culture and a substantive change in legislative output. The latter type of argument assumes that this diversity in terms of social recruitment reflects diversity in terms of values, priorities and styles. Finally, a legitimacy rise is also expected, not only due to a substantive diversification but also due to the assembly's mirroring of society (for theoretical and/or empirical research on utilitarian arguments, see, among others: Mill (1991a, b); Haavio-Mannila (1985); Dahlerup (1988); Skjeie (1988); Edwards (1995); Karvonen and Selle (1995); Philips (1995, 1998); Beilstein (1996); Norris (1996); Karam (1998); Lovenduski and Karam (1998); Sapiro (1998); Sawer (2000); Tremblay and Pelletier (2000); Wängnerud (1998, 2000); Chaney and Fevre (2002); Mateo Diaz (2002); Studlar and McAllister (2002).

REFERENCES

Beilstein, J.C. (1996): *Women in Political Decision-Making: Progress Towards a 'Critical Mass'*, New York: UN.
Beveridge F., S. Nott and K. Stephen (eds.) (2000): *Making Women Count. Integrating Gender into Law and Policy-making*, Dartmouth: Ashgate.
Chaney, P. and R. Fevre (2002): 'Is there a Demand for Descriptive Representation? Evidence from the UK's Devolution Programme', *Political Studies* 50/5, pp.897–915.

Dahlerup, D. (1988): 'From a Small to a Large Minority: Women in Scandinavian Politics', *Scandinavian Political Studies* 11/4, pp.275–98.

Edwards, M. (1995): *Participation des femmes et changement politique: le cas de la Suède* [The Participation of Women in Political Change: The Swedish Case], *La place des femmes: les enjeux de l'identité et de l'égalité au regard des sciences sociales*, Paris: Ed. de la Découverte.

Freedman, J. (2002): 'Women in the European Parliament', *Parliamentary Affairs* 55/1, pp.179–88.

Haavio-Mannila, E. (1985): *Unifinished Democracy: Women in Nordic Politics*, Oxford: Pergamon Press.

Karam, A. (ed.) (1998): *Women in Parliament: Beyond Numbers*, Stockholm: International Institute for Democracy and Electoral Assistance.

Karvonen, L. and P. Selle (eds.) (1995): *Women in Nordic Politics: Closing the Gap*, Aldershot: Dartmouth.

Leon, M., M. Mateo Diaz, and S. Millns (2003): 'Engendering the Convention: Women and the future of the European Union', *Constitutional Online Essays* No.6/03; www.fedtrust.co.uk/eu_constitution.htm.

Lovenduski, J. and A. Karam (1998): 'Women in Parliament Making a Difference', *Women in Parliament Beyond Numbers*, Sweden: IDEA, pp.125–58.

Manin, B. (1996): *Principes Du Gouvernement Représentatif*, France: Flammarion.

Mateo Diaz, M. (2002): *Are Women In Parliament Representing Women? From Descriptive to Substantive Representation ... And Back Again?*, Louvain-la-Neuve: Presses Universitaires de Louvain, No.399.

Mill, J.S. (1991a) [1863]: 'Utilitarianism', in J. Gray (ed.), *John Stuart Mill: On Liberty and Others Essays*, Oxford: Oxford University Press, pp.130–203.

Mill, J.S. (1991b) [1869]: 'On the Subjection of Women', in Gray (ed.), *John Stuart Mill*, pp.471–581.

Norris, P. (1996): 'Women Politicians: Transforming Westminister?', in J. Lovenduski and P. Norris (eds.), *Women in Politics*, Oxford: Oxford University Press, pp.91–104.

Norris, P. and J. Lovenduski (1995): *Political Recruitment. Gender, Race and Class in the British Parliament*, Cambridge: Cambridge University Press.

Phillips, A. (1995): *The Politics of Presence*, Oxford: Clarendon Press.

Phillips, A. (1998): 'Democracy and Representation: Or, Why Should it Matter Who our Representatives Are?', in A. Phillips (ed.), *Feminism and Politics*, Oxford: Oxford University Press, pp.224–40.

Sapiro, V. (1998): 'When are Interests Interesting? The Problem of Political Representation of Women', in Phillips (ed.), *Feminism and Politics*, pp.161–92.

Sawer, M. (2000): 'Parliamentary Representation of Women: From Discourses of Justice to Strategies of Accountability', *International Political Science Review* 21/4, pp.361–80.

Shaw, J. (2002): *Process, Responsibility and Inclusion in EU Constitutionalism: The Challenge for the Convention on the Future of the Union*, London: The Federal Trust for Education and Research, www.fedtrust.co.uk/EU_constitution.

Skjeie, H. (1988): *The Feminisation of Power: Norway's Political Experiment (1986–??)*, Oslo: Institute for Social Research.

Studlar, D.T. and I.McAllister (2002): 'Does a Critical Mass Exist? A Comparative Analysis of Women's Legislative Representation since 1950', *European Journal of Political Research* 41/2, pp.233–53.

Tremblay, M. and R.Pelletier (2000): 'More Women or More Feminists? Descriptive and Substantive Representations of Women in the 1997 Canadian Federal Elections', *International Political Science Review* 21/4, pp.381–405.

Wängnerud, L. (1998): *Politikens andra sida: om kvinnorepresentation i Sveriges riksdag* [The Second Face of Democracy. Women's Representation in the Swedish Parliament], Gothenburg: Statsvetenskapliga institutionen.

Wängnerud, L. (2000): 'Testing the Politics of Presence: Women's Representation in the Swedish Riksdag', *Scandinavian Political Studies* 23/1, pp.67–91.

Official Records

Official Journal of the European Communities (2001/C 80/01), *Treaty of Nice Amending the Treaty on European Union, the Treaties Establishing the European Communities and Certain Related Acts.*

Preliminary draft of the Constitutional Treaty drawn up by the Praesidium, presented by the president at the plenary session on 28 October 2002 (CONV 369/02).

The European Convention, www.european-convention.eu.int, as of 15 October 2002.

Inter-parliamentary Union, *Women in National Parliaments,* www.ipu.org/wmn-e/classif.htm, as of 25 November 2002.

Annex 1
Laeken Declaration on the Future of the European Union

(ANNEX 1 TO THE PRESIDENCY CONCLUSIONS, EUROPEAN COUNCIL MEETING IN LAEKEN, 14–15 DECEMBER 2001)

EUROPE AT A CROSSROADS

For centuries, peoples and states have taken up arms and waged war to win control of the European continent. The debilitating effects of two bloody wars and the weakening of Europe's position in the world brought a growing realization that only peace and concerted action could make the dream of a strong, unified Europe come true. In order to banish once and for all the demons of the past, a start was made with a coal and steel community. Other economic activities, such as agriculture, were subsequently added in. A genuine single market was eventually established for goods, persons, services and capital, and a single currency was added in 1999. On 1 January 2002 the euro is to become a day-to-day reality for 300 million European citizens.

The European Union has thus gradually come into being. In the beginning, it was more of an economic and technical collaboration. Twenty years ago, with the first direct elections to the European Parliament, the Community's democratic legitimacy, which until then had lain with the Council alone, was considerably strengthened. Over the last ten years, construction of a political union has begun and cooperation been established on social policy, employment, asylum, immigration, police, justice, foreign policy and a common security and defence policy.

The European Union is a success story. For over half a century now, Europe has been at peace. Along with North America and Japan, the Union forms one of the three most prosperous parts of the world. As a result of mutual solidarity and fair distribution of the benefits of economic development, moreover, the standard of living in the Union's weaker regions has increased enormously and they have made good much of the disadvantage they were at.

South European Society & Politics, Vol.9, No.1, Summer 2004, pp.223–238
ISSN 1360-8746 print/ISSN 1743-9612 online
DOI: 10.1080/13608740410001681352   © 2004 Taylor & Francis Ltd

Fifty years on, however, the Union stands at a crossroads, a defining moment in its existence. The unification of Europe is near. The Union is about to expand to bring in more than ten new Member States, predominantly central and eastern European, thereby finally closing one of the darkest chapters in European history: the Second World War and the ensuing artificial division of Europe. At long last, Europe is on its way to becoming one big family, without bloodshed, a real transformation clearly calling for a different approach from 50 years ago, when six countries first took the lead.

The Democratic Challenge Facing Europe

At the same time, the Union faces twin challenges, one within and the other beyond its borders. Within the Union, the European institutions must be brought closer to its citizens. Citizens undoubtedly support the Union's broad aims, but they do not always see a connection between those goals and the Union's everyday action. They want the European institutions to be less unwieldy and rigid and, above all, more efficient and open. Many also feel that the Union should involve itself more with their particular concerns, instead of intervening, in every detail, in matters by their nature better left to Member States' and regions' elected representatives. This is even perceived by some as a threat to their identity. More importantly, however, they feel that deals are all too often cut out of their sight and they want better democratic scrutiny.

Europe's New Role in a Globalized World

Beyond its borders, in turn, the European Union is confronted with a fast-changing, globalized world. Following the fall of the Berlin Wall, it looked briefly as though we would for a long while be living in a stable world order, free from conflict, founded upon human rights. Just a few years later, however, there is no such certainty. The eleventh of September has brought a rude awakening. The opposing forces have not gone away: religious fanaticism, ethnic nationalism, racism and terrorism are on the increase, and regional conflicts, poverty and underdevelopment still provide a constant seedbed for them.

What is Europe's role in this changed world? Does Europe not, now that it is finally unified, have a leading part to play in a new world order, that of a power able both to have a stabilizing role worldwide and to point the way ahead for many countries and peoples? Europe as the continent of humane values, the Magna Carta, the Bill of Rights, the French Revolution and the fall of the Berlin Wall; the continent of liberty, solidarity and above all diversity, meaning respect for others' languages, cultures and traditions. The European Union's one boundary is democracy and human rights. The Union is open only to countries which uphold basic values such as free elections, respect for minorities and respect for the rule of law.

Now that the Cold War is over and we are living in a globalized, yet also highly fragmented world, Europe needs to shoulder its responsibilities in the governance of globalization. The role it has to play is that of a power resolutely doing battle against all violence, all terror and all fanaticism, but which also does not turn a blind eye to the world's heartrending injustices. In short, a power wanting to change the course of world affairs in such a way as to benefit not just the rich countries but also the poorest. A power seeking to set globalization within a moral framework, in other words to anchor it in solidarity and sustainable development.

The Expectations of Europe's Citizens

The image of a democratic and globally engaged Europe admirably matches citizens' wishes. There have been frequent public calls for a greater EU role in justice and security, action against cross-border crime, control of migration flows and reception of asylum seekers and refugees from far-flung war zones. Citizens also want results in the fields of employment and combating poverty and social exclusion, as well as in the field of economic and social cohesion. They want a common approach on environmental pollution, climate change and food safety, in short, all transnational issues which they instinctively sense can only be tackled by working together. Just as they also want to see Europe more involved in foreign affairs, security and defence, in other words, greater and better coordinated action to deal with trouble spots in and around Europe and in the rest of the world.

At the same time, citizens also feel that the Union is behaving too bureaucratically in numerous other areas. In coordinating the economic, financial and fiscal environment, the basic issue should continue to be proper operation of the internal market and the single currency, without this jeopardizing Member States' individuality. National and regional differences frequently stem from history or tradition. They can be enriching. In other words, what citizens understand by 'good governance' is opening up fresh opportunities, not imposing further red tape. What they expect is more results, better responses to practical issues and not a European superstate or European institutions inveigling their way into every nook and cranny of life. In short, citizens are calling for a clear, open, effective, democratically controlled Community approach, developing a Europe which points the way ahead for the world. An approach that provides concrete results in terms of more jobs, better quality of life, less crime, decent education and better health care. There can be no doubt that this will require Europe to undergo renewal and reform.

CHALLENGES AND REFORMS IN A RENEWED UNION

The Union needs to become more democratic, more transparent and more efficient. It also has to resolve three basic challenges: how to bring citizens, and primarily the young, closer to the European design and the European institutions, how to organize politics and the European political area in an enlarged Union and how to develop the Union into a stabilizing factor and a model in the new, multipolar world. In order to address them a number of specific questions need to be put.

A Better Division and Definition of Competence in the European Union

Citizens often hold expectations of the European Union that are not always fulfilled. And vice versa they sometimes have the impression that the Union takes on too much in areas where its involvement is not always essential. Thus the important thing is to clarify, simplify and adjust the division of competence between the Union and the Member States in the light of the new challenges facing the Union. This can lead both to restoring tasks to the Member States and to assigning new missions to the Union, or to the extension of existing powers, while constantly bearing in mind the equality of the Member States and their mutual solidarity.

A first series of questions that needs to be put concerns how the division of competence can be made more transparent. Can we thus make a clearer distinction between three types of competence: the exclusive competence of the Union, the competence of the Member States and the shared competence of the Union and the Member States? At what level is competence exercised in the most efficient way? How is the principle of subsidiarity to be applied here? And should we not make it clear that any powers not assigned by the Treaties to the Union fall within the exclusive sphere of competence of the Member States? And what would be the consequences of this?

The next series of questions should aim, within this new framework and while respecting the *acquis communautaire*, to determine whether there needs to be any reorganization of competence. How can citizens' expectations be taken as a guide here? What missions would this produce for the Union? And, vice versa, what tasks could better be left to the Member States? What amendments should be made to the Treaty on the various policies? How, for example, should a more coherent common foreign policy and defence policy be developed? Should the Petersberg tasks be updated? Do we want to adopt a more integrated approach to police and criminal law cooperation? How can economic policy coordination be stepped up? How can we intensify cooperation in the field of social inclusion, the environment, health and food safety? But then, should not the day-to-day administration and implementation of the Union's policy be left more emphatically to the Member States and, where their constitutions so provide, to the regions? Should they not be provided with guarantees that their spheres of competence will not be affected?

Lastly, there is the question of how to ensure that a redefined division of competence does not lead to a creeping expansion of the competence of the Union or to encroachment upon the exclusive areas of competence of the Member States and, where there is provision for this, regions. How are we to ensure at the same time that the European dynamic does not come to a halt? In the future as well the Union must continue to be able to react to fresh challenges and developments and must be able to explore new policy areas. Should Articles 95 and 308 of the Treaty be reviewed for this purpose in the light of the *acquis jurisprudentiel*?

Simplification of the Union's Instruments

Who does what is not the only important question; the nature of the Union's action and what instruments it should use are equally important. Successive amendments to the Treaty have on each occasion resulted in a proliferation of instruments, and directives have gradually evolved towards more and more detailed legislation. The key question is therefore whether the Union's various instruments should not be better defined and whether their number should not be reduced.

In other words, should a distinction be introduced between legislative and executive measures? Should the number of legislative instruments be reduced: directly applicable rules, framework legislation and non-enforceable instruments (opinions, recommendations, open coordination)? Is it or is it not desirable to have more frequent recourse to framework legislation, which affords the Member States more room for manoeuvre in achieving policy objectives? For which areas of competence are open coordination and mutual recognition the most appropriate instruments? Is the principle of proportionality to remain the point of departure?

More Democracy, Transparency and Efficiency in the European Union

The European Union derives its legitimacy from the democratic values it projects, the aims it pursues and the powers and instruments it possesses. However, the European project also derives its legitimacy from democratic, transparent and efficient institutions. The national parliaments also contribute towards the legitimacy of the European project. The declaration on the future of the Union, annexed to the Treaty of Nice, stressed the need to examine their role in European integration. More generally, the question arises as to what initiatives we can take to develop a European public area.

The first question is thus how we can increase the democratic legitimacy and transparency of the present institutions, a question which is valid for the three institutions.

How can the authority and efficiency of the European Commission be enhanced? How should the President of the Commission be appointed: by the European Council, by the European Parliament or should he be directly elected by the citizens? Should the role of the European Parliament be strengthened? Should we extend the right of co-decision or not? Should the way in which we elect the members of the European Parliament be reviewed? Should a European electoral constituency be created, or should constituencies continue to be determined nationally? Can the two systems be combined? Should the role of the Council be strengthened? Should the Council act in the same manner in its legislative and its executive capacities? With a view to greater transparency, should the meetings of the Council, at least in its legislative capacity, be public? Should citizens have more access to Council documents? How, finally, should the balance and reciprocal control between the institutions be ensured?

A second question, which also relates to democratic legitimacy, involves the role of national parliaments. Should they be represented in a new institution, alongside the Council and the European Parliament? Should they have a role in areas of European action in which the European Parliament has no competence? Should they focus on the division of competence between Union and Member States, for example through preliminary checking of compliance with the principle of subsidiarity?

The third question concerns how we can improve the efficiency of decision-making and the workings of the institutions in a Union of some 30 Member States. How could the Union set its objectives and priorities more effectively and ensure better implementation? Is there a need for more decisions by a qualified majority? How is the co-decision procedure between the Council and the European Parliament to be simplified and speeded up? What of the six-monthly rotation of the Presidency of the Union? What is the future role of the European Parliament? What of the future role and structure of the various Council formations? How should the coherence of European foreign policy be enhanced? How is synergy between the High Representative and the competent Commissioner to be reinforced? Should the external representation of the Union in international fora be extended further?

Towards a Constitution for European Citizens

The European Union currently has four Treaties. The objectives, powers and policy instruments of the Union are currently spread across those Treaties. If we are to have greater transparency, simplification is essential.

Four sets of questions arise in this connection. The first concerns simplifying the existing Treaties without changing their content. Should the distinction between the Union and the Communities be reviewed? What of the division into three pillars?

Questions then arise as to the possible reorganization of the Treaties. Should a distinction be made between a basic treaty and the other treaty provisions? Should this distinction involve separating the texts? Could this lead to a distinction between the amendment and ratification procedures for the basic treaty and for the other treaty provisions?

Thought would also have to be given to whether the Charter of Fundamental Rights should be included in the basic treaty and to whether the European Community should accede to the European Convention on Human Rights.

The question ultimately arises as to whether this simplification and reorganization might not lead in the long run to the adoption of a constitutional text in the Union. What might the basic features of such a constitution be? The values which the Union cherishes, the fundamental rights and obligations of its citizens, the relationship between Member States in the Union?

CONVENING OF A CONVENTION ON THE FUTURE OF EUROPE

In order to pave the way for the next Intergovernmental Conference as broadly and openly as possible, the European Council has decided to convene a Convention composed of the main parties involved in the debate on the future of the Union. In the light of the foregoing, it will be the task of that Convention to consider the key issues arising for the Union's future development and try to identify the various possible responses.

The European Council has appointed Mr V. Giscard d'Estaing as Chairman of the Convention and Mr G. Amato and Mr J.L. Dehaene as Vice-Chairmen.

Composition

In addition to its Chairman and Vice-Chairmen, the Convention will be composed of 15 representatives of the Heads of State or Government of the Member States (one from each Member State), 30 members of national parliaments (two from each Member State), 16 members of the European Parliament and two Commission representatives. The accession candidate countries will be fully involved in the Convention's proceedings. They will be represented in the same way as the current Member States (one government representative and two national parliament members) and will be able to take part in the proceedings without, however, being able to prevent any consensus which may emerge among the Member States.

The members of the Convention may only be replaced by alternate members if they are not present. The alternate members will be designated in the same way as full members.

The Praesidium of the Convention will be composed of the Convention Chairman and Vice-Chairmen and nine members drawn from the Convention (the representatives of all the governments holding the Council Presidency during the Convention, two national parliament representatives, two European Parliament representatives and two Commission representatives).

Three representatives of the Economic and Social Committee with three representatives of the European social partners; from the Committee of the Regions: six representatives (to be appointed by the Committee of the Regions from the regions, cities and regions with legislative powers), and the European Ombudsman will be invited to attend as observers. The Presidents of the Court of Justice and of the Court of Auditors may be invited by the Praesidium to address the Convention.

Length of Proceedings

The Convention will hold its inaugural meeting on 1 March 2002, when it will appoint its Praesidium and adopt its rules of procedure. Proceedings will be completed after a year, that is to say in time for the Chairman of the Convention to present its outcome to the European Council.

Working Methods

The Chairman will pave the way for the opening of the Convention's proceedings by drawing conclusions from the public debate. The Praesidium will serve to lend impetus and will provide the Convention with an initial working basis.

The Praesidium may consult Commission officials and experts of its choice on any technical aspect which it sees fit to look into. It may set up ad hoc working parties.

The Council will be kept informed of the progress of the Convention's proceedings. The Convention Chairman will give an oral progress report at each European Council meeting, thus enabling Heads of State or Government to give their views at the same time.

The Convention will meet in Brussels. The Convention's discussions and all official documents will be in the public domain. The Convention will work in the Union's 11 working languages.

Final Document

The Convention will consider the various issues. It will draw up a final document which may comprise either different options, indicating the degree of support which they received, or recommendations if consensus is achieved.

Together with the outcome of national debates on the future of the Union, the final document will provide a starting point for discussions in the Intergovernmental Conference, which will take the ultimate decisions.

Forum

In order for the debate to be broadly based and involve all citizens, a Forum will be opened for organizations representing civil society (the social partners, the business world, non-governmental organizations, academia, etc.). It will take the form of a structured network of organizations receiving regular information on the Convention's proceedings. Their contributions will serve as input into the debate. Such organizations may be heard or consulted on specific topics in accordance with arrangements to be established by the Praesidium.

Secretariat

The Praesidium will be assisted by a Convention Secretariat, to be provided by the General Secretariat of the Council, which may incorporate Commission and European Parliament experts.

ANNEX 2
Composition of the Convention and South European Participation[1]

PRAESIDIUM

President
Presidente Valéry GISCARD d'ESTAING

Vice-Presidents
Mr Giuliano AMATO
Mr Jean-Luc DEHAENE

Members drawn from the Convention (*below):
(i) the representatives of all the governments holding the Council Presidency during the Convention:
Mr Alfonso Dastis
Mr Hennig Christophersen
Mr Georges Papandreou

(ii) two national parliament representatives
Mr John Bruton
Mrs Gisela Stuart

(iii) two European Parliament representatives
Mr Klaus Hänsch
Mr Iñigo Mendez de Vigo

(iv) two Commission representatives
Mr Michel Barnier
Mr Antònio Vitorino

Invited
Mr Alojz Peterle

---

[1]South European participants are in bold. Members of the Commission are not included (given the fact that they do not represent their country nor their fellow citizens). The table does not take into account the turnover of representatives, mentioning only the last ones. However, in the case of the South European countries, turnovers are indicated in the footnotes.

REPRESENTATIVES OF STATE OR GOVERNMENT

Member State	Member	Alternate member
België/Belgique	Mr. Louis MICHEL	Mr Pierre CHEVALIER
*Danmark	Mr Henning CHRISTOPHERSEN	Mr Poul SCHLÜTER
Deutschland	Mr Joschka FISCHER	Mr Hans Martin BURY
*Ellas	Mr Georges PAPANDREOU[2]	Mr Georges KATIFORIS
*España	Mr Alfonso DASTIS	Mrs Ana PALACIO
France	Mr Dominique de VILLEPIN	Mrs Pascale ANDREANI
Ireland	Mr Dick ROCHE	Mr Bobby McDONAGH
Italia	Mr Gianfranco FINI	Mr Francesco E. SPERONI
Luxembourg	Mr Jacques SANTER	Mr Nicolas SCHMIT
Nederland	Mr Gijs de VRIES	Mr Thom de BRUIJN
Österreich	Mr Hannes FARNLEITNER	Mr Gerhard TUSEK
Portugal	Mr Ernâni LOPES	Mr Manuel Lobo ANTUNES
Suomi/Finland	Mrs Teija TIILIKAINEN	Mr Antti PELTOMÄKI
Sverige	Mrs Lena HJELM-WALLÉN	Mr Sven-Olof PETERSSON
United Kingdom	Mr Peter HAIN	Baroness Scotland of Asthal

REPRESENTATIVES OF NATIONAL PARLIAMENTS

Member State Member Alternate Member	Member	Alternate member
België/Belgique	Mr Karel DE GUCHT Mr Elio DI RUPO	Mr Danny PIETERS Mrs Marie NAGY
Danmark	Mr Peter SKAARUP Mr Henrik DAM KRISTENSEN	Mr Per DALGAARD Mr Niels HELVEG PETERSEN
Deutschland	Mr Jürgen MEYER Mr Erwin TEUFEL	Mr Peter ALTMAIER Mr Wolfgang GERHARDS
Ellas	Mr Paraskevas AVGERINOS Mrs Marietta GIANNAKOU	Mr Nikolaos CONSTANTOPOULOS Mr Evripidis STILIANIDES
España	Mr Josep BORRELL FONTELLES Mr Gabriel CISNEROS LABORDA	Mr Diego LÓPEZ GARRIDO Mr Alejandro MUÑOZ ALONSO

---

[2]Until... the Government Representative was George Katiforis, with Panayotis Ioakimidis as Alternate.

France	Mr Pierre LEQUILLER Mr Hubert HAENEL	Mr Jacques FLOCH Mr Robert BADINTER
Ireland	*Mr John BRUTON Mr Proinsias DE ROSSA	Mr Pat CAREY Mr John GORMLEY
Italia	Mr Marco FOLLINI Mr Lamberto DINI	Mr Valdo SPINI Mr Filadelfio Guido BASILE
Luxembourg	Mr Paul HELMINGER Mr Ben FAYOT	Mr Gaston GIBERYEN Mrs Renée WAGENER
Nederland	Mr René van der LINDEN Mr Frans TIMMERMANS	Mr Wim VAN EEKELEN Mr Jan Jacob VAN DIJK
Österreich	Mr Caspar EINEM Mr Reinhard Eugen BÖSCH	Mrs Evelin LICHTENBERGER Mr Eduard MAINONI
Portugal	Mr Alberto COSTA Mrs Eduarda AZEVEDO	Mr Guilherme d'OLIVEIRA MARTINS Mr António NAZARÉ-PEREIRA
Suomi/Finland	Mr Kimmo KILJUNEN Mr Jari VILÉN	Mr Hannu TAKKULA Mr Esko HELLE
Sverige	Mr Sören LEKBERG Mr Göran LENNMARKER	Mr Kenneth KVIST Mr Ingvar SVENSSON
United Kingdom	*Mrs Gisela STUART Mr David HEATHCOAT- AMORY	Lord TOMLINSON Lord MACLENNAN OF ROGART

REPRESENTATIVES OF THE EUROPEAN PARLIAMENT

Member	Alternate Member
Mr Elmar BROK (D)	Mrs Teresa ALMEIDA GARRETT (P)
Mr Timothy KIRKHOPE (UK)	Mr John CUSHNAHAN (IRL)
Mr Alain LAMASSOURE (F)	Mrs Piia-Noora KAUPPI (FI)
Mrs Hanja MAIJ-WEGGEN (NL)	Mr Reinhard RACK (ÖS)
*Mr Íñigo MÉNDEZ DE VIGO Y MONTOJO (ES)	The Earl of STOCKTON (UK)
Mr Antonio TAJANI (IT)	Mr Joachim WUERMELING (D)
*Mr Klaus HÄNSCH (D)	Mrs Pervenche BERÈS (F)
Mr Olivier DUHAMEL (F)	Mrs Maria BERGER (ÖS)
Mr Luís MARINHO (P)	Mr Carlos CARNERO GONZÁLEZ (ES)
Mrs Linda McAVAN (UK)	Mrs Elena PACIOTTI (IT)
Mrs Anne VAN LANCKER (B)	Mrs Helle THORNING-SCHMIDT (DK)
Mr Andrew Nicholas DUFF (UK)	Mrs Lone DYBKJAER (DK)
Mr Johannes VOGGENHUBER (ÖS)	Mr Neil MacCORMICK (UK)
Mrs Sylvia-Yvonne KAUFMANN (D)	Mr Esko SEPPÄNEN (FI)
Mrs Cristiana MUSCARDINI (IT)	Mr Luís QUEIRÓ (P)
Mr Jens-Peter BONDE (DK)	Mr William ABITBOL (F)

REPRESENTATIVES OF THE EUROPEAN COMMISSION

Member	Alternate Member
*Mr Michel BARNIER	Mr David O'Sullivan
*Mr António VITORINO	Mr Paolo Ponzano

REPRESENTATIVES OF STATE OR GOVERNMENT OF THE APPLICANT COUNTRIES

Country	Member	Alternate Member
Κύπρος (Cyprus)	Mr Michael ATTALIDES	Mr Theophilos V. THEOPHILOU
Malta	Mr Peter SERRACINO-INGLOTT	Mr John INGUANEZ
Magyarorszàg (Hungary)	Mr Péter BALÁZS	Mr Péter GOTTFRIED
Polska (Poland)	Mrs Danuta HÜBNER	Mr Janusz TRZCIŃSKI
România (Rumania)	Mrs Hildegard Carola PUWAK	Mr Constantin ENE
Slovensko (Slovakia)	Mr Ivan KORČOK	Mr Juraj MIGAŠ
Latvija (Latvia)	Mrs Sandra KALNIETE	Mr Roberts ZILE
Eesti (Estonia)	Mr Lennart MERI	Mr Henrik HOLOLEI
Lietuva (Lithuania)	Mr Rytis MARTIKONIS	Mr Oskaras JUSYS
Българиа (Bulgaria)	Mrs Meglena KUNEVA	Mrs Neli KUTSKOVA
Česká Republika (Czech Republic)	Mr Jan KOHOUT	Mrs Lenka Anna ROVNA
Slovenija (Slovenia)	Mr Dimitrij RUPEL	Mr Janez LENARČIČ
Türkiye (Turkey)	Mr Abdullah Gül[3]	Mr Oğuz DEMİRALP[4]

REPRESENTATIVE OF THE NATIONAL PARLIAMENTS OF THE APPLICANT COUNTRIES

Country	Member	Alternate Member
Κύπρος (Cyprus)	Mrs Eleni MAVROU Mr Panayiotis DEMETRIOU	Mr Marios MATSAKIS Mrs Androula VASSILIOU
Malta	Mr Michael FRENDO Mr Alfred SANT	Mrs Dolores CRISTINA Mr George VELLA
Magyarorszàg (Hungary)	Mr József SZÁJER	Mr András KELEMEN
	Mr Pál VASTAGH	Mr István SZENT-IVÁNYI

---

[3]From May to December 2002 the member was Mr Mesut Yılmaz; from December 2002 to March 2003 the member was Mr. Yaşar Yakış.
[4]From May to August 2002 the alternate member was Mr. Nihat Akyol.

Polska (Poland)	Mr Jozef OLEKSY	Mrs Marta FOGLER
	Mr Edmund WITTBRODT	Mrs Genowefa GRABOWSKA
România (Romania)	Mr Alexandru ATHANASIU	Mr Péter ECKSTEIN-KOVACS
	Mr Puiu HASOTTI	Mr Adrian SEVERIN
Slovensko (Slovakia)	Mr Jan FIGEL	Mrs Zuzana MARTINAKOVA
	Mrs Irena BELOHORSKÁ	Mr Boris ZALA
Latvija (Latvia)	Mr Rihards PIKS	Mr Guntars KRASTS
	Mrs Liene LIEPINA	Mr Arturs Krisjanis KARINS
Eesti (Estonia)	Mr Tunne KELAM	Mrs Liina TÕNISSON
	Mr Rein LANG	Mr Urmas REINSALU
Lietuva (Lithuania)	Mr Vytenis ANDRIUKAITIS	Mr Gintautas ŠIVICKAS
	Mr Algirdas GRICIUS	Mr Eugenijus MALDEIKIS
Бъллария (Bulgaria)	Mr Daniel VALCHEV	Mr Alexander ARABADJIEV
	Mr Nikolai MLADENOV	Mr Nesrin UZUN
Česká Republika (Czech Republic)	Mr Jan ZAHRADIL	Mr Petr NEČAS
	Mr Josef ZIELENIEC	Mr Frantiřek KROUPA
Slovenija (Slovenia)	Mr Jelko KACIN	Mr Franc HORVAT
	*Mr Alojz PETERLE	Mr Mihael BREJC
Türkiye (Turkey)	Mr Zekeriya AKCAM[5]	Mr Ibrahim ÖZAL
	Mr Kemal DERVIŞ[6]	Mr Necdet BUDAK

OBSERVERS

Committee of the Regions

Mr Josef CHABERT
Mr Manfred DAMMEYER
Mr Patrick DEWAEL
Mrs Claude DU GRANRUT
Mr Claudio MARTINI
Mr Ramón Luis VALCÁRCEL SISO

Economic and Social Committee

Mr Göke FRERICHS
Mr Roger BRIESCH
Mrs Anne-Marie SIGMUND

European Social Parties

Mr Emilio GABAGLIO
Mr João CARDONA CRAVINHO
Mr Georges JACOBS

European Ombudsman

Mr Nikiforos DIAMANDOUROS[7]

---

[5]From May to December 2002 the member was Mr. Ali Tekin, while the alternate was Mr. Kürşat Eser.

[6]From May to December 2002 the member was Mrs. Ayfer Yılmaz, while the alternate was Mr. Emre Kocaoğlu.

[7]Since 1 April 2004.

Annex 3
South European Participation in the Working Groups

I
Subsidiarity (Italy: Lamberto Dini; Portugal: Alberto Costa, Ernâni Lopes since May 2002, Luís Marinho; Malta: Serracino Inglott; Ellas: Paraskevas Avgerinos; Espana: Iñigo Mendez de Vigo.)

II
Charter/ECHR (Italy: Gianfranco Fini, Claudio Martini, Elena Paciotti; Portugal: João Cravinho; Manuel Lobo Antunes; Turkey: Mr. Emre Kocaoğlu; Cyprus: Marios Matsakis, Eleni Mavrou; Espana: Gabriel Cisneros, Diego Lopez Garrido.)

III
Legal personality (Italy: Giuliano Amato, Cristina Muscardini, Paolo Ponzano, Antonio Tafani; Portugal: Teresa Almeida Garrett; Ellas: Panayotis Ioakimidis; Espana: Carlos Carnero, Ana Palacio.)

IV
National parliaments (Italy: Filadelfio Guido Basile; Portugal: Eduarda Azevedo, Luís Queiró; Malta: John Inguanez, Dolores Cristina; Turkey: Mr. Kürşat Eser, Mr. Ali Tekin; Cyprus: Panayotis Demetriou; Ellas: Evripidis Stilianidis.)

V
Complementary Competencies (Italy Francesco Speroni; Portugal: Osvaldo de Castro -until June 2002, Guilherme d'Oliveira Martins - from June 2002; Malta: M Frendo; Cyprus: Michael Attalides, Androula Vassiliou; Ellas: Marietta Giannakou.)

VI
Economic Governance (Italy: Marco Follini, Emilio Gabaglio, Valdo Spini; Portugal: António Nazaré Pereira; Turkey: Mrs. Ayfer Yılmaz; Ellas: Georges Katiforis; Espana: Josep Borrell.)

VII
External Action (Italy: Lamberto Dini, Gianfranco Fini, Marco Follini, Claudio Martini; Portugal: Ernâni Lopes since May 2002, Teresa Almeida Garrett, António Nazaré Pereira; Cyprus: Theophilos Theophilou, Michael Attalides; Ellas: Evripidis Stilianidis; Espana: Alfonso Dastis, Josep Borrell.)

VIII
Defence (Portugal: Eduarda Azevedo, Manuel Lobo Antunes; Cyprus: Marios Matsakis; Italy: Valdo Spini; Ellas: Marietta Giannakou, Panayotis Ioakimidis, Giorgos Katiforis; Espana: Alejandro Muñoz Alonso, Diego Lopez Garrido; Malta: John Inguanez, Michael Frendo; Turkey: Oğuz Demiralp.)

IX
Simplification (Italy: Giuliano Amato, Cristiana Muscardini, Paolo Ponzano, Filadelfio Basile; Portugal: Guilherme d'Oliveira Martins, Luís Marinho; Espana: Carlos Carnero, Gabriel Cisneros.)

X
Freedom, Security and Justice (Italy: Elena Paciotti, Antonio Tajani; Portugal: Alberto Costa, Luís Queiró; Turkey: Mr. Emre Kocaoğlu; Cyprus: Panayotis Demetiou, Androula Vassiliou; Espana: Iñigo Mendez de Vigo, Ana Palacio.)

XI
Social Europe (Italy: Filadelfio Guido Basile, Emilio Gabaglio, Valdo Spini; Portugal: Eduarda Azevedo, Alberto Costa, Luís Marinho, João Cravinho.)

INDEX

ABGS *see Avrupa Birliği Genel Sekreterliği*
academic networks: Convention debate 197; Greece 137; Italy 55–6; Malta 145, 147–8; Portugal 110, 115; Spain 82, 84–5, 86–7; *see also* intellectuals
acceptance position: Portugal 106
accession candidate countries: Assembly representation 2; Convention method 153; general public 169; member states contrast 7; sex-composition of Convention 211, 213–15; *see also* applicant countries
accession negotiations: Turkey 173–5
Accession Treaty, Athens 143, 148–9, 151
acquis communautaire 167, 168–9
ACs *see* Autonomous Communities
Adalet ve Kalkınma Partisi (AKP) 174, 180, 181–2, 188
adaptation pressure: domestic politics 157
AEGEE *see Association des Etats Generaux des Etudiants de l'Europe*
Africa-Brazil axis 105
Agapiou-Josephides, Kalliope 152–72
Akçam, Zekeriya 180
AKP *see Adalet ve Kalkınma Partisi*
alternates in Convention 211–14
Alternattiva Demokratika Party 147
Amato, Giuliano 42, 43, 50, 51–2, 58
Amsterdam Treaty 129
analytical framework of Convention 154–6
Anavatan Partisi (ANAP) 173

Annan Plan 167
applicant countries 7, 11, 17–19; *see also* accession candidate countries
arguing activities 24–5, 29, 32–4
Assembly composition 2–3
Association des Etats Generaux des Etudiants de l'Europe (AEGEE) 183–4
Atatürk, Mustafa Kemal 175
Autonomous Communities (ACs) 63, 65, 67–9, 78, 85, 93
Avrupa Birliği Genel Sekreterliği (ABGS) 178
awareness: Spanish public 71–2, 75
Aznar, José María 46, 63, 64, 88, 90
Azores 111

'BAB' (Blair, Aznar, Berlusconi) 46
The Balkans 133, 136
barometers 71–5, 116–17, 133–4; *see also* Eurobarometers
Basile, Filadelfio 42, 49
Basque Country 68–9, 70, 78; Convention debate 197–8; intellectual debate 85; radicalism 205; regional agenda 200; *see also* Spain
Belgium 194
Berlusconi, Silvio 10–11, 17, 41, 43–6, 58
Blair, Tony 46
Borrell, Josep 64, 70
Bossi, Umberto 47
bottom-up approach 6–9, 32; *see also* process-based approach

239

implementation in the regions 204–5
inclusion: women 208–10
incrementalism: treaty reform 154
innovation 1, 4, 14–16, 34–6; see also
ideational innovation
institutional balance: Cyprus 163
institutional changes: Portugal
97–120
institutional legacies 31–3
institutional reforms: Spain 74, 93–4
Instituto de España 84–5
integration: Cyprus 152–3, 162–4,
167, 170; governmental
transformations 195–6; Greek
opinions 123–5, 134–5; Portugal's
stance 98–101, 116; Turkey 186–8
intellectuals 12–13; attitudes 87–9;
channels 85–6; horizontal essays 8;
Italian civil society 55–6; Malta 22;
Portugal 110; roles 86–95; Spain 70,
82–96
interest groups 75–7, 109–10, 128; see
also trade unions
intergovernmental conferences (IGCs)
1, 5; conceptual and analytical
framework 154–6; Italian
mobilization 10–11, 41, 46;
Portugal's stance 99
international politics 6, 9–10
Internet see online resources
Iraq crisis 9–10, 17, 89, 121, 182
Italy 41–62; country reports 7;
domestication 17; governments
10–11, 42–6; intellectuals 12–13;
membership 42–6; positions 46–53;
press coverage 53–4; regions 194,
197–8, 200, 206; work at the
Convention 50–1
'Ithaca' 170, 171

Jean Monnet Chair in European
Political Integration 164–5
Jean Monnet Project 76
Joint Committee Senate/Congress:
Spain 64
journals 55–6, 85–6

Karamanlis, K. 126, 127, 133
Kasoulides, Ioannis 161
Keating, Michael 192–207

Kirişci, Kemal 173–91
Komunistiko Koma Elladas (KKE)
122, 125, 127–8, 134

Labour Party: Malta 142–5, 146–50
Laeken Declaration 28–30, 153, 166,
209
Laeken European Council 2, 177
Lamassoure, Alain 205
Länder see German Länder
Latvia 211, 215
launching the Convention 158–9
lawyers: Spain 86–7, 90
left-wing constitutional debate 89
Lega Nord 47
legal approaches 24
legal-political analysis 5
legitimacy: Convention method
153–4; integration 170;
participatory democracy 35–6,
138; women representatives
218–19
León, Margarita 63–81
Lionarakis, Nikitas 130
Llorente, Rubio 91
local authorities: Cyprus 168–9
local level of governance 31–2, 35
Lopes, Ernâni 103, 119
Lucarelli, Sonia 1–23

Madeira 111
maintenance position: Portugal 106
Malta 142–51; country reports 7;
debate 144–9; intellectuals 22;
youth mobilization 12
Malta–EU Information Centre (MIC)
144–5
Martini, Claudio 43
Maziotis, D. 131
media coverage 13–14; Cyprus 153–4,
159, 165; Greece 131–2; Italy 53–4,
57; Malta 143, 147, 149–50;
Portugal 97, 112–13, 114–15; Spain
69–75, 86, 88; Turkey 173, 178,
186; see also press coverage
member states: applicants contrast 7,
11; Assembly representation 2;
Convention method 153; sex-
composition of Convention 211–12,
214–15

For Product Safety Concerns and Information please contact our EU
representative GPSR@taylorandfrancis.com
Taylor & Francis Verlag GmbH, Kaufingerstraße 24, 80331 München, Germany

www.ingramcontent.com/pod-product-compliance
Lightning Source LLC
Chambersburg PA
CBHW050415280326
41932CB00013BA/1868